FACTS AND VALUES
Studies in Ethical Analysis

FACTS and VALUES

Studies in Ethical Analysis

by Charles L. Stevenson

New Haven and London: Yale University Press, 1963

To the memory of Paul Henle

Preface

The present volume deals with various problems that arise in deciding what is good or bad, or what ought or ought not to be done —problems that are familiar in everyday discussions, and which range from idle bits of gossip about this or that man's character to prolonged and serious discussions of international politics. It has far less to say about the *summum bonum* of the philosophers than about the judgments of the ordinary man as he finishes reading the morning's newspaper. But the volume is nevertheless concerned with issues that belong to traditional ethics, and issues that in recent years have been considered central to ethics. So to make clear its philosophical status, and to point out its deliberately limited scope, I want to "place" the volume within ethics as a whole—as I can best do by mentioning the three branches into which the subject is commonly divided.

First there is "descriptive" ethics, which studies the moral practices and convictions that have been current among these or those peoples, and thus studies what has been implicitly or explicitly *considered* good, obligatory, etc. At the present time this part of ethics is developed less by philosophers (though philosophers must of course study it) than by social scientists.

Second, there is "normative" ethics, which seeks to reach conclusions about the justice of this or that law, for instance, or the value of this or that type of conduct, and which often (though not always) attempts to systematize these conclusions under general principles, such as the greatest happiness principle of Bentham and Mill, or the categorical imperative of Kant. Normative ethics differs from descriptive ethics in an obvious way: it does not seek conclusions about what others have implicitly or explicitly *considered* good, etc., but instead seeks well founded conclusions that are intended to supplement, back up, or stand in opposition to what others have considered good. In a somewhat similar way, a research worker in medicine does not recount what others have considered to be cures for a disease, but instead seeks well founded conclusions that supplement, back up, or stand in opposition to what others have considered cures.

Third, there is a branch of ethics that *surveys* normative ethics with the intent of clarifying its problems and its terminology, and with the intent, in particular, of examining the sorts of reasons by which its conclusions can be supported. It is called "analytical" ethics, though it also goes under alternative names such as "meta-ethics" and "critical" ethics. Socrates was engaged in analytical ethics when he asked, for instance, whether virtue is knowledge, or whether virtue, like knowledge, can be taught. It is accordingly an old branch of the subject; and writers on normative ethics have rarely been content to ignore it, simply because normative ethics has been thought to need the near-logical discipline that analytical ethics has sought to provide.

Now the present volume, as its title will suggest, is concerned with analytical ethics. It touches on questions of descriptive ethics only in passing. And it makes no effort to answer (as distinct from survey) the questions of normative ethics—withholding answers to them because, in the interest of a temporary division of labor, it must restrict attention to its selected tasks.

The need of such a specialized approach to ethics is readily seen. When we say that so and so is good, etc., we usually try to avoid dogmatism by giving reasons for what we say; and in many cases we have a dependable half-knowledge of how to go about this. But we are not always aware of the potential complexity of the reasons, or of the extent to which the reasons we manage to give can be supplemented by further reasons. Nor do we clearly understand just what is involved in saying that our reasons "justify" our conclusions. An analytical study, temporarily letting us see our issues in a neutral perspective, is needed to provide us with something rather more than this sort of half-knowledge—doing so not by attempting to give further support to some given conclusion, but rather by pointing out what general kind of support is possible.

An unanalyzed half-knowledge may have one of two effects. It may lead us to an illusory conviction of having said the last word on a normative issue, this conviction being attended by a contempt for those who fail to see the "obvious cogency" of our arguments. Or it may lead us, when controversies attending our "last word" eventually become discouraging, to a growing conviction that reasoning about ethical matters is never really worthwhile. Such convictions are not easilly dispelled; but it is not too much to say, I think, that they spring in good measure from ignorance, and from a kind of ignorance that analytical ethics can hope to correct.

I have been emphasizing the question, "what sort of reasons can be given for normative conclusions?" and that, in my opinion, is a question of central importance. But it is inseparable, in practice, from two other questions, namely, "how, if at all, do the problems of normative ethics differ from the problems of the sciences?" and "how, if at all, do the key terms of ethics differ in meaning from those of the sciences?" Taken together, these three questions make up the greater part of analytical ethics; and it is with them exclusively that the present volume is concerned.

Of the eleven essays that make up the volume, ten have been previously published, and apart from minor changes are reproduced here in the form in which they initially appeared. Essay XI, previously unpublished, has been included partly in order to introduce some needed corrections, and partly to round out the volume and relate it to trends in ethics that have developed during the past few years.

The essays are all closely related to my *Ethics and Language*, which was published by the Yale University Press in 1944. Some of them were preliminary sketches for that work, and others were attempts to restate its views in clearer form. But the essays do not presuppose a familiarity with *Ethics and Language* and can be considered as much an introduction to it as an elaboration and defense of it. In writing *Ethics and Language* I felt it necessary to develop points of a somewhat technical character and accordingly addressed my remarks to professional philosophers. It is my hope that *Facts and Values* will be of interest not only to philosophers but to the general reader as well. It is a set of variations, as it were, on the same, always recognizable theme; and perhaps the variations will help to show that the theme, bare though it may initially seem, is rich in its possibilities.

I list below the periodicals or books in which the previously published essays first appeared—the order being that in which they were written, and not, it will be noted, the order in which they were published or occur in the present volume.

"The Emotive Meaning of Ethical Terms," *Mind*, *46* (1937); "Ethical Judgments and Avoidability," *Mind*, *47* (1938); "Persuasive Definitions," *Mind*, *47* (1938); "The Nature of Ethical Disagreement," *Sigma*, *8-9* (1948) [written in 1941]; "Moore's Arguments against Certain Forms of Ethical Naturalism," in *The Philosophy of G. E. Moore*, ed. Paul Schilpp, Northwestern University Press, 1942; "Some Relations between Philosophy and the Study of Language," *Analysis*, *8* (1946) [written in 1943]; "Meaning Descriptive and Emotive," *The Philosophical Review*, *57* (1948); "The Emotive Conception of Ethics and its Cognitive Implications," *The Philosophical Review*, *69* (1950); "Reflections on John Dewey's Ethics," *Proceedings of the Aristotelian Society*, *62* (1961-62) [written in 1959, as a part of a series of lectures arranged by Brandeis University in honor of the Dewey Centennial]; "Relativism and Nonrelativism in the Theory of Value," *Proceedings of the American Philosophical Association* (1961-62) [Presidential address to the Western Division of the Association, May, 1962].

I want to thank the various editors who have permitted me to republish these essays. I want also to thank my colleagues and students at the University of Michigan for many stimulating discussions, and in particular to thank William Frankena, who read most of the essays when they were still in manuscript and invariably made helpful suggestions. Funds to aid publication of this volume were provided through the generosity of the Ford Foundation.

C.L.S.

Ann Arbor, Michigan
December 31, 1962

Table of Contents

1. The Nature of Ethical Disagreement

When people disagree about the value of something—one saying that it is good or right and another that it is bad or wrong—by what methods of argument or inquiry can their disagreement be resolved? Can it be resolved by the methods of science, or does it require methods of some other kind, or is it open to no rational solution at all?

The question must be clarified before it can be answered. And the word that is particularly in need of clarification, as we shall see, is the word "disagreement."

Let us begin by noting that "disagreement" has two broad senses: In the first sense it refers to what I shall call "disagreement in belief." This occurs when Mr. A believes *p*, when Mr. B believes *not-p*, or something incompatible with *p*, and when neither is content to let the belief of the other remain unchallenged. Thus doctors may disagree in belief about the causes of an illness; and friends may disagree in belief about the exact date on which they last met.

In the second sense the word refers to what I shall call "disagreement in attitude." This occurs when Mr. A has a favorable attitude to something, when Mr. B has an unfavorable or less favorable attitude to it, and when neither is content to let the other's attitude remain unchanged. The term "attitude" is here used in much the same sense that R. B. Perry uses "interest"; it designates any psychological disposition of being *for* or *against* something. Hence love and hate are relatively specific kinds of attitudes, as are approval and disapproval, and so on.

This second sense can be illustrated in this way: Two men are planning to have dinner together. One wants to eat at a restaurant that the other doesn't like. Temporarily, then, the men cannot "agree" on where to dine. Their argument may be trivial, and perhaps only half serious; but in any case it represents a disagreement *in attitude*. The men have divergent preferences and each is trying to redirect the preference of the other—though normally, of course, each is willing to revise his own preference in the light of what the other may say.

Further examples are readily found. Mrs. Smith wishes to cultivate only the four hundred; Mr. Smith is loyal to his old poker-playing friends. They accordingly disagree, in attitude, about whom to invite to their party. The progressive mayor wants modern school buildings and large parks; the older citizens are against these "new-fangled" ways; so they disagree on civic policy. These cases differ from the one about the restaurant only in that the clash of attitudes is more serious and may lead to more vigorous argument.

The difference between the two senses of "disagreement" is essentially this: the first involves an opposition of beliefs, both of which cannot be true, and the second involves an opposition of attitudes, both of which cannot be satisfied.

Let us apply this distinction to a case that will sharpen it. Mr. A believes that most voters will favor a proposed tax and Mr. B disagrees with him. The disagreement concerns attitudes—those of the voters—but note that A and B are *not* disagreeing in attitude. Their disagreement is *in belief about* attitudes. It is simply a special kind of disagreement in belief, differing from disagreement in belief about head colds only with regard to subject matter. It implies not an opposition of the actual attitudes of the speakers but only of their beliefs about certain attitudes. Disagreement *in* attitude, on the other hand, implies that the very attitudes of the speakers are opposed. A and B may have opposed beliefs about attitudes without having opposed attitudes, just as they may have opposed beliefs about head colds without having opposed head colds. Hence we must not, from the fact that an argument is concerned with attitudes, infer that it necessarily involves disagreement *in* attitude.

2

We may now turn more directly to disagreement about values, with particular reference to normative ethics. When people argue about what is good, do they disagree in belief, or do they disagree in attitude? A long tradition of ethical theorists strongly suggest, whether they always intend to or not, that the disagreement is one *in belief*. Naturalistic theorists, for instance, identify an ethical judgment with some sort of scientific statement, and so make normative ethics a branch of science. Now a scientific argument typically exemplifies disagreement in belief, and if an ethical argument is simply a scientific one, then it too exemplifies disagreement in belief. The usual naturalistic theories of ethics that stress attitudes —such as those of Hume, Westermarck, Perry, Richards, and so many others—stress disagreement in belief no less than the rest. They imply, of course, that disagreement about what is good is disagreement *in belief* about attitudes; but we have seen that that is simply one sort of disagreement in belief, and by no means the same as disagreement *in* attitude. Analyses that stress disagreement *in* attitude are extremely rare.

If ethical arguments, as we encounter them in everyday life, involved disagreement in belief exclusively—whether the beliefs were about attitudes or about something else—then I should have no quarrel with the ordinary sort of naturalistic analysis. Normative judgments could be taken as scientific statements and amenable to the usual scientific proof. But a moment's attention will readily show that disagreement in belief has not the exclusive role that theory has so repeatedly ascribed to it. It must be readily granted that ethical arguments usually involve disagreement in belief; but they *also* involve disagreement in attitude. And the conspicuous role of disagreement in attitude is what we usually take, whether we realize it or not, as the distinguishing feature of ethical arguments. For example:

Suppose that the representative of a union urges that the wage level in a given company ought to be higher—that it is only right that the workers receive more pay. The company representative urges in reply that the workers ought to receive no more than they get. Such an argument clearly represents a disagreement in attitude. The union is *for* higher wages; the company is *against* them, and neither is content to let the other's attitude remain unchanged. *In addition* to this disagreement in attitude, of course, the argument may represent no little disagreement in belief. Perhaps the parties disagree about how much the cost of living has risen and how much the workers are suffering under the present wage scale. Or perhaps they disagree about the company's earnings and the extent to which the company could raise wages and still operate at a profit. Like any typical ethical argument, then, this argument involves both disagreement in attitude and disagreement in belief.

It is easy to see, however, that the disagreement in attitude plays a unifying and predominating role in the argument. This is so in two ways:

In the first place, disagreement in attitude determines what beliefs are *relevant* to the argument. Suppose that the company affirms that the wage scale of fifty years ago was far lower than it is now. The union will immediately urge that this contention, even though true, is irrelevant. And it is irrelevant simply because information about the wage level of fifty years ago, maintained under totally different circumstances, is not likely to affect the present attitudes of either party. To be relevant, any belief that is introduced into the argument must be one that is likely to lead one side or the other to have a different attitude, and so reconcile disagreement in attitude. Attitudes are often functions of beliefs. We often change our attitudes to something when we change our beliefs about it; just as a child ceases to *want* to touch a live coal when he comes to *believe* that it will burn him. Thus in the present argument any beliefs that are at all likely to alter attitudes, such as those about the increasing cost of living or the financial state of the company, will be considered by both sides to be relevant to the argument. Agreement in belief on these matters may lead to agreement in attitude toward the wage scale. But beliefs that are likely to alter the attitudes of neither side will be declared irrelevant. They will have no bearing on the disagreement in attitude, with which both parties are primarily concerned.

In the second place, ethical argument usually terminates when disagreement in attitude terminates, even though a certain amount of disagreement in belief remains. Suppose, for instance, that the company and the union continue to disagree in belief about the increasing cost of living, but that the company, even so, ends by favoring the higher wage scale. The union will then be content to end the argument and will cease to press its point about living costs. It may bring up that point again, in some future argument of the same sort, or in urging the righteousness of its victory to the newspaper columnists; but for the moment the fact that the company has agreed in attitude is sufficient to terminate the argument. On the other hand: suppose that both parties agreed on all beliefs that were introduced into the argument, but even so continued to disagree in attitude. In that case neither party would feel that their dispute had been successfully terminated. They might look for other beliefs that could be introduced into the argument. They might use words to play on each other's emotions. They might agree (in attitude) to submit the case to arbitration, both feeling that a decision, even if strongly adverse to one party or the other, would be preferable to a continued impasse. Or, perhaps, they might abandon hope of settling their dispute by any peaceable means.

In many other cases, of course, men discuss ethical topics without having the strong, uncompromising attitudes that the present example has illustrated. They are often as much concerned with redirecting their own attitudes, in the light of greater knowledge, as with redirecting the attitudes of others. And the attitudes involved are often altruistic rather than selfish. Yet the above example will serve, so long as that is understood, to suggest the nature of ethical disagreement. Both disagreement in attitude and disagreement in belief are involved, but the former predominates in that (1) it determines what sort of disagreement in belief is relevantly disputed in a given ethical argument, and (2) it determines by its continued presence or its resolution whether or not the argument has been settled. We may see further how intimately the two sorts of disagreement are related: since attitudes are often functions of beliefs, an agreement in belief may lead people, as a matter of psychological fact, to agree in attitude.

3

Having discussed disagreement, we may turn to the broad question that was first mentioned, namely: By what methods of argument or inquiry may disagreement about matters of value be resolved?

It will be obvious that to whatever extent an argument involves disagreement in belief, it is open to the usual methods of the sciences. If these methods are the *only* rational methods for supporting beliefs —as I believe to be so, but cannot now take time to discuss—then scientific methods are the only rational methods for resolving the disagreement in *belief* that arguments about values may include.

But if science is granted an undisputed sway in reconciling beliefs, it does not thereby acquire, without qualification, an undisputed sway in reconciling attitudes. We have seen that arguments about values include disagreement in attitude, no less than disagreement in belief, and that in certain ways the disagreement in attitude predominates. By what methods shall the latter sort of disagreement be resolved?

The methods of science are still available for that purpose, but only in an indirect way. Initially, these methods have only to do with establishing agreement in belief. If they serve further to establish agreement in attitude, that will be due simply to the psychological fact that altered beliefs may cause altered attitudes. Hence scientific methods are conclusive in ending arguments about values only to the extent that their success in obtaining agreement in belief will in turn lead to agreement in attitude.

In other words: the extent to which scientific methods can bring about agreement on values depends on the extent to which a commonly accepted body of scientific beliefs would cause us to have a commonly accepted set of attitudes.

How much is the development of science likely to achieve, then, with regard to values? To what extent *would* common beliefs lead to common attitudes? It is, perhaps, a pardonable enthusiasm to *hope* that science will do everything—to hope that in some rosy future, when all men know the consequences of their acts, they will all have common aspirations and live peaceably in complete moral accord. But if we speak not from our enthusiastic hopes but from our present knowledge, the answer must be far less exciting. We usually *do not know*, at the beginning of any argument about values, whether an agreement in belief, scientifically established, will lead to an agreement in attitude or not. It is logically possible, at least, that two men should continue to disagree in attitude even though they had all their beliefs in common, and even though neither had made any logical or inductive error, or omitted any relevant evidence. Differences in temperament, or in early training, or in social status, might make the men retain different attitudes even though both were possessed of the complete scientific truth. Whether this logical possibility is an empirical likelihood I shall not presume to say; but it is unquestionably a possibility that must not be left out of account.

To say that science can always settle arguments about value, we have seen, is to make this assumption: Agreement in attitude will always be consequent upon complete agreement in belief, and science can always bring about the latter. Taken as purely heuristic, this assumption has its usefulness. It leads people to discover the discrepancies in their beliefs and to prolong enlightening argument that *may* lead, as a matter of fact, from commonly accepted beliefs to commonly accepted attitudes. It leads people to reconcile their attitudes in a rational, permanent way, rather than by rhapsody or exhortation. But the assumption is *nothing more*, for present knowledge, than a heuristic maxim. It is wholly without any proper foundation of probability. I conclude, therefore, that scientific methods cannot be guaranteed the definite role in the so-called normative sciences that they may have in the natural sciences. Apart from a heuristic assumption to the contrary, it is possible that the growth of scientific knowledge may leave many disputes about values permanently unsolved. Should these disputes persist, there are nonrational methods for dealing with them, of course, such as impassioned, moving oratory. But the purely intellectual methods of science, and, indeed, *all* methods of reasoning, may be insufficient to settle disputes about values even though they may greatly help to do so.

For the same reasons I conclude that normative ethics is not a branch of any science. It deliberately deals with a type of disagreement that science deliberately avoids. Ethics is not psychology, for instance; for although psychologists may, of course, agree or disagree in belief about attitudes, they need not, as psychologists, be concerned with whether they agree or disagree with one another *in* attitude. Insofar as normative ethics draws from the sciences, in order to change attitudes *via* changing people's beliefs, it *draws* from *all* the sciences; but a moralist's peculiar aim—that of *redirecting* attitudes—is a type of activity, rather than knowledge, and falls within no science. Science may study that activity and may help indirectly to forward it; but is not *identical* with that activity.

4

I can take only a brief space to explain why the ethical terms, such as "good," "wrong," "ought," and so on, are so habitually used to deal with disagreement in attitude. On account of their repeated occurrence in emotional situations they have acquired a strong emotive meaning. This emotive meaning makes them serviceable in initiating changes in a hearer's attitudes. Sheer emotive impact is not likely, under many circumstances, to change attitudes in any permanent way; but it *begins* a process that can then be supported by other means.

There is no occasion for saying that the meaning of ethical terms is *purely* emotive, like that of "alas" or "hurrah." We have seen that ethical *arguments* include many expressions of *belief,* and the rough rules of ordinary language permit us to say that some of these beliefs are expressed by an ethical judgment itself. But the beliefs so expressed are by no means always the same. Ethical terms are notable for their ambiguity, and opponents in an argument may use them in different senses. Sometimes this leads to artificial issues, but it usually does not. So long as one person says "this is good" with emotive praise, and another says "no, it is bad," with emotive condemnation, a disagreement in attitude is manifest. Whether or not the beliefs that these statements express are logically incompatible may not be discovered until later in the argument; but even if they are actually compatible, disagreement in attitude will be preserved by emotive meaning; and this disagreement, so central to ethics, may lead to an argument that is certainly not artificial in its issues so long as it is taken for what it is.

The many theorists who have refused to identify ethical statements with scientific ones have much to be said in their favor. They have seen that ethical judgments mold or alter attitudes, rather than describe them, and they have seen that ethical judgments can be guaranteed no definitive scientific support. But one need not on that account provide ethics with any extramundane, sui generis *subject matter.* The distinguishing features of an ethical judgment can be preserved by a recognition of emotive meaning and disagreement in attitude, rather than by some nonnatural quality—and with far greater intelligibility. If a unique subject matter is *postulated,* as it usually is, to preserve the important distinction between normative ethics and science, it serves no purpose that is not served by the very simple analysis I have here suggested. Unless nonnatural qualities can be defended by positive arguments, rather than as an "only resort" from the acknowledged weakness of ordinary forms of naturalism, they would seem nothing more than the invisible shadows cast by emotive meaning.

II. The Emotive Meaning of Ethical Terms

Ethical questions first arise in the form "is so and so good?" or "is this alternative better than that?" These questions are difficult partly because we don't quite know what we are seeking. We are asking, "is there a needle in the haystack?" without even knowing just what a needle is. So the first thing to do is to examine the questions themselves. We must try to make them clearer, either by defining the terms in which they are expressed or by any other method that is available.

The present essay is concerned wholly with this preliminary step of making ethical questions clear. In order to help answer the question "is X good?" we must *substitute* for it a question that is free from ambiguity and confusion.

It is obvious that in substituting a clearer question we must not introduce some utterly different kind of question. It won't do (to take an extreme instance of a prevalent fallacy) to substitute for "is X good?" the question "is X pink with yellow trimmings?" and then point out how easy the question really is. This would beg the original question, not help answer it. On the other hand, we must not expect the substituted question to be strictly "identical" with the original one. The original question may embody hypostatization, anthropomorphism, vagueness, and all the other ills to which our ordinary discourse is subject. If our substituted question is to be clearer it must remove these ills. The questions will be identical only in the sense that a child is identical with the man he later becomes. Hence we must not demand that the substitution strike us, on immediate introspection, as making no change in meaning.

Just how, then, must the substituted question be related to the original? Let us assume (inaccurately) that it must result from replacing "good" by some set of terms that define it. The question then resolves itself to this: How must the defined meaning of "good" be related to its original meaning?

I answer that it must be *relevant*. A defined meaning will be called "relevant" to the original meaning under these circumstances: Those who have understood the definition must be able to say all that they then want to say by using the term in the defined way. They must never have occasion to use the term in the old, unclear sense. (If a person did have to go on using the word in the old sense, then to this extent his meaning would not be clarified and the philosophical task would not be completed.) It frequently happens that a word is used so confusedly and ambiguously that we must give it *several* defined meanings, rather than one. In this case only the whole set of defined meanings will be called "relevant," and any one of them will be called "partially relevant." This is not a rigorous treatment of *relevance*, by any means, but it will serve for the present purposes.

Let us now turn to our particular task—that of giving a relevant definition of "good." Let us first examine some of the ways in which others have attempted to do this.

The word "good" has often been defined in terms of *approval*, or similar psychological attitudes. We may take as typical examples: "good" means *desired by me* (Hobbes); and "good" means *approved by most people* (Hume, in effect).[1] It will be convenient to refer to

1. The definition ascribed to Hume is oversimplified, but not, I think, in a way that weakens the force of the observations that I am about to make. Perhaps the same should be said of Hobbes.

A more accurate account of Hume's Ethics is given in *Ethics and Language* (New Haven, 1944), pp. 273–76.

definitions of this sort as "interest theories," following R. B. Perry, although neither "interest" nor "theory" is used in the most usual way.[2]

Are definitions of this sort relevant?

It is idle to deny their *partial relevance*. The most superficial inquiry will reveal that "good" is exceedingly ambiguous. To maintain that "good" is *never* used in Hobbes' sense, and never in Hume's, is only to manifest an insensitivity to the complexities of language. We must recognize, perhaps, not only these senses, but a variety of similar ones, differing both with regard to the kind of interest in question and with regard to the people who are said to have the interest.

But that is a minor matter. The essential question is not whether interest theories are *partially* relevant, but whether they are *wholly* relevant. This is the only point for intelligent dispute. Briefly: Granted that some senses of "good" may relevantly be defined in terms of interest, is there some *other* sense which is *not* relevantly so defined? We must give this question careful attention. For it is quite possible that when philosophers (and many others) have found the question "is X good?" so difficult, they have been grasping for this *other* sense of "good" and not any sense relevantly defined in terms of interest. If we insist on defining "good" in terms of interest, and answer the question when thus interpreted, we may be begging *their* question entirely. Of course this *other* sense of "good" may not exist, or it may be a complete confusion; but that is what we must discover.

Now many have maintained that interest theores are *far* from being completely relevant. They have argued that such theories neglect

2. In *General Theory of Value* (New York, 1926) Perry used "interest" to refer to any sort of favoring or disfavoring, or any sort of disposition to be for or against something. And he used "theory" where he might, alternatively, have used "proposed definition," or "proposed analysis of a common sense meaning."

In most of the (chronologically) later essays in the present volume the term "interest" systematically gives place to the term "attitude." The purpose of the change was solely to provide a more transparent terminology: it was not intended to repudiate Perry's *conception* of interest.

the very sense of "good" that is most typical of ethics. And certainly, their arguments are not without plausibility.

Only—what *is* this typical sense of "good"? The answers have been so vague and so beset with difficulties that one can scarcely determine.

There are certain requirements, however, with which the typical sense has been expected to comply—requirements which appeal strongly to our common sense. It will be helpful to summarize these, showing how they exclude the interest theories:

In the first place, we must be able sensibly to *disagree* about whether something is "good." This condition rules out Hobbes' definition. For consider the following argument: "This is good." "That isn't so; it's not good." As translated by Hobbes, this becomes: "I desire this." "That isn't so, for *I* don't." The speakers are not contradicting one another, and think they are only because of an elementary confusion in the use of pronouns. The definition, "good" means *desired by my community*, is also excluded, for how could people from different communities disagree?[3]

In the second place, "goodness" must have, so to speak, a magnetism. A person who recognizes X to be "good" must ipso facto acquire a stronger tendency to act in its favor than he otherwise would have had. This rules out the Humian type of definition. For according to Hume, to recognize that something is "good" is simply to recognize that the majority approve of it. Clearly, a man may see that the majority approve of X without having, himself, a stronger tendency to favor it. This requirement excludes any attempt to define "good" in terms of the interest of people *other* than the speaker.[4]

In the third place, the "goodness" of anything must not be verifiable solely by use of the scientific method. "Ethics must not be psychology." This restriction rules out all of the traditional interest theories without exception. It is so sweeping a restriction that we must examine its plausibility. What are the methodological implications of interest theories which are here rejected?

3. See G. E. Moore, *Philosophical Studies* (New York, 1922), pp. 332–34.
4. See G. C. Field, *Moral Theory* (London, 1921) pp. 52, 56–57.

According to Hobbes' definition a person can prove his ethical judgments with finality by showing that he is not making an introspective error about his desires. According to Hume's definition one may prove ethical judgments (roughly speaking) by taking a vote. *This* use of the empirical method, at any rate, seems highly remote from what we usually accept as proof and reflects on the complete relevance of the definitions that imply it.

But are there not more complicated interest theories that are immune from such methodological implications? No, for the same factors appear; they are only put off for a while. Consider, for example, the definition: "X is good" means *most people would approve of X if they knew its nature and consequences.* How, according to this definition, could we prove that a certain X was good? We should first have to find out, empirically, just what X was like and what its consequences would be. To this extent the empirical method as required by the definition seems beyond intelligent objection. But what remains? We should next have to discover whether most people would approve of the sort of thing we had discovered X to be. This could not be determined by popular vote—but only because it would be too difficult to explain to the voters, beforehand, what the nature and consequences of X really were. Apart from this, voting would be a pertinent method. We are again reduced to counting noses as a *perfectly final* appeal.

Now we need not scorn voting entirely. A man who rejected interest theories as irrelevant might readily make the following statement: "If I believed that X would be approved by the majority, when they knew all about it, I should be strongly *led* to say that X was good." But he would continue: "*Need* I say that X was good, under the circumstances? Wouldn't my acceptance of the alleged 'final proof' result simply from my being democratic? What about the more aristocratic people? They would simply say that the approval of most people, even when they knew all about the object of their approval, simply had nothing to do with the goodness of anything, and they would probably add a few remarks about the low state of people's interests." It would indeed seem, from these considerations, that the definition we have been considering has presupposed democratic ideals from the start; it has dressed up democratic propaganda in the guise of a definition.

The omnipotence of the empirical method, as implied by interest theories and others, may be shown unacceptable in a somewhat different way. G. E. Moore's familiar objection about the open question is chiefly pertinent in this regard. No matter what set of scientifically knowable properties a thing may have (says Moore, in effect), you will find, on careful introspection, that it is an open question to ask whether anything having these properties is *good*. It is difficult to believe that this recurrent question is a totally confused one, or that it seems open only because of the ambiguity of "good." Rather, we must be using some sense of "good" which is not definable, relevantly, in terms of anything scientifically knowable. That is, the scientific method is not sufficient for ethics.[5]

These, then, are the requirements with which the "typical" sense of "good" is expected to comply: (1) goodness must be a topic for intelligent disagreement; (2) it must be "magnetic"; and (3) it must not be discoverable solely through the scientific method.

2

I can now turn to my proposed analysis of ethical judgments. First let me present my position dogmatically, showing to what extent I vary from tradition.

I believe that the three requirements given above are perfectly sensible, that there is some *one* sense of "good" which satisfies all three requirements, and that no traditional interest theory satisfies them all. But this does not imply that "good" must be explained in terms of a Platonic Idea, or of a categorical imperative, or of a unique, unanalyzable property. On the contrary, the three requirements can be met by a *kind* of interest theory. *But we must give up a presupposition that all the traditional interest theories have made.*

5. See G. E. Moore, *Principia Ethica* (Cambridge, 1903), ch. 1. I am simply trying to preserve the spirit of Moore's objection and not the exact form of it.

Traditional interest theories hold that ethical statements are *descriptive* of the existing state of interests—that they simply *give information* about interests. (More accurately, ethical judgments are said to describe what the state of interests is, was, or will be, or to indicate what the state of interests *would* be under specified circumstances.) It is this emphasis on description, on information, which leads to their incomplete relevance. Doubtless there is always *some* element of description in ethical judgments, but this is by no means all. Their major use is not to indicate facts but to *create an influence*. Instead of merely describing people's interests they *change* or *intensify* them. They *recommend* an interest in an object, rather than state that the interest already exists.

For instance: When you tell a man that he ought not to steal, your object is not merely to let him know that people disapprove of stealing. You are attemping, rather, to get *him* to disapprove of it. Your ethical judgment has a quasi-imperative force which, operating through suggestion and intensified by your tone of voice, readily permits you to begin to *influence*, to *modify*, his interests. If in the end you do not succeed in getting *him* to disapprove of stealing, you will feel that you have failed to convince him that stealing is wrong. You will continue to feel this, even though he fully acknowledges that you disapprove of it and that almost everyone else does. When you point out to him the consequences of his actions—consequences which you suspect he already disapproves of—these *reasons* which support your ethical judgment are simply a means of facilitating your influence. If you think you can change his interests by making vivid to him how others will disapprove of him, you will do so, otherwise not. So the consideration about other people's interest is just an additional means you may employ in order to move him and is not a part of the ethical judgment itself. Your ethical judgment does not merely describe interests to him, it directs his very interests. The difference between the traditional interest theories and my view is like the difference between describing a desert and irrigating it.

Another example: A munitions maker declares that war is a good thing. If he merely meant that he approved of it, he would not have to insist so strongly nor grow so excited in his argument. People would be quite easily convinced that he approved of it. If he merely meant that most people approved of war, or that most people would approve of it if they knew the consequences, he would have to yield his point if it were proved that his was not so. But he would not do this, nor does consistency require it. He is not *describing* the state of people's approval; he is trying to *change* it by his influence. If he found that few people approved of war, he might insist all the more strongly that it was good, for there would be more changing to be done.

This example illustrates how "good" may be used for what most of us would call bad purposes. Such cases are as pertinent as any others. I am not indicating the *good* way of using "good." I am not influencing people but am describing the way this influence sometimes goes on. If the reader wishes to say that the munitions maker's influence is bad—that is, if the reader wishes to awaken people's disapproval of the man, and to make him disapprove of his own actions—I should at another time be willing to join in this undertaking. But this is not the present concern. I am not using ethical terms but am indicating how they *are* used. The munitions maker, in his use of "good," illustrates the persuasive character of the word just as well as does the unselfish man who, eager to encourage in each of us a desire for the happiness of all, contends that the supreme good is peace.

Thus ethical terms are *instruments* used in the complicated interplay and readjustment of human interests. This can be seen plainly from more general observations. People from widely separated communities have different moral attitudes. Why? To a great extent because they have been subject to different social influences. Now clearly this influence does not operate through sticks and stones alone; words play a great part. People praise one another to encourage certain inclinations and blame one another to discourage others. Those of forceful personalities issue commands which weaker people, for complicated instinctive reasons, find it difficult to disobey, quite apart from fears of consequences. Further influence is brought to bear by writers and orators. Thus social influence is exerted, to an enormous extent, by means that have nothing to do with physical force or material reward. The ethical terms facilitate such influence. Being suited for use in *suggestion*, they are a means by which men's attitudes may be led this way or that. The reason, then, that we find a greater similarity in the moral attitudes of one community than in those of different communities is largely this: ethical judgments propagate themselves. One man says "this is good"; this may influence the approval of another person, who then makes the same ethical judgment, which in turn influences another person, and so on. In the end, by a process of mutual influence, people take up more or less the same attitudes. Between people of widely separated communities, of course, the influence is less strong; hence different communities have different attitudes.

These remarks will serve to give a general idea of my point of view. We must now go into more detail. There are several questions which must be answered: How does an ethical sentence acquire its power of influencing people—why is it suited to suggestion? Again, what has this influence to do with the *meaning* of ethical terms? And finally, do these considerations really lead us to a sense of "good" which meets the requirements mentioned in the preceding section?

Let us deal first with the question about *meaning*. This is far from an easy question, so we must enter into a preliminary inquiry about meaning in general. Although a seeming digression this will prove indispensable.

3

Broadly speaking, there are two different *purposes* which lead us to use language. On the one hand we use words (as in science) to record, clarify, and communicate *beliefs*. On the other hand we use words to give vent to our feelings (interjections), or to create moods (poetry), or to incite people to actions or attitudes (oratory).

The first use of words I shall call "descriptive," the second, "dynamic." Note that the distinction depends solely upon the *purpose* of the *speaker*.

When a person says "hydrogen is the lightest known gas," his purpose *may* be simply to lead the hearer to believe this, or to believe that the speaker believes it. In that case the words are used descriptively. When a person cuts himself and says "damn," his purpose is not ordinarily to record, clarify, or communicate any belief. The word is used dynamically. The two ways of using words, however, are by no means mutually exclusive. This is obvious from the fact that our purposes are often complex. Thus when one says "I want you to close the door," part of his purpose, ordinarily, is to lead the hearer to believe that he has this want. To that extent the words are used descriptively. But the major part of one's purpose is to lead the hearer to *satisfy* the want. To that extent the words are used dynamically.

It very frequently happens that the same sentence may have a dynamic use on one occasion and not on another, and that it may have different dynamic uses on different occasions. For instance: A man says to a visiting neighbor, "I am loaded down with work." His purpose may be to let the neighbor know how life is going with him. This would *not* be a dynamic use of words. He may make the remark, however, in order to drop a hint. This *would* be dynamic usage (as well as descriptive). Again, he may make the remark to arouse the neighbor's sympathy. This would be a *different* dynamic usage from that of hinting.

Or again, when we say to a man, "of course you won't make those mistakes any more," we *may* simply be making a prediction. But we are more likely to be using "suggestion," in order to encourage him and hence *keep* him from making mistakes. The first use would be descriptive, the second, mainly dynamic.

From these examples it will be clear that we can not determine whether words are used dynamically or not merely by reading the dictionary—even assuming that everyone is faithful to dictionary meanings. Indeed, to know whether a person is using a word dynamically we must note his tone of voice, his gestures, the general circumstances under which he is speaking, and so on.

We must now proceed to an important question: What has the dynamic use of words to do with their *meaning*? One thing is clear —we must not define "meaning" in a way that would make meaning vary with dynamic usage. If we did, we should have no use for the term. All that we could say about such "meaning" would be that it is very complicated and subject to constant change. So we must certainly distinguish between the dynamic use of words and their meaning.

It does not follow, however, that we must define "meaning" in some nonpsychological fashion. We must simply restrict the psychological field. Instead of identifying meaning with *all* the psychological causes and effects that attend a word's utterance, we must identify it with those that it has a *tendency* (causal property, dispositional property) to be connected with. The tendency must be of a particular kind, moreover. It must exist for all who speak the language; it must be persistent and must be realizable more or less independently of determinate circumstances attending the word's utterance. There will be further restrictions dealing with the interrelations of word in different contexts. Moreover, we must include, under the psychological responses which the words tend to produce, not only immediately introspectable experiences but *dispositions* to react in a given way with appropriate stimuli. I hope to go into these matters in a subsequent essay.[6] Suffice it now to say that I think "meaning" may be thus defined in a way to include "propositional" meaning as an important kind.

The definition will readily permit a distinction between meaning and dynamic use. For when words are accompanied by dynamic purposes, it does not follow that they *tend* to be accompanied by them

6. The "subsequent essay" became, instead, Chapter 3 of *Ethics and Language*, which among other points defends those that follow:

(1) When used in a generic sense that emphasizes what C. W. Morris calls the *pragmatic* aspects of language, the term "meaning" designates a tendency of words to express or evoke states of mind in the people who use the words. The tendency is of

in the way mentioned above. E.g. there need be no tendency re-alizable more or less independently of the determinate circumstances under which the words are uttered.

There will be a kind of meaning, however, in the sense above defined, which has an intimate relation to dynamic usage. I refer to "emotive" meaning (in a sense roughly like that employed by Ogden and Richards).[7] The emotive meaning of a word is a tendency of a word, arising through the history of its usage, to produce (result from) *affective* responses in people. It is the imme-diate aura of feeling which hovers about a word.[8] Such tendencies to produce affective responses cling to words very tenaciously. It would be difficult, for instance, to express merriment by using the interjection "alas." Because of the persistence of such affective

a special kind, however, and many qualifications are needed (including some that bear on syntax) to specify its nature.

(2) When the states of mind in question are cognitive, the meaning can con-veniently be called *descriptive*; and when they are feelings, emotions, or attitudes, the meanings can conveniently be called *emotive*.

(3) The states of mind (in a rough and tentative sense of that term) are normally quite complicated. They are not necessarily images or feelings but may in their turn be further tendencies—tendencies to respond to various stimuli that may subsequently arise. A word may have a constant meaning, accordingly, even though it is accom-panied, at various times that it is used, by different images or feelings.

(4) Emotive meaning is sometimes more than a by-product of descriptive meaning. When a term has both sorts of meaning, for example, a change in its descriptive mean-ing may not be attended by a change in emotive meaning.

(5) When a speaker's use of emotive terms evokes an attitude in a hearer (as it sometimes may not, since it has only a *tendency* to do so), it must not be conceived as merely adding to the hearer's attitude in the way that a spark might add its heat to the atmosphere. For a more appropriate analogy, in many cases, we must think rather of a spark that ignites tinder.

7. See C. K. Ogden and I. A. Richards, *The Meaning of Meaning* (2nd ed. London, 1927). On p. 125 there is a passage on ethics which is the source of the ideas embodied in this essay.

8. In *Ethics and Language* the phrase "aura of feeling" was expressly repudiated. If the present essay had been more successful in anticipating the analysis given in that later work, it would have introduced the notion of emotive meaning in some such way as this:

The emotive meaning of a word or phrase is a strong and persistent tendency, built up in the course of linguistic history, to give direct expression (quasi-interjectionally) to certain of the speaker's feelings or emotions or attitudes; and it is also a tendency to evoke (quasi-imperatively) corresponding feelings, emotions, or attitudes in those to tendencies (among other reasons) it becomes feasible to classify them as "meanings."

Just *what* is the relation between emotive meaning and the dynamic use of words? Let us take an example. Suppose that a man tells his hostess, at the end of a party, that he thoroughly enjoyed himself, and suppose that he was in fact bored. If we consider his remark an innocent one, are we likely to remind him, later, that he "lied" to his hostess? Obviously not, or at least, not without a broad smile; for although he told her something that he believed to be false, and with the intent of making her believe that it was true—those being the ordinary earmarks of a lie—the expression, "you lied to her," would be emotively too strong for our purposes. It would seem to be a reproach, even if we intended it not to be a reproach. So it will be evident that such words as "lied" (and many parallel examples could be cited) become suited, on account of their emotive meaning, to a certain kind of dynamic use—so well suited, in fact, that the hearer is likely to be misled when we use them in any other way. The more pronounced a word's emotive meaning is, the less likely people are to use it purely descriptively. Some words are suited to encourage people, some to discourage them, some to quiet them, and so on.

Even in these cases, of course, the dynamic purposes are not to be identified with any sort of meaning; for the emotive meaning accompanies a word much more persistently than do the dynamic purposes. But there is an important contingent relation between emotive meaning and dynamic purpose: the former assists the latter. Hence if we define emotively laden terms in a way that neglects their emotive meaning, we become seriously confused. *We lead people to think that the terms defined are used dynamically less often than they are.*

whom the speaker's remarks are addressed. It is the emotive meaning of a word, accordingly, that leads us to characterize it as *laudatory* or *derogatory*—that rather generic characterization being of particular importance when we are dealing with terms like "good" and "bad" or "right and wrong." But emotive meanings are of great variety: they may yield terms that express or evoke horror, amazement, sadness, sympathy, and so on.

4

Let us now apply these remarks in defining "good." This word may be used morally or nonmorally. I shall deal with the nonmoral usage almost entirely, but only because it is simpler. The main points of the analysis will apply equally well to either usage.

As a preliminary definition let us take an inaccurate approximation. It may be more misleading than helpful but will do to begin with. Roughly, then, the sentence "X is good" means *we like X.* ("We" includes the hearer or hearers.)

At first glance this definition sounds absurd. If used, we should expect to find the following sort of conversation: A. "This is good." B. "But I *don't* like it. What led you to believe that I did?" The unnaturalness of B's reply, judged by ordinary word usage, would seem to cast doubt on the relevance of my definition.

B's unnaturalness, however, lies simply in this: he is assuming that "we like it" (as would occur implicitly in the use of "good") is being used descriptively. This will not do. When "we like it" is to take the place of "this is good," the former sentence must be used not purely descriptively, but dynamically. More specifically, it must be used to promote a very subtle (and for the nonmoral sense in question, a very easily resisted) kind of *suggestion.* To the extent that "we" refers to the hearer it must have the dynamic use, essential to suggestion, of leading the hearer to *make* true what is said, rather than merely to believe it. And to the extent that "we" refers to the speaker, the sentence must have not only the descriptive use of indicating belief about the speaker's interest, but the quasi-interjectory, dynamic function of giving direct expression to the interest. (This immediate expression of feelings assists in the process of suggestion. It is difficult to disapprove in the face of another's enthusiasm.)

For an example of a case where "we like this" is used in the dynamic way that "this is good" is used, consider the case of a mother who says to her several children, "one thing is certain, *we all like to be neat.*" If she really believed this, she would not bother to say so. But she is not using the words descriptively. She is *encouraging* the children to like neatness. By telling them that they like neatness, she will lead them to *make* her statement true, so to speak. If, instead of saying "we all like to be neat" in this way, she had said "it's a good thing to be neat," the effect would have been approximately the same.

But these remarks are still misleading. Even when "we like it" is used for suggestion, it is not quite like "this is good." The latter is more subtle. With such a sentence as "this is a good book," for example, it would be practically impossible to use instead "we like this book." When the latter is used it must be accompanied by so exaggerated an intonation, to prevent its becoming confused with a descriptive statement, that the force of suggestion becomes stronger and ludicrously more overt than when "good" is used.

The definition is inadequate, further, in that the definiens has been restricted to dynamic usage. Having said that dynamic usage was different from meaning, I should not have to mention it in giving the *meaning* of "good."

It is in connection with this last point that we must return to emotive meaning. The word "good" has a laudatory emotive meaning that fits it for the dynamic use of suggesting favorable interest. But the sentence "we like it" has no such emotive meaning. Hence my definition has neglected emotive meaning entirely. Now to neglect emotive meaning serves to foster serious confusions, as I have previously intimated; so I have sought to make up for the inadequacy of the definition by letting the restriction about dynamic usage take the place of emotive meaning. What I should do, of course, is to find a definiens whose emotive meaning, like that of "good," simply does *lead* to dynamic usage.

Why did I not do this? I answer that it is not possible if the definition is to afford us increased clarity. No two words, in the first place, have quite the same emotive meaning. The most we can hope for is a rough approximation. But if we seek for such an approximation for "good," we shall find nothing more than synonyms, such as "desirable" or "valuable"; and these are profitless because they do not clear up the connection between "good" and favorable interest. If we reject such synonyms, in favor of nonethical terms, we shall be highly misleading. For instance "this is good" has something like the meaning of "I *do* like this; do so as well." But this is certainly not accurate. For the imperative makes an appeal to the conscious efforts of the hearer. Of course he cannot like something just by trying. He must be led to like it through suggestion. Hence an ethical sentence differs from an imperative in that it enables one to make changes in a much more subtle, less fully conscious way. Note that the ethical sentence centers the hearer's attention not on his interests but on the object of interest, and thereby facilitates suggestion. Because of its subtlety, moreover, an ethical sentence readily permits counter-suggestion and leads to the give and take situation that is so characteristic of arguments about values.

Strictly speaking, then, it is impossible to define "good" in terms of favorable interest if emotive meaning is not to be distorted. Yet it is possible to say that "this is good" is *about* the favorable interest of the speaker and the hearer or hearers, and that it has a laudatory emotive meaning which fits the words for use in suggestion. This is a rough description of meaning, not a definition. But it serves the same clarifying function that a definition ordinarily does, and that, after all, is enough.

A word must be added about the moral use of "good." This differs from the above in that it is about a different kind of interest. Instead of being about what the hearer and speaker *like*, it is about a stronger sort of approval. When a person *likes* something, he is pleased when it prospers and disappointed when it does not. When a person *morally approves* of something he experiences a rich feeling of security when it prospers and is indignant or "shocked" when it does not. These are rough and inaccurate examples of the many factors which one would have to mention in distinguishing the two kinds of interest. In the moral usage, as well as in the nonmoral, "good" has an emotive meaning which adapts it to suggestion.

And now, are these considerations of any importance? Why do I stress emotive meanings in this fashion? Does the omission of them really lead people into errors? I think, indeed, that the errors resulting from such omissions are enormous. In order to see this, however, we must return to the restrictions, mentioned in Section 1, with which the typical sense of "good" has been expected to comply.

5

The first restriction, it will be remembered, had to do with disagreement. Now there is clearly some sense in which people disagree on ethical points, but we must not rashly assume that all disagreement is modeled after the sort that occurs in the natural sciences. We must distinguish between "disagreement in belief" (typical of the sciences) and "disagreement in interest." Disagreement in belief occurs when A believes p and B disbelieves it. Disagreement in interest occurs when A has a favorable interest in X and when B has an unfavorable one in it. (For a full-bodied disagreement, neither party is content with the discrepancy.)

Let me give an example of disagreement in interest. A. "Let's go to a cinema tonight." B. "I don't want to do that. Let's go to the symphony." A continues to insist on the cinema, B on the symphony. This is disagreement in a perfectly conventional sense. They cannot agree on where they want to go, and each is trying to redirect the other's interest. (Note that imperatives are used in the example.)

It is disagreement in *interest* which takes places in ethics. When C says "this is good," and D says "no, it's bad," we have a case of suggestion and counter-suggestion. Each man is trying to redirect the other's interest. There obviously need be no domineering, since each may be willing to give ear to the other's influence; but each is trying to move the other none the less. It is in this sense that they disagree. Those who argue that certain interest theories make no provision for disagreement have been misled, I believe, simply because the traditional theories, in leaving out emotive meaning, give the impression that ethical judgments are used descriptively only; and of course when judgments are used purely descriptively, the only disagreement that can arise is disagreement *in belief*. Such disagreement may be disagreement in belief *about* interests, but this is not the same as disagreement *in* interest. My definition does not provide for disagreement in belief about interests any more than does Hobbes'; but that is no matter, for there is no reason to believe, at least on common sense grounds, that this kind of disagreement exists. There is only disagreement *in* interest. (We shall see in a moment that disagreement in interest does not remove ethics from sober argument—that this kind of disagreement may often be resolved through empirical means.)

The second restriction, about "magnetism," or the connection between goodness and actions, requires only a word. This rules out only those interest theories that do *not* include the interest of the speaker in defining "good." My account does include the speaker's interest, hence is immune.

The third restriction, about the empirical method, may be met in a way that springs naturally from the above account of disagreement. Let us put the question in this way: When two people disagree over an ethical matter, can they completely resolve the disagreement through empirical considerations, assuming that each applies the empirical method exhaustively, consistently, and without error?

I answer that sometimes they can and sometimes they cannot, and that at any rate, even when they can, the relation between empirical knowledge and ethical judgments is quite different from the one that traditional interest theories seem to imply.

This can best be seen from an analogy. Let us return to the example where A and B could not agree on a cinema or a symphony. The example differed from an ethical argument in that imperatives were used, rather than ethical judgments, but was analogous to the extent that each person was endeavoring to modify the other's interest. Now how would these people argue the case, assuming that they were too intelligent just to shout at one another?

Clearly, they would give "reasons" to support their imperatives. A might say, "but you know, Garbo is at the Bijou." His hope is that B, who admires Garbo, will acquire a desire to go to the cinema when he knows what film will be there. B may counter, "but Toscanini is guest conductor tonight, in an all-Beethoven program." And so on. Each supports his imperative (*"let's* do so and so") by reasons which may be empirically established.

To generalize from this: disagreement in interest may be rooted in disagreement in belief. That is to say, people who disagree in interest would often cease to do so if they knew the precise nature and consequences of the object of their interest. To this extent disagreement in interest may be resolved by securing agreement in belief, which in turn may be secured empirically.

This generalization holds for ethics. If A and B, instead of using imperatives, had said, respectively, "it would be *better* to go to the cinema," and "it would be better to go to the symphony," the reasons which they would advance would be roughly the same. They would each give a more thorough account of the object of interest, with the purpose of completing the redirection of interest which was begun by the suggestive force of the ethical sentence. On the whole, of course, the suggestive force of the ethical statement merely exerts enough pressure to start such trains of reasons, since the reasons are much more essential in resolving disagreement in interest than the persuasive effect of the ethical judgment itself.

Thus the empirical method is relevant to ethics simply because our knowledge of the world is a determining factor to our interests. But note that empirical facts are not inductive grounds from which the ethical judgment problematically follows. (This is what traditional interest theories imply.) If someone said "close the door," and added the reason "we'll catch cold," the latter would scarcely be called an inductive ground of the former. Now imperatives are related to the reasons which support them in the same way that ethical judgments are related to reasons.

Is the empirical method *sufficient* for attaining ethical agreement? Clearly not. For empirical knowledge resolves disagreement in interest only to the extent that such disagreement is rooted in disagreement in belief. Not all disagreement in interest is of this sort. For instance: A is of a sympathetic nature and B is not. They are arguing about whether a public dole would be good. Suppose that they discovered all the consequences of the dole. Is it not possible, even so, that A will say that it is good and B that it is bad? The disagreement in interest may arise not from limited factual knowledge but simply from A's sympathy and B's coldness. Or again, suppose in the above argument that A was poor and unemployed and that B was rich. Here again the disagreement might not be due to different factual knowledge. It would be due to the different social positions of the men, together with their predominant self-interest.

When ethical disagreement is not rooted in disagreement in belief, is there *any* method by which it may be settled? If one means by "method" a *rational* method, then there is no method. But in any case there is a "way." Let us consider the above example again, where disagreement was due to A's sympathy and B's coldness. Must they end by saying, "well, it's just a matter of our having different temperaments"? Not necessarily. A, for instance, may try to *change* the temperament of his opponent. He may pour out his enthusiasms in such a moving way—present the sufferings of the poor with such appeal—that he will lead his opponent to see life through different eyes. He may build up by the contagion of his feelings an influence which will modify B's temperament and create in him a sympathy for the poor which did not previously exist. This is often the only way to obtain ethical agreement, if there is any way at all. It is persuasive, not empirical or rational; but that is no reason for neglecting it. There is no reason to scorn it, either, for it is only by such means that our personalities are able to grow, through our contact with others.

The point I wish to stress, however, is simply that the empirical method is instrumental to ethical agreement only to the extent that disagreement in interest is rooted in disagreement in belief. There is little reason to believe that all disagreements is of this sort. Hence the empirical method is not sufficient for ethics. In any case, ethics is not psychology, since psychology does not endeavour to *direct* our interests; it discovers facts about the ways in which interests are or can be directed, but that is quite another matter.

To summarize this section: my analysis of ethical judgments meets the three requirements for the typical sense of "good" that were mentioned in Section 1. The traditional interest theories fail to meet these requirements simply because they neglect emotive meaning. This neglect leads them to neglect dynamic usage, and the sort of disagreement that results from such usage, together with the method of resolving the disagreement. I may add that my analysis answers Moore's objection about the open question. Whatever scientifically knowable properties a thing may have, it *is* always open to question whether a thing having these (enumerated) qualities is good. For to ask whether it is good is to ask for *influence*. And whatever I may know about an object, I can still ask, quite pertinently, to be influenced with regard to my interest in it.

6

And now, have I really pointed out the "typical" sense of "good"?

I suppose that many will still say "no," claiming that I have simply failed to set down *enough* requirements that this sense must meet, and that my analysis, like all others given in terms of interest, is a way of begging the issue. They will say: "When we ask 'is X good?' we don't want mere influence, mere advice. We decidedly don't want to be influenced through persuasion, nor are we fully content when the influence is supported by a wide scientific knowledge of X. The answer to our question will, of course, modify our interests. But this is only because a unique sort of truth will be revealed to us—a truth that must be apprehended a priori. We want our interests to be guided by this truth and by nothing else. To substitute for this special truth mere emotive meaning and mere factual truth is to conceal from us the very object of our search."

I can only answer that I do not understand. What is this truth to be *about*? For I recollect no Platonic Idea, nor do I know what to *try* to recollect. I find no indefinable property nor do I know what to look for. And the "self-evident" deliverances of reason, which so many philosophers have mentioned, seem on examination to be deliverances of their respective reasons only (if of anyone's) and not of mine.

I strongly suspect, indeed, that any sense of "good" which is expected both to unite itself in synthetic a priori fashion with other concepts and to influence interests as well, is really a great confusion. I extract from this meaning the power of influence alone, which I find the only intelligible part. If the rest is confusion, however, then it certainly deserves more than the shrug of one's shoulders. What I should like to do is to *account* for the confusion—to examine the psychological needs which have given rise to it and show how these needs may be satisfied in another way. This is *the* problem, if confusion is to be stopped at its source. But it is an enormous problem and my reflections on it, which are at present worked out only roughly, must be reserved until some later time.

I may add that if "X is good" has the meaning that I ascribe to it, then it is not a judgment that professional philosophers and only professional philosophers are qualified to make. To the extent that ethics predicates the ethical terms of anything, rather that explains their meaning, it becomes more than a purely intellectual study. Ethical judgments are social instruments. They are used in a cooperative enterprise that leads to a mutual readjustment of human interests. Philosophers have a part in this; but so too do all men.

III. Persuasive Definitions

A "persuasive" definition is one which gives a new conceptual meaning to a familiar word without substantially changing its emotive meaning, and which is used with the conscious or unconscious purpose of changing, by this means, the direction of people's interests.[1]

The object of this paper is to show that persuasive definitions are often used in philosophy and that the widespread failure to recognize them for what they are—the temptation to consider them as definitions which merely abbreviate, or which analyze common concepts —has led to important philosophical confusions.

Before considering philosophical examples, however, it will be helpful to consider some simpler ones, which will serve to make clearer what persuasive definitions are.

As an initial example let us take a definition of the word "culture." It will be convenient to invent pure fictions about the linguistic habits of the people to whom the definition is addressed, for this will typify the actual situation in a way that is free from complicating irrelevancies. Let us consider, then, a hypothetical community in which "culture" began by having an almost purely conceptual meaning. Let us sketch the development of its emotive meaning, show

1. In this essay, as in Essay II, the term "interest" has R. B. Perry's sense, which elsewhere in the present volume is expressed by the term "attitude." See note 2, p. 12.

why the emotive meaning led certain people to redefine the word, and examine the way in which this redefinition achieved its purpose.

There was once a community in which "cultured" meant *widely read and acquainted with the arts*.

In the course of time these qualities came into high favor. If one man wanted to pay another a compliment he would dwell at length upon his culture. It became unnatural to use "culture" in any but a laudatory tone of voice. Those who lacked culture used the word with awe, and those who possessed it used the word with self-satisfaction, or perhaps with careful modesty. In this way the word acquired a strong emotive meaning. It awakened feelings not only because of its conceptual meaning, but more directly, in its own right; for it recalled the gestures, smiles, and tone of voice that so habitually accompanied it. A public speaker, for instance, was never introduced as "a man widely read and acquainted with the arts." He was described, rather, as "a man of culture." The latter phrase had no different conceptual meaning than the former but was more suitable for awakening in the audience a favorable attitude.

As the emotive meaning of the word grew more pronounced, the conceptual meaning grew more vague. This was inevitable, for the emotive meaning made the word suitable for use in metaphors. Men who were not cultured, literally, were often called so, particularly when they were admired for having *some* of the defining qualities of "culture." At first people readily distinguished these metaphorical compliments from literal statements; but as the metaphors grew more frequent the distinction became less clear. People weren't quite sure whether a person *must* know about the arts in order to be literally cultured. Perhaps some other kind of knowledge would serve as a substitute.

Let us now suppose that one member of the community had no wholehearted regard for mere reading or mere acquaintance with the arts but valued them only to the extent that they served to develop imaginative sensitivity. He felt that they were not always a reliable means to that end, and on no account the only means. It was his constant source of regret that such mechanical procedures as reading, or visiting museums, should win instant praise, and that sensitivity should scarcely be noticed. For this reason he proceeded to give "culture" a new meaning. "I know," he insisted, "that so and so is widely read and acquainted with the arts; but what has that to do with culture? The real meaning of 'culture,' the true meaning of 'culture,' is *imaginative sensitivity*." He persisted in this statement in spite of the fact that "culture" had never before been used in exactly this sense.

It will now be obvious that this definition was no mere abbreviation; nor was it intended as an analysis of a common concept. Its purpose, rather, was to redirect people's interests. "Culture" had and would continue to have a laudatory emotive meaning. The definition urged people to stop using the laudatory term to refer to reading and the arts and to use it, instead, to mean imaginative sensitivity. In this manner it sought to place the former qualities in a poor light and the latter in a fine one, and thus to redirect people's admiration. When people learn to call something by a name rich in pleasant associations, they more readily admire it; and when they learn not to call it by such a name, they less readily admire it. The definition made use of this fact. It changed interests by changing names.

The past history of "culture" facilitated the change. The emotive meaning of the word, it is true, had grown up because of the old conceptual meaning; but it was now so firmly established that it would persist even though the conceptual meaning were somewhat altered. The old conceptual meaning was easily altered, since it had been made vague by metaphorical usage. The definition could effect a change in conceptual meaning, then, which left the emotive meaning unaltered. Thanks again to vagueness the change seemed a "natural" one, which, by escaping the attention of the hearers, did not remind them that they were being influenced and so did not stultify them by making them self-conscious. The effectiveness of the definition lay partly in this and partly in the fact that it made its results permanent by embedding them in people's very linguistic habits.

The definition may be called "persuasive," then, in a quite conventional sense. Like most persuasive definitions it was in fact doubly persuasive. It at once dissuaded people from indiscriminately admiring one set of qualities (wide reading and acquaintance with the arts) and induced them to admire another (imaginative sensitivity). The speaker wished to attain both of these ends and was enabled, by his definition, to work for both at the same time.

There are hundreds of words which, like "culture," have both a vague conceptual meaning and a rich emotive meaning. The conceptual meaning of them all is subject to constant redefinition. The words are prizes which each man seeks to bestow on the qualities of his own choice.

In the nineteenth century, for instance, critics sometimes remarked that Alexander Pope was "not a poet." The foolish reply would be, "it's a mere matter of definition." It is indeed a matter of definition, but not a "mere" one. The word "poet" was used in an extremely narrow sense. This, so far from being idle, had important consequences; it enabled the critics to deny to Pope a laudatory name and so to induce people to disregard him. A persuasive definition, tacitly employed, was at work in redirecting interests. Those who wish to decide whether Pope was a poet must decide whether they will yield to the critics' influence—whether they will come to dislike Pope enough to allow him to be deprived of an honorary title. This decision will require a knowledge of Pope's works and a knowledge of their own minds. Such are the important matters which lie behind the acceptance of the tacitly proposed, narrow definition of "poet." It is not a matter of "merely arbitrary" definition, then, nor is any persuasive definition "merely arbitrary," if that phrase is taken to imply "suitably decided by the flip of a coin."

Persuasive definitions are often recognizable from the words "real" or "true," employed in a metaphorical sense. The speaker in our first example, for instance, was telling us what "real" culture was, as distinct from the "shell" of culture. The following are additional examples: "charity," in the true sense of the word, means the giving not merely of gold but of understanding; true love is the communion between minds alone; "courage," in the true sense, is strength against adverse public opinion. Each of these statements is a way of redirecting interests by leaving the emotive meaning of the words unchanged and wedding it to a new conceptual one. Similarly we may speak of the true meaning of "sportsmanship," "genius," "beauty," and so on. Or we may speak of the true meaning of "selfishness" or "hypocrisy," using persuasive definitions of these derogatory terms to blame rather than to praise. "True," in such contexts, is obviously not used literally. Since people usually accept what they consider true, "true" comes to have the persuasive force of "to be accepted." This force is utilized in the metaphorical expression "true meaning." The hearer is induced to accept the new meaning which the speaker introduces.

Outside the confinements of philosophical theory the importance of persuasive definitions has often been recognized. In philology they receive occasional stress. Or rather, although little attention is given to persuasive definitions, much is said about the broad heading under which a study of them would fall: the interplay between emotive and conceptual meanings in determining linguistic change, and its correlation with interests.

Leonard Bloomfield presents us with a particularly clear example: "The speculative builder has learned to appeal to every weakness, including the sentimentality, of the prospective buyer; he uses the speech forms whose content will turn the hearer in the right direction. In many locutions 'house' is the colorless, and 'home' the sentimental word. Thus the salesman comes to use the word 'home' for an empty shell that has never been inhabited, and the rest of us follow his style."[2]

Hanns Oertel, having stated that "the emotional element greatly influences the fate of some words," points out that "amica" came to have one sense which was synonymous with "concubina."[3] To be sure there are several reasons for this. "Concubina" had become

2. *Language* (New York, 1933), p. 442.
3. *Lectures on the Study of Language* (New York, 1902), pp. 304, 305.

slightly profane, too strong for delicate ears. And "amica" permitted a convenient ambiguity. Any shocking thoughts could always be ascribed to those who chose to understand the word in its less innocent sense. But a persuasive factor must also have been involved. Tact often required people to refer to concubines without expressing contempt. The word "amica," which retained part of its old laudatory emotive meaning in spite of its new sense, was useful in making concubines appear less contemptible.

Persuasive definitions are too frequently encountered, however, to have been noticed solely by the philologists. An extremely penetrating account, in spite of its cynical turn, is given by Aldous Huxley in his *Eyeless in Gaza*:

"But if you want to be free, you've got to be a prisoner. It's the condition of freedom—true freedom."

"True freedom!" Anthony repeated in the parody of a clerical voice. "I always love that kind of argument. The contrary of a thing isn't the contrary; oh, dear me, no! It's the thing itself, but as it *truly* is. Ask any diehard what conservatism is; he'll tell you it's *true* socialism. And the brewer's trade papers; they're full of articles about the beauty of true temperance. Ordinary temperance is just gross refusal to drink; but true temperance, *true* temperance is something much more refined. True temperance is a bottle of claret with each meal and three double whiskies after dinner.

"What's in a name?" Anthony went on. "The answer is, practically everything, if the name's a good one. Freedom's a marvellous name. That's why you're so anxious to make use of it. You think that, if you call imprisonment true freedom, people will be attracted to the prison. And the worst of it is you're quite right." [4]

2

As has been intimated the study of persuasive definitions falls under a much broader heading: the correlation between terminology and interests. This correlation is highly complicated. A few observations will serve to show that our account of persuasive definitions deals with a severely limited aspect of it.

A change in meaning may be either a cause or an effect of a

4. (New York, 1936), p. 90.

change in interest; and persuasive definitions figure only when the change in meaning is a cause. When it is an effect, as when our growing disapproval of conditions in Germany in the 1930s caused us to use "fascist" as an epithet, there is not in this situation itself any element of persuasion; although once the word has acquired its derogatory associations, it may be used in persuasion later on.

Our subject is still more limited in scope than this. We are concerned with *definitions* which change interests. And it is important to note that we are concerned only with *some* of these definitions. Many definitions which redirect interests are not persuasive. Interests tend to be redirected by *any* definition, so long as it at all changes the meaning of a term or selects some one sense to the exclusion of others. When a scientist introduces a technical term, in no matter how detached a manner, he indicates his interest in what he names—his estimation of the importance of talking about it or of predicting its occurrence—and he often leads his readers to have a similar interest. It would be quite misleading to call such definitions "persuasive." How, then, are they to be distinguished from persuasive definitions?

The distinction depends upon whether the term defined has a strong emotive meaning and whether the speaker employs the emotively laden word with dynamic purposes—with the predominating *intention* of changing people's interests. Men sometimes say, "I do not care what word you use, so long as you make my distinction"; and again, "If you are not interested in my distinction, well and good; I shall confine my remarks to the limited set of people who are." Definitions given in such a spirit are not persuasive; for although they indicate the speaker's interests, and may happen to influence the hearer's interests, they do not make use of emotive meaning in a deliberate effort to sway interests.

Such a distinction is inconveniently stringent, however, and must be slightly qualified. When a definition is given mainly for the purposes of distinction or classification, when it is used to guide only those interests which (like *curiosity*) are involved in making the classification understood, and when it in no way suggests that this is *the one* legitimate sort of classification, then the definition will not be called persuasive. (This is not meant to imply that persuasive definitions are never used in scientific writings, nor that nonpersuasive definitions are based on some rock foundation, nor that persuasive definitions are less respectable than others.)

We must now proceed to a further point. Persuasive definitions redirect interests by changing only the conceptual meaning of an emotively laden term, allowing the emotive meaning to remain roughly constant. Clearly, the opposite change is equally important and prevalent: the emotive meaning may be altered, the conceptual meaning remaining constant. This latter device is no less persuasive. In fact, the same persuasive force can often be obtained either by the one linguistic change or by the other. In our initial example of "culture," for instance, the speaker used a persuasive definition. He might equally well have reiterated statements such as this: "Culture is only fool's gold; the true metal is imaginative sensitivity." This procedure would have permitted "culture" to retain its old conceptual meaning but would have tended to make its emotive meaning derogatory; and it would have added to the laudatory emotive meaning of "imaginative sensitivity." The same purpose would have been served in this way that was served by the persuasive definition. The qualities commonly referred to by "culture" would still be placed in a poor light and imaginative sensitivity in a fine one; but this would have been effected by a change in emotive meaning rather than in conceptual meaning.

Cases of this last sort must be excluded from our account of persuasive definitions. Although persuasive they are not secured through definition, but rather by one's gestures and tone of voice, or by rhetorical devices such as similes and metaphors. It is expedient to restrict the word "definition" to cases where conceptual meaning alone is being determined, or where, at least, this aspect predominates. We must not forget, however, that many statements which change mainly the emotive meaning of words may, in a wider sense, be called "definitions"; and that they, no less than persuasive definitions in our strict sense, may easily be confused with statements that are not persuasive. (For example, "by 'conscience' is meant the voice of destiny.")

The remarks of the last several pages may be summarized as follows: Persuasive definitions, so far from explaining the whole interrelationship between terminology and interests, deal only with the cases where change in terminology *causes* change in interest, where emotive meaning and dynamic usage are involved, and where the terminological change is in conceptual meaning only.

There is one further clarifying remark that deserves mention. The redirection of people's interests obviously depends upon much more than emotive meaning. It depends as well upon dynamic usage: upon the vigor of the speaker, his gestures, his tone of voice, the cadence of his accompanying sentences, his figures of speech, and so on. It is further conditioned by the temperament of the hearers, their respect for the speaker, their susceptibility to suggestion, their latent prejudices and ideals—and indeed, by their factual beliefs, for a sudden change in men's beliefs prepares the way (though often with a "lag") for a redirection of interests. Persuasion is seldom effective unless the hearers are already on the point of changing their interests. A persausive definition may then be important as a final impetus to the change and as a mnemonic device, imbedded in language, for keeping the change permanent. In dwelling upon definitions, then, and upon the function of emotive meaning, we have stressed but one aspect of persuasive situations. There are excellent reasons for this stress, however. Emotive meaning is a fairly stable element amid the widely varying set of factors upon which effective persuasion depends and, although a partial factor, is often essential. When a man redefines an emotively laden term, moreover, he is *very* frequently endeavoring to persuade and takes care that the other factors necessary to successful persuasion are fulfilled. Emotive meaning is a reliable *sign* of persuasion—permits it to be noticed. This is important in the case of definitions, where persuasion, however legitimate and vital in itself, can so easily acquire a spurious appeal by masking itself in the guise of a logical analysis.

3

Having explained what persuasive definitions are, let us now see how they are important to philosophy.

We can readily begin by considering philosophic definitions of the word "philosophy" itself. Ramsey defines it as a system of definitions. Van der Leeuw defines it as an attempt to penetrate behind appearances. Their divergence is no terminological accident. "Philosophy" is a dignified term, and each man reserves it for the inquiry he most wishes to dignify.

Consider the word "reality." Philosophers often seek not reality, but Reality, or rather, true Reality. But "true Reality," like "true culture," is easily defined in many different ways, with many different persuasive effects. Were the shadows in Plato's cave "real" shadows? Were there "real" shadows of horses and men as distinct from the imaginary shadows of centaurs? It will not do to express it so. "Real" is too impressive a term to be used in describing shadows and flux; so it must be given a restricted sense which makes it predicable only of the eternal patterns. (When "Reality" is used by the mystics the effects of a tacit persuasive definition become even more obvious.)

Why did Spinoza, so anxious to free thinking from anthropomorphism, nevertheless tempt his readers to anthropomorphism by using the word "God"? Why did he not speak always of "The One Substance"? One points, of course, to the political and social forces of the times, which made a semblance of orthodoxy imperative. But assuredly this is not all. The word "God" arouses, as if by magic, the very deepest of feelings. By giving the word a new conceptual meaning Spinoza was enabled to direct its emotional force away from the old anthropomorphic fictions and center it upon Substance, which he so earnestly thought would be a more rewarding object for all our wonder and humility. Had he said, "there is no God; nothing but Substance and its Modes," he would have said what he believed, provided "God" was used in the popular sense. But this would have been poor economy of the emotions. It would have taken away the object of men's wonder and humility, providing no substitute; and so these feelings would have died, to the great impoverishment of emotional life. The persuasive definition of a word was needed to preserve emotional vitality. The change in the meaning of "God" was too abrupt, however, to escape notice. Spinoza "the atheist" was long in giving place to Spinoza "the God-intoxicated man"; for the supporters of orthodoxy were not slow to see that his God was God in emotive meaning only.

These remarks are not to be misconstrued as cynical. To point out persuasion is not necessarily to condemn it, nor to identify all persuasion with that of a mob-orator. It *is* imperative, however, to distinguish between persuasion and rational demonstration.

Let us now proceed to a more recent issue. Positivism achieved its wide appeal before Carnap's "principle of tolerance" and achieved it largely through the statement, "metaphysics is without meaning." But isn't this remark surprisingly like that of the nineteenth-century critics who said that Pope was "not a poet"? The positivists were stating an unquestionable truth in their sense of "meaning," just as the nineteenth-century critics were in their sense of "poet." The truth of such statements, however, is utterly beside the point. Controversy hinges on the emotive words that are used. Shall we define "meaning" narrowly, so that science alone will receive this laudatory title and metaphysics the correspondingly derogatory one of "nonsense"? Shall our terminology show science in a fine light and metaphysics in a poor one? Shall we, in short, accept this *persuasive* definition of "meaning"? This is the question, though well concealed by the dictum that definitions are "merely arbitrary."

But this conclusion deserves careful qualification. We must remember that the nineteenth-century critics, to return to the analogy, were not condemning Pope with sheer bombast. They were also making a distinction. Their narrow sense of "poet" had the function of stressing, in the reader's attention, certain features common to most poetry, but lacking in Pope's. Perhaps they meant to say this: "We have long been blind to fundamental differences between Pope's work and that of a Shakespeare or Milton. It is because of this blindness alone that we have been content to give Pope a laudatory title. Let us note the difference, then, and deprive him of the title." The contention of the positivists will easily bear the same interpretation. Perhaps they meant to say: "We have long been blind to the fundamental differences between the use of sentences in science and their use in metaphysics. It is because of this blindness alone that we have been content to dignify metaphysics with such titles as 'meaningful.' Let us define 'meaning,' then, in a way that will at once stress these fundamental differences and deprive metaphysics of its title." When thus stated the positivistic thesis has not only heat but light and is not to be scorned. And yet, perhaps there is still too much heat for the amount of light. It is of no little service to stress the ways in which metaphysics has been confused with science; and to the extent that posivitists have done this, their "conquest of metaphysics" has not depended upon exhortation. But do their distinctions take us more than *half way* to a full rejection of metaphysics? Are we led to go the other half by the word "nonsense," defined so that it may cast its objectionable emotive meaning upon metaphysics without being predicated of it untruthfully?

The same question arises even when metaphysics is denied "cognitive" meaning only. "Cognitive" is used to mean "empirically verifiable or else analytic," and with exclusive laudatory import. Hence the positivistic contention reduces to this: "Metaphysical statements are neither empirically verifiable nor analytic; hence they are not respectable." If metaphysicians answer, "our statements, even though neither empirically verifiable nor analytic, are still respectable," they are scarcely to be led away from their position by mere exhortation.

Metaphysical impulses are too strong for hortatory treatment; they are inhibited by it without being removed. If metaphysics is wholly to give place to science in our esteem this can come only from a closer scrutiny of both metaphysics and science. Inquiries into verification and syntax make a good beginning, but they are not the only points for study. It would be well to consider how words which suggest graphic images and metaphors are used in the sciences, and contrast their function there with their function in metaphysics; or to examine the psychological needs and specific confusions which lead people to think that metaphysics is necessary. Such inquiries would direct our attitudes toward metaphysics in a more permanent and illuminating fashion; they would shape our attitudes by clarifying and augmenting our beliefs. If an adverse attitude to metaphysics were prepared for in this manner, the word "nonsense," persuasively defined, would be helpful in crystallizing the attitude. Such a program seems more promising than that of the metaphysicians. It is a pity, then, to hide its real complexity by using a persuasive definition prematurely.

4

Let us now turn to ethics, with particular attention to the word "justice," as defined in Plato's *Republic*.

The first book of the *Republic*, it will be remembered, is largely taken up with an argument between Socrates and Thrasymachus. Socrates is the victor and yet he is not content. "I have gone from one subject to another," he says, "without having discovered what I sought first, the nature of justice. I left that inquiry and turned away to consider whether justice is virtue and wisdom, or evil and folly" (354, Jowett).

Was this argument about the "virtue or evil" of justice really an unwarranted digression? In the light of our previous discussion we cannot agree that it was. The argument had the important function of determining whether or not "justice" was to retain its laudatory emotive meaning, and this was essential to the subsequent developments of the dialogue. When a man is about to give a persuasive definition (and we shall see in a moment that Socrates was) he must make sure that the emotive meaning of the term defined is well established. Otherwise a definition which was intended to illuminate a conceptual meaning under a laudatory title will end by obscuring it under a derogatory one. The word "justice," which is a little too stern to be wholly pleasing, is in danger of becoming derogatory, and particularly so when men like Thrasymachus (with a persuasive technique like that mentioned on page 39 above) are using their oratorical ability to *make* the word derogatory. Socrates must praise justice, then, before he defines "justice."

The question about the meaning of "justice" reappears in the fourth book. The two intervening books have redirected our interests by a moving description of the ideal state. These new interests must be rendered permanent. This can be done by dignifying the more significant aspects of the state under laudatory titles. Of the four laudatory terms which Socrates mentions, "wisdom," "courage," "temperance," and "justice," the first three are readily made to serve this purpose without great change in their conceptual meaning. The remaining term must be reserved for whatever else needs dignity. And so the definition of "justice" is found. "Justice of the state consists of each of the three classes doing the work of its own class" (441).

The persuasive character of this definition—the fact that it forms a part of a spirited plea for a new class system, a beautiful and inspired kind of aristocratic propaganda—can scarcely be denied. The usual meanings of "justice" must give place to the "true" one, to the meaning which needs the dignity of a laudatory name.

This account would strike Plato as decidedly unfamiliar. Yet he would disagree with it much less fundamentally than may at first appear. Let us follow his own account, stressing such points as bear analogy to the present one.

Plato would have agreed that the usual meaning of "justice" was only a point for departure. We must fashion our definition not after the common conception of justice but after justice itself—after the eternal Idea of justice, which we have beheld in a life before birth, and can now know only through careful *recollection*. A definition based on common usage would disclose merely the imperfect recollection of the Idea, as grasped by men bound to the world of opinion.

This point of agreement seems slight and outweighed by the theory of recollection. But let us look more closely. How did Plato decide whether his recollection was correct? Did he consider it correct when he reached a conception which satisfied his deepest, inmost aspirations? Did the dialectical method serve only to clarify his mind so that his aspirations could be directed to something articulate? It is difficult to think of any other answer. Plato aspired to the Ideas; but this was not a consequence of some miraculous power of attraction which the Ideas possessed. It was a matter of analytic necessity. Anything that was not an object of his aspirations was not called an Idea. If this is so, then our account is again close to his. If he had consciously been making a persuasive definition, he would still have selected, as the conceptual meaning of "justice," the object of these same aspirations. Nothing else would have been granted the laudatory name. We have retained the factors which led Plato to make his definition without retaining the poetic realm of the Ideas, whose functions, indeed, was only to adorn his procedure, not to alter its outcome.

If Plato's work had been less utopian, more satirical, he would have had recollections not from one realm of Ideas but from two. The first realm would have been the dwelling place of the gods, as described in the *Phaedrus*; and the second the dwelling place of the "author of evil" who makes his unexpected appearance in the tenth book of the *Laws*. Just as aspirations would be the criteria for correct recollection from the first realm, so aversions would be the criteria for correct recollection from the second. The theory of definition would then be less closely confined to the laudatory terms. Recollection could function likewise for the derogatory ones. But it would be of vital importance in defining the derogatory terms to confine the recollection to the second realm. The most serious philosophical errors would come from a failure to recollect from the "correct" realm, where the correctness of the realm would depend on the emotive meaning of the term defined.

We must return, however, to the definition of "justice." Plato's definition was persuasive; but this is far from being exceptional. Later definitions of "justice," with but few exceptions, are equally persuasive. They exert a different kind of influence, of course. Not all philosophers are aristocrats. But they do exert an influence.

Let us consider Bentham's definition. " 'Justice,' in the only sense which has meaning [!], is an imaginary personage, feigned for the convenience of discourse, whose dictates are the dictates of utility, applied to certain particular cases."[5] More simply stated, "this is a just law" is a hypostatic way of saying, "this law contributes to the greatest happiness of the greatest number." Such a definition may not immediately strike us as being persuasive since so many of us are willing to be led in its direction. Yet its stress on mere numbers, its stress on counting the poor man's happiness side by side with the rich man's, clearly marks a plea for greater democracy. The definition propagated the ideals of a great liberal.

By a "just" wage for laborers, it may be suggested, is meant the wage that anticipates what laborers would get eventually, through operation of the laws of supply and demand, if only there were a perfect market in the economic sense. This definition conceals its persuasion quite well, making it seem to have the detachment of a purely scientific economics. But it is a plea, though slightly compromised, for the operation not of economic laws but of "natural" economic laws—that is to say, for the operation of economic laws as they *could* be stated *if* the purely competitive, "devil take the hindmost" aspects of industry were guaranteed. So you will find this definition more pleasing to those who thrive under the present industrial conditions than to those who do not.

"Justice" can be defined in a great many ways, always without shocking the lexicographers. An eye for an eye, and a tooth for a tooth? The keeping of contracts, merely? The king's will? The distribution of social wealth in accordance with the amount of *labor* that each man does? We have a wide choice of meanings and freedom, within wide conventional limits, to invent new ones. Which meaning we choose, however, is no trivial matter, for we shall dignify that meaning by a laudatory title. To choose a meaning is to take sides in a social struggle.

It is curious to note that theorists have all been perturbed by the uncertainty of ethics and have caught glimpses, even in moments of

5. *Principles of Morals and Legislation* (1789), ch. 10, sect. 40, n. 2.

philosophical calm, of the element of persuasion involved. They sought to avoid this by defining their terms, hoping to give greater rigor and rationality to their inquiries. Yet, ironically enough, these very definitions involved the same persuasion, and in a way that veiled and confused it by making it appear to be purely intellectual analysis.

5

The examples we have considered, whether from metaphysics, theology, epistemology, or ethics, indicate that persuasive definitions are far from rare in philosophy and that failure to recognize their persuasive character has been responsible for much confusion. But what, essentially, is the nature of this confusion? Largely this: Blindness to persuasion has fostered a misunderstanding of the *kind of disagreement* that motivates many disputes, and in consequence has led people to support their contentions by far too simple a *method*, or to seek a definitive method of proof where none is possible.

These methodological confusions have so far been evident only by implication and must now be treated more explicitly. Let us proceed by indicating the *actual* complexity in methodology which persuasive definitions introduce, for the extent to which this complexity has been overlooked will then become obvious without further mention. It will be convenient to confine our attention to the example of "justice"; but it must be remembered, of course, that the same considerations arise for any case which involves a term that is subject to persuasive definition.

The summary of methodology will be parallel to that given in the previous essay (p. 27 ff). The pattern of analysis there exemplified by "good," however, is slightly different from the one here exemplified by "justice." The same methodological considerations reappear, but we must recognize them in their new guise and amid additional complications.

Two men disagree about whether a certain law is just. Let us examine the several forms which their argument may take.

(1) Suppose that both men use "just" with the same conceptual

meaning, namely: *leading to consequences A and B.* The argument may then be resolved by use of the empirical method. The disputants have only to see whether the law in question leads to these consequences.

This simple case is seldom found, however. We have seen that "justice" is constantly subject to persuasive definition, with the result that different people come to use it in different senses.

(2) Suppose, then, that the first man uses "just" to refer to A and B, and the second man uses it to refer to B and C. Suppose further that B is the only point of disagreement. In this case the disputants will probably proceed without noticing the discrepancy in their terminology and will again find the empirical method adequate. The outcome of the argument will depend upon whether the law is or is not found to lead to B.

(3) Let us next make the same supposition as immediately above, save that C, rather than B, is the sole point of disagreement. The discrepancy in terminology will then probably be realized. Yet the argument may proceed and in *some* cases may be settled empirically. If the second man, who uses "just" to refer to B and C, is the one who denies the justice of the law, his opponent may refute him by showing empirically that the law does lead to C. (B is already agreed upon, by hypothesis.) "You are refuted," the first man will say, "even according to your own faulty conception of justice."

This case raises a point which demands particular attention. The first disputant did not refer to C, in his initial statement, and the second disputant denied the justice of the law on account of C alone. Hence the initial statement of the first man was at no time contradicted by his opponent. Yet the first man will feel, even after the discrepancy in terminology is clearly realized, that he has been opposed from the very beginning. He will feel the need of refuting his opponent's statement as though this were necessary to support his own. Why is this the case?

This question seems puzzling only because we have attended exclusively to conceptual meaning. We have been tacitly assuming that the disputants were pure scientists, motivated by a detached curiosity. If our example is to be typical of the majority of actual ones, this assumption is wholly unwarranted. The use of "just" and "unjust" clearly indicated that one disputant was *for* the law and the other *against* it. They argued for this reason, not because they were statistically minded. They were *disagreeing in interest*. Each had a different kind of interest in the law, and neither was content to let the other's interest remain unchanged.[6] This kind of disagreement is evident more from emotive meaning than from conceptual meaning. The fact, then, that the conceptual meaning of the first disputant was not contradicted did not lead him to feel that his position was unchallenged. He wanted his opponent not merely to acknowledge certain consequences of the law but likewise to praise it; and his opponent would not be praising it if he called it "unjust," no matter what conceptual meaning he assigned to the term.

The disagreement in interest is most easily seen in cases like (3), but a moment's consideration will show that it is equally present in cases (1) and (2). The use of the laudatory term "just" in the earlier cases indicated that they too were concerned with whether or not the law was to be favored. A, B, and C were involved, of course, but no more so than in the third case, and they were relevant for the same reason—relevant because the disagreement in interest, which motivated the argument, was rooted in a disagreement in belief. In other words the disputants would have the same kind of interest in the law if only they resolved their opposing beliefs about these consequences of it. In the first cases these opposing beliefs were about consequences which *both* disputants referred to conceptually by the word "just." In this third case they were about something which only one referred to by "just." This is the main point of difference between the cases and it is unimportant. The disagreement was of a sort that would terminate only when both disputants had the same kind of interest in the law. Beliefs were relevant only to the extent that they redirected interests. Which beliefs did so, and whether they were expressed in the initial statements of both

6. See Essays II and I, pp. 26 f. and 1 ff.

opponents, determined merely the complexity of the argument and not its fundamental character.

These remarks prepare us for a further case:

(4) Suppose, as before, that the first man uses "just" to refer to A and B, and the second man (who denies the justice of the law) uses "just" to refer to B and C. Suppose further that both have fully established that the law does lead to A and B, and that it does not lead to C. Conceptually speaking, of course, they have as yet located no point of disagreement, nor is there the possibility, as in (3), of one man's refuting the other "even according to the opponent's faulty conception of justice." Yet they may still argue about the justice of the law. The laudatory force of "just" and the derogatory force of "unjust" are still indicative of a disagreement in interest.

With regard to methodology this case is of particular importance. It represents a disagreement which the *empirical method may be wholly incapable of resolving*.

This will be clear if we again consider, at the expense of partial repetition, why the empirical method *was* decisive in the first three cases. In each of the earlier cases the initial judgment of one disputant was false. This was guaranteed either by the law of contradiction or by explicit hypothesis. Each disputant moreover, would have had a favorable interest in the law only so long as he believed that "just," in his sense, was truthfully predicable of it; for otherwise he would have used the laudatory term in a different conceptual sense. For these reasons the disputants had only to look to the truth of their initial statements, and this would lead them to have the same kind of interest in the law. In short, the disagreement in interest, which was the mainspring of the argument, was rooted in a disagreement in belief—in some belief which at least one of the opponents had falsely expressed in his initial statement. The empirical method, by upsetting this belief, would likewise resolve the disagreement in interest.

In case (4), however, the initial statements of the opponents are both true. The men are disposed, as above, to favor or disfavor the law in accordance with whether "just" and "unjust," in the dis-

parate senses which they employ, are truthfully predicable of it; but
an empirical inquiry will serve to *support both* of their statements.
Hence the first man will continue to call the law "just," with favor,
and the second "unjust," with disfavor. Their disagreement is not
rooted in some belief which either is expressing and may be due
solely to their different temperaments. Since the empirical method
alters interests only through altering beliefs, how can it be used to
resolve this disagreement?

It is immediately clear that the empirical method has not the same
direct application in (4) that it had in the earlier cases. Yet we shall
conclude too hastily if we say that there is no room for it here at all.
Let us examine further.

If case (4) continues to be disputed, persuasive definitions, which
hitherto have been responsible only for the ambiguity of "just," will
come to play a more overt and important role. Each man, in order
to influence the other's interests, will insist upon his own definition.
They will argue about whether the law is just in the *true* sense of
"just." Until they agree upon the sense of the word they will
not agree upon their fundamental issue, namely: whether the law is
to be described by a name that indicates their praise.

The empirical method, however unavailing it may be in altering
the truth of the conceptual predications which the disputants first
made, may reappear as a means of supporting their persuasive definitions. The second disputant, for instance, may be led to discover that
C, to which he refers by "just," has the further consequences, F, G,
and H. If he has an unfavorable interest in these consequences he
may no longer wish to define "just" in terms of C. If he is led to discover that A has the further consequences I, J, and K, in which he
has a favorable interest, he may decide to use "just" to refer to A. In
other words he may accept the definition upon which his opponent
has been insisting. Both men will then come to agree that the law is
just in a mutually accepted sense of "just." This sense will be a product of their wider empirical knowledge, and it will terminate their
argument not merely because they both believe that it is truthfully
predicable of the law, but because their mutual acceptance of it

indicates that they no longer disagree in interest, but both favor the law.

The argument in case (4) *may* be resolved, then, in an empirical fashion, but we must remember that it also may not. Even if the disputants know all the relevant consequences of the law, one of them may still wish to praise it and the other to condemn it. They will be led to no common conceptual sense of "just," and although neither man need be stating anything false about the law, they will continue to disagree about its justice. The disagreement will be one in interest, not rooted in any sort of disagreement in belief. If resolved at all it will be resolved only by exhortation.

It is a general truth that the empirical method can resolve ethical disagreement, or any other kind of disagreement in interest, only when this is rooted in a disagreement in belief. The present outline of methodology has become complicated only with regard to *which* beliefs are at the root of the disagreement in interest—whether there are any, and if so, to what extent they are expressed in the initial judgments. Such considerations are essential in clarifying the nature of the argument, but they are of no additional importance. This is obvious from the fact that arguments of this sort spring from the emotive meaning of the initial judgments more than from the conceptual meaning. It is evident from a further consideration: In actual practice "just" is used so vaguely that neither disputant will be sure which consequences are included in the definition of "just," and which psychologically guide him to make this definition.

The present pattern of analysis is conveniently applicable to all of the more specific ethical terms and likewise to "beautiful." The pattern of analysis exemplified elsewhere by "good"[7] is conveniently applicable only to the more generic ethical terms. (It does not provide any ready means of indicating *differentiae*.) But which of these patterns of analysis we seclect for any ethical term is largely a matter of technical convenience. "Just" could perhaps be treated after the manner of "good" and distinguished from "good" by the kind of

---

7. Essay II, Sect. 4. But see also Essay XI, Sect. 9, where with regard to "the more specific ethical terms" a somewhat different view is presented.

interest involved—though present psychological terminology does not provide a means of making the distinction accurately. "Good" could doubtless be treated after the manner of "just." Moritz Schlick made a beginning of this,[8] but his failure to stress disagreement in interest, and all that it implies, largely vitiates his account. The same may be said, although with several qualifications, of the original account given by Ogden and Richards[9] and of the account given by C. D. Broad.[10]

The ethical terms are used so vaguely that many different patterns of analysis are relevant to the conventional usage. It is idle to select some one of these as *the* pattern of analysis. All that is required is that the analysis clarify, whether in one way or another, the essential features of ethical arguments. These are emotive meaning, dynamic usage, disagreement in interest, and an important but not definitive role for the empirical method.

8. *Fragen der Ethik* (Vienna, 1930), ch. 1.

9. *The Meaning of Meaning*, p. 149.

10. "Is Goodness the Name of a Simple, Non-natural Quality?" *Proceedings of the Aristotelian Society*, n.s. *34* (1933–34), 249–68.

IV. The Emotive Conception of Ethics and its Cognitive Implications

In discussing emotive meaning and its place in ethics, I wish to begin not with an analysis of the ethical terms but with a description of the practical situations in which they are used. And in particular I wish to deal with situations that involve a "personal decision."

I shall say that a man's ethical decision is "personal," as distinct from "interpersonal," when he makes it in the privacy of his own reflections. In judging what is good or bad, right or wrong, he is not consulting others and is not advising them but is merely settling the issue in his own mind. Such a decision is not, of course, typical of the whole of an ethical problem. Sooner or later any man is likely to let his personal problem become interpersonal: he will discuss it with others, either in the hope of revising his judgment in the light of what they say, or else in the hope of leading them to revise their judgments. But for brevity I must ignore the interpersonal aspects of the problem. I have dealt with them elsewhere in considering the methods that are available for resolving a disagreement in attitude; and in the present essay I think it may be of interest to view ethics from a somewhat different perspective.

My conception of a personal decision will not be new: I shall borrow most of it from John Dewey and the rest from such writers as Hobbes, Spinoza, and Hume. My hope is simply to see this old conception in a new relationship. Some may feel that an emotive analysis of ethics, of the sort I shall later defend, is too simple—that it must be insensitive, in particular, to the role of cognition in ethics. Now I think that is far from the case. So I shall take a conception of a personal decision which, by common consent, has cognitive elements that are highly complex; and I shall then endeavor to show than an emotive analysis, so far from ignoring them, is actually of interest in throwing them into sharper relief.

2

Suppose, then, that a man is making a personal decision about an ethical issue. Just what is he trying to do?

A part of my answer is this: he is trying to make up his mind whether to approve or disapprove of something. So at first—though, as we shall see, only at first—his attitudes have a more conspicuous role in his problem than do his thoughts or beliefs. So long as he is ethically undecided his attitudes are in a psychological state of *conflict*; half of him approves of a certain object or action, and the other half of him disapproves of it. And only when he has resolved his conflict, making his attitudes, at least in greater degree, speak with one voice, will he have made his decision. As we commonly put it, he is making up his mind about "what he really approves of."[1]

To see the cognitive aspects of such a decision we need look only a little further: When a man has conflicting attitudes he is virtually forced to think—to recall to mind whatever he knows about the alternatives before him and to learn as much more about them as he can. For between his thoughts and his attitudes there is an intimate relationship. A change in his thoughts is likely to *bring about* a change in his attitudes and, in particular, is likely to end or minimize his conflict by strengthening, weakening, or redirecting one of the

---

1. He is also deciding whether he wants others to *share* his approval—a point which I must here ignore for simplicity. There will also be an interplay, of course, between an individual's decision and the "mores" of his community, as I have explained in Essay XI, end of Sect. 5, and in *Ethics and Language*, p. 97.

attitudes involved. The man may not know this in the sense of holding it as an articulate theory of psychology; but at least he will act, in some degree, as if he knew it. Hence his problem of resolving his conflict will also be a problem of establishing, cognitively, the varied beliefs that may *help* him to resolve it.

Just how does this influence of thoughts upon attitudes take place? A full explanation, of course, is far more than I am prepared to undertake; but a small part of it is given by this familiar psychological principle: our approval of anything is strengthened or weakened depending on whether we approve or disapprove of its consequences. Suppose, for instance, that a man has conflicting attitudes toward X, and suppose that he later comes to believe that X causes Y. Now if he approves of Y (and for simplicity I shall consider that possibility only) he will thereupon approve of X more strongly. And his strengthened approval of X, outweighing the partial disapproval that he also has for it, will tend to make him resolve his conflict in X's favor.

The role of thought or cognitive inquiry in this example will be obvious: it establishes the ordinary causal proposition that X leads to Y. But we have still to explain why a belief of this proposition does anything more than satisfy a scientific curiosity. Why does it strengthen the man's approval of X? One cannot easily hold, I think, that the belief has any power *in itself* to do this. It strengthens the man's approval of X only because Y too is an object of his approval. If Y were indifferent to him he would feel that any question about the relation of X to Y was foreign to his problem. His reasoning serves, then, purely as an *intermediary* between his attitudes: by connecting his thought of X with his thought of Y it also connects his attitude toward X with his attitude toward Y, letting the one be reinforced by the other. And by serving as an intermediary—not this one time, of course, but over and over again—his reasoning fulfills an ethical function. It is an instance of "practical reason" in the only sense of that term that seems to me intelligible: it is ordinary reasoning made practical by its psychological context. But let us note, and with full attention, that its function remains an essential, pervasive one. Without such reasoning each attitude would be compartmentalized from the others, and the net result would not even be conflict, it would be psychological chaos.

When a personal decision in ethics is conceived in this way its cognitive elements are of the utmost variety. They belong not to some one science but rather to all sciences.

At first glance they may seem to belong exclusively to psychology, but in fact they do not. I have said, to be sure, that they spring from a conflict in attitudes, which in turn introduces beliefs that mediate between these attitudes and others; and that much can properly be described and explained by a psychologist. But a psychologist's problem is not the ethical problem that provides the *subject* of his study. The ethical problem lies in *resolving* the conflict, not in describing or explaining it. And the beliefs that help an individual to resolve it, though themselves psychological phenomena, are not beliefs *about* psychological phenomena, necessarily, and hence not beliefs whose *truth* is tested by psychologists. They may be beliefs about economic phenomena, political phenomena, sociological phenomena, physical phenomena, and so on; for all of these, being potentially the objects of an individual's attitudes, may have to be related to the given object that he is evaluating. Some of the beliefs, of course, *may* be about psychological phenomena, hence psychology is relevant to an ethical problem just as the other sciences are. But it simply takes its place *beside* these other sciences. It has no special privileges.

3

I have been discussing "ethics" in a broad sense of the term. I have not distinguished between a decision about what is *morally good* and a decision about what is simply *valuable*. Now such a distinction can obviously be made, and, although I have doubts as to whether it is very important, I suspect it deserves our passing attention. There are several ways of making it, the most important way, as I see it, depending on the sort of attitudes that are in question and hence on the sort of conflict that is being resolved.

Some of our attitudes are "peculiarly moral," in contrast not to those that are "immoral" but only to those that are "nonmoral." The peculiarly moral attitudes manifest themselves to introspection by feelings of guilt, remorse, indignation, shock, and so on, or else (when their object prospers rather than fails to prosper) by a specially heightened feeling of security and internal strength. These introspective manifestations, of course, are indicative of various other characteristics, of which I shall mention only one: When we act in accordance with a peculiarly moral approval we have a secondary approval, so to speak, which makes us proud to recognize our primary one. And when we yield to what we call "temptation"—or, in other words, when the strength of this peculiarly moral approval is outweighed by our nonmoral disapproval—we have a strong inclination to conceal our conduct from our introspection. When we cannot do this, as is often the case, we then have the sense of being victimized by forces which, in retrospect, we wish we had been able to control. "If we had the power to live our life over again," we say to ourselves in effect, "we should take care to inhibit these other attitudes before they had time to become ingrained into our personality."

Now when an individual has a conflict between one peculiarly moral attitude and another, and when he is attempting to make these attitudes, and only these, speak with one voice, then his personal decision, too, can be called "peculiarly moral," and will belong to "ethics" in a quite narrow sense of the term. But if some or all of the attitudes involved are not of this sort, then his decision, though still evaluative, is not "peculiarly moral" and belongs to "ethics" in a broad sense of the term only.

So the distinction in question can readily be made. But, as I have intimated, I suspect it of being unimportant. I doubt whether any of us will have much interest in a man's peculiarly moral decision unless it involves attitudes that predominate over his ordinary preferences. For suppose to the contrary: suppose that a monk has fully decided that it is his duty to be chaste. His peculiarly moral attitudes are not in conflict with one another; they direct him with one voice to follow the straight and narrow path. But suppose that his ordinary preferences constantly outweigh his peculiarly moral attitudes, leading him along a path that is not so straight and not so narrow. I suspect, in that case, that we shall be interested less in his code of morality than in his code of preference. In short, if ethics is to be "practical" philosophy and not a mockery of what is practical, it must be prepared to look beyond the peculiarly moral attitudes and consider all those other attitudes by which a man's conduct may be directed.

So in what follows I shall include as "ethical" any decision that makes an important difference to conduct—no matter whether the attitudes involved are peculiarly moral or not. But perhaps the reader need not reject my views even if he feels that I define "ethical" too broadly. For no matter whether a decision is peculiarly moral or simply preferential, it will involve the resolution of conflict; and it will also involve the many cognitive elements that I have mentioned—the many beliefs which, mediating between attitudes, become relevant to the conflict. So if the reader wishes to restrict the topic to peculiarly moral decisions, he will not, as I see it, be revealing new forces that influence their outcome; he will simply be viewing the forces I have mentioned in a smaller field of operation.

4

Having discussed the nature of a personal decision I can now go on to the topic of ethical language. The point I wish to make is this:

An ethical analysis that puts emotive meaning to one side and pays attention only to descriptive meaning is very likely to *under*estimate the cognitive content of ethics. One of the main reasons, then, for paying attention to emotive meaning is that it enables one to avoid this error and to recognize the cognitive content in its full variety. Thus I wish to show that an emotive conception of ethics, so often criticized for depriving ethics of its thoughtful, reflective elements, has actually just the opposite effect.

Let me begin by criticizing the nonemotive views. I cannot be at all complete, for many of my objections would depend upon my conception of interpersonal problems, whereas I must here limit my attention to those that are personal. But perhaps a partial criticism will be sufficient.

Consider the following statement, which is typical of the evolutionary school of analysis: *The degree to which anything is good or bad depends upon the degree to which it increases or decreases the power of society to win out in the struggle for survival.* I shall assume that this statement is in quasi-syntactical idiom and hence can be considered as a definition. Now what will be the effect of this definition if it is introduced into a situation where any one of us, troubled by conflicting attitudes toward a given object or action, X, is trying to make an ethical decision?

There can be little doubt that it will introduce a *part* of what is cognitively relevant. It will lead us to inquire about the effects of X on social survival; and, since we may be presumed to have a strong approval of the latter, which will transfer to X if we find that X leads to it, our inquiry will be relevant to our conflict. But note that the definition will also do something else: it will lead us to suppose that the effect of X on social survival is *all* that we have to consider. And, if our problem is one of resolving a conflict, that may easily be false. As I have previously remarked the considerations relevant to resolving a conflict are of the greatest variety. So although the definition introduces certain topics it excludes others and ends with a conception of ethics that is cognitively impoverished.

That *other* cognitive topics are relevant is evident from this possibility: Having found that X would maximize social survival, suppose we also found that it would produce a society like that of Aldous Huxley in his *Brave New World*—a society that is secure enough, to be sure, but so lacking in poetic imagination that literature degenerates into the pithy but banal slogans of advertisers. I think most of us would being to fear that the proposed X would purchase survival at too high a price: we should feel that the price, too, had to be reckoned with. And should anyone argue that the price was irrelevant, being foreign to the evolutionary definition of "good," I think we should answer: "So much the worse for the definition."

My objection holds not merely against this one definition but against any definition of the form, " 'X is valuable' means that X is conducive to E," where E need not be social survival, but can be the social integration of interests, or the greatest happiness of the greatest number, or the maximal presence of a unique, indefinable quality, or any other impersonal aim. Such a definition implies that one need only, in making an evaluative decision about X, examine its consequences upon E. It implies that one need *not* examine the consequences of X upon things unrelated to E and need not examine the consequences of E itself. But in fact a person may have *doubts* as to whether E will resolve the conflict from which the need of his evaluative decision arose. He may wonder whether his approval of E is strong enough to outweigh his disapproval of the other consequences I have mentioned. Now the very possibility of these *doubts* shows that the definition is insensitive to the magnitude of his problem; for to settle the doubts he must examine these other consequences, which the definition declares to be irrelevant.

All but a very few nonemotive analyses, in my opinion, are open to an objection which, if not identical with this, is closely parallel to it. And I suspect that the analyses which are free from the objection immediately run into difficulties of another kind. For example:

Consider the definition, " 'X is good' means the same as 'If I knew all about the nature and consequences of X, any conflict that I now may have about it would be resolved in its favor.' " This is a nonemotive definition; and, being made to order, as it were, to fit my conception of a personal decision, it is free from the above objection. But since it introduces the pronoun, "I," it does not make clear how two spectators can disagree: when one says "X is good" and the other says "X is not good" each is talking about himself and each may be telling the truth. An emotive conception, on the other hand, can easily avoid this difficulty, as I have shown elsewhere in contrasting disagreement in belief about attitudes with disagreement in attitude.[2] This point would lead us away from the personal to the interpersonal aspects of an ethical problem, however, so I shall keep within my prescribed limits and say no more about it.

The view of John Dewey, who has been so sensitive to the cognitive complexity of ethics, raise a somewhat different question. I am greatly indebted to Dewey, as this essay readily indicates. And yet I cannot believe that he has been successful in analyzing the ethical terms. He is content to say that they affect conduct and satisfaction by being predictive. But, since all predictive statements tend to affect conduct and satisfaction, and since not all of them, presumably, are ethical, we must ask what *sort* of predictions are in question. And to this Dewey gives no precise answer.

Nor do I see how Dewey could succeed—apart from introducing emotive meaning in the way I shall presently discuss—in repairing his analysis. The cognitive elements that are relevant to a conflict are no less varied than the attitudes between which they mediate. I should suppose, moreover, that they are different for different individuals; and I should suppose that, even for a given individual, they would vary with different problems. Now Dewey wants to pack all these elements into the very meaning of an ethical term: he wants them to be relevant to an ethical judgment *by definition*. But they are so complicated that he is unable to specify what they are. So he can give only the genus of a definition, without the needed differentiae.

5

Let me now turn to the more constructive part of this essay. I hope to show that emotive meaning is likely to succeed where cognitive meaning is likely to fail, that it will restore the thoughtful and reflective elements of ethics to their rightful place.

The precise definition of "emotive meaning" is itself a complicated matter; but the various details will not, I think, greatly affect the simple point I am about to make. So I shall assume that "emotive meaning," whatever else, refers to a tendency of certain words to

2. Essays I and II, pp. 1 ff. and 26 f., and *Ethics and Language*, chs. 1 and 8.

express or evoke attitudes; and I shall assume that it is one thing to express or evoke attitudes and another thing to designate them. That is to say, the interjection, "alas," which expresses or evokes sorrow, functions rather differently from the noun "sorrow" itself, which designates sorrow.

It will be unnecessary for me to show, I trust, that the ethical terms have an emotive meaning—so long, that is, as I do not insist that it is their only sort of meaning. The controversy has been concerned not with this point but rather with the *importance* of their emotive meaning. Is it to be mentioned only to be put to one side so that it will not distract us from what is really essential; or is it itself an essential factor?

When we limit attention to problems of the sort I have been emphasizing—evaluative decisions that a man makes in private rather than in discussions with other people—the emotive meaning of the ethical terms may at first seem trivial. It may remind us merely that ethical decisions are sometimes attended by self-exhortation. Although self-exhortation is interesting enough, it is scarcely a matter to be dwelt upon.

There is another respect, however, in which attention to emotive meaning is more rewarding. It helps us, in cases where a man is making a decision, to see how his language reflects his problem—how it reflects his effort to make his attitudes speak with one voice. It does so in this simple way:

Suppose that the man first withholds such terms as "good" and "bad"; that he next uses them somewhat tentatively, or else alternates between the one term and the other; and that finally he uses one of them only, and with conviction. If we take his ethical terms as emotive, and hence as expressing his attitudes, we can easily explain the fact that they are verbal clues to the nature of his problem; for at first he has no unimpeded attitude to express, being in a state of conflict; and, as his attitudes speak more and more with one voice, he expresses them more and more freely.

Let me here emphasize a point that I feel to be of central importance. If we take the man's ethical terms as *expressing* his attitudes, we can become sensitive to the nature of his problem without difficulty. But if we take them as merely *designating* his attitudes, we are likely to miss the very aspect of his problem that makes it an evaluative one.

For suppose we were to insist that his ethical judgment was no more than attitude-designating, like the statement, "Careful introspection assures me that I approve of this." That would immediately suggest to us that the man's problem was one of describing his own state of mind and hence a problem in psychology. Whereas we have seen that it is something else. The man is trying to *resolve* a conflict, and the process of resolving it is much more complicated than the introspective process of describing it. In other words the attitude-designating terms would be twice removed from his problem; they would formulate beliefs that were *about* it. And by emphasizing *these* beliefs, instead of the many others that he is really concerned with, they would suggest that he is simply *looking at* his conflict. But in fact he is *living through* it and all the activities that attend its resolution, the task of looking at it being comparatively inessential.

To restore the correct emphasis, then, we must take the ethical terms not as attitude-designating but as attitude-expressing and hence as emotive. For in the latter capacity the terms are only once removed from the man's attitudes; they are related to his attitudes by a direct route and not by the indirect route of expressing beliefs about them. By causing us to look to the attitudes themselves, rather than to beliefs that do no more than describe them, emotive meaning frees us from the tendency of supposing that an evaluative decision is somehow an exercise in introspective psychology. It reminds us that the man's efforts throughout his decision are to change his very attitudes. He must actually make this change and not merely describe it as a self-conscious spectator, as if all the work were being done for him by somebody else.

Thus emotive meaning, once it is taken into account, makes us more sensitive to the nature of an ethical problem. And yet we have seen only its negative importance: we have seen only how it prevents us from making too much of the beliefs that are comparatively *in*essential—the individual's introspective beliefs that are *about* his attitudes. We have still to see how emotive meaning bears positively on cognition, how it introduces the beliefs that really are essential— those that *mediate between* an individual's attitudes and thus cause his attitudes to change.

I can best deal with this latter topic by taking a simple example. Suppose that a man says that X is good. By itself this is only a beginning; he is likely to go on, giving what are called *reasons* for his judgment. "It is good," he says, "because it leads to Y and Z." And if we ask him, "Are those the only reasons you need to consider?" he will be likely to say, "No, I suppose not." Perhaps he will then go on to consider other consequences of X, or of Y and Z. And so on.

This example, which simply puts an ethical judgment in its wider context, is sufficient to show that the cognitive elements in an ethical problem are well taken care of by statements that contain no ethical terms at all. They are taken care of by the *reasons for* the ethical judgment. The latter statements, though they do indeed, in such a context, deal with beliefs that mediate between attitudes, remain ordinary cognitive statements, open to all the tests of inductive or deductive logic. So the question that arises is this: since the reasons that attend the ethical judgment will introduce the cognitive issues, to what extent must their work be anticipated by the ethical judgment itself?

My answer is this: there can be no objection, so far as the cognitive richness of an ethical problem is concerned, to an analysis that delegates *all* the relevant beliefs to the reasons, allowing the judgment to keep none of them. I do not say that that is mandatory from a linguistic point of view, but I do say that it is feasible. For the important thing, after all, is that our language be conceived as introducing, in one way or another, the varied cognitive elements which an ethical problem does in fact bring with it. And how can an analysis be thought to impoverish ethics if, having recognized no cognitive elements in an ethical judgment itself, it immediately recognizes them among the reasons by which the ethical judgment can be supported?

To be sure, such an analysis must not stop at that point. It must explain why the ethical judgment, once made, introduces a situation to which the reasons become relevant. It must explain why the judgment feels naked, so to speak, when the reasons are not given. But that is easily explained, and the explanation simply takes us back to emotive meaning and to the living context in which the emotive terms are used.

A man's willingness to say that X is good, and hence to express his approval, will depend partly on his beliefs—his beliefs serving, as usual, to mediate between his attitude to X and his attitudes to other things. Unless he is rather less than a rational animal, then, he will not express his approval without stopping to think. And the reasons that he gives for his judgment enable him to formulate what he is stopping to think *about*. In that simple way the relation between his judgment and his reasons can be explained. His reasons do not "entail" his expression of approval, of course, or make it "probable." An expression of attitude cannot stand in these logical relationships to descriptive statements but only in causal relationships. But the reasons do make a difference: they help to determine whether the man will continue to make his judgment, or qualify it, or replace it by an unfavorable one. So they can be called "reasons" in a perfectly familiar sense of that term.

It is because the ethical terms are emotive, then, that they introduce the varied cognitive elements into an ethical problem. Although emotive meaning does not supply these elements by itself it introduces a situation that shows them to be relevant. This will be true if we take the ethical terms to be *purely* emotive. That is not, actually, my own view; but, since my own view cannot be briefly summarized, I shall be content to defend it by showing that even an extreme view is immune to an all too familiar objection. Whatever else the emotive conception of ethics may do it does not imply that evaluative decisions must be thoughtless.

Let me now argue that an emotive view cannot only be sensitive to the complexities of an ethical problem but is likely to be *more* sensitive to them than any nonemotive view.

If we think back on the nonemotive views I have criticized we can easily see that they too are trying to account for the reasons that support an ethical judgment. But how can they *relate* the judgment to the reasons? They cannot, of course, do this in the way I have done it, for they ignore emotive meaning from the start. So they do what at first glance seems plausible. They conceive of the judgment as somehow containing in its own meaning all the cognitive factors that the reasons deal with. They suppose that the reasons simply do over again, explicitly, the cognitive work that the judgment has done implicitly.

But this procedure, as we have seen, is an impossible one. The reasons are too complicated to permit it. So one of several things will happen. In attemping to make clear what an ethical judgment means a nonemotive analyst will have to leave something out; he will have to mention some too limited factor, like survival, and ignore all the others—thus impoverishing ethics. Or else he will be adequate to personal problems at the expense of ignoring interpersonal ones. Or else, like Dewey, he will be unable to complete his analysis. This last alternative is no less distressing than the others, in my opinion, since it gives the impression that the ethical terms are somehow unfit for use until all their meaning is specified and hence that they remain suspect until analysis achieves the impossible.

When the reasons are conceived as causally related to an *emotive* judgment, however, these difficulties vanish. The full set of reasons need not be "there" in the ethical judgment itself. We can add them piecemeal. And that is how, in practice, we do add them. For we do not know in advance all the reasons that will bear upon our problem, just as we do not know in advance the nature of our varied attitudes between which the reasons mediate. We progressively become aware of them as our evaluative decision gets under way.

6

I have been limiting my attention to personal decisions, even though the *inter*personal aspects of ethics are of equal or greater importance. And as I have said I cannot here develop the latter topic. But I feel that I should make one remark about it to avoid stating the cognitive claims of an emotive ethics in an exaggerated form.

In making a personal decision a man is very likely to find that his reasons, if carefully developed, will resolve his conflict to a significant degree and hence lead him to a definite judgment. For the chance of his being evenly divided against himself, when all his attitudes come into play, is scarcely worth considering. In an interpersonal problem, however, the case may be different. When controversial, such a problem involves disagreement in attitude—which is roughly a conflict "writ large." Two men disagree in the sense that their attitudes cannot both be satisfied. Now will reasoning, by its causal effect on their attitudes, resolve such a disagreement and lead both men to value the same things?

I suspect that it often will, but I cannot be sure that it always will. For the question is a complicated, psychological one: If men come to share a great number of beliefs about X, will they have the same attitude to X? On a question of such magnitude it is difficult even to weigh the probabilities.

So in spite of the cognitive richness of the emotive conception of ethics, I cannot be sure that it will make all the questions of normative ethics theoretically open to a unique, reasoned answer. And perhaps the reader will consider that a ground for seeking some other conception of ethics. When seen only in relation to personal decisions, he may say, the emotive conception of ethics seems defensible, but for interpersonal issues it is cognitively weak and must be rejected.

If that is his objection then I can only wonder what more acceptable analysis he can find. For however he may care to define the ethical terms, he will be able to mention nothing that I cannot recognize among the *reasons* that support an emotive judgment. And his subject matter either will or will not be an object of people's approval. To find out about this he must raise the complicated psychological question that I have just mentioned; and he too will not know the answer.

But perhaps the reader does not care whether his ethical subject matter is an object of approval. In that case he will have this to consider: having convinced certain men by reasoning that X is good, in his sense, he may find that in consequence they have a much greater desire to destroy X. His ethics may be totally "unsanctioned," as Bentham and Mill would say. But how could such an ethics be of interest to anybody? Why, indeed, would one study ethics at all, in preference to some pleasantly innocuous subject, like the stamp issues of Andorra? It will not help him to rest content in the assurance that all men *ought*, in his unsanctioned sense, to approve of what he finds good. They may admit that too, and thereupon take a special pride in doing what, in his sense, they oughtn't to do.

The uncertainty of a rationally obtainable convergence of attitudes will arise, then, for *any* ethics that actually works. And that being so, the seeming objection to the emotive conception is rather an objection to the complexities of social life. So I hold to my central thesis: the emotive conception of ethics, so far from depriving ethics of its thoughtful, reflective elements, in fact preserves them in all their variety.

V. Relativism and Nonrelativism in the Theory of Value

I

The term "relativism," like most other "isms," can safely be used only when it is first defined; so in the introductory part of this essay I shall clarify a sense that is in reasonable accord with philosophical English. I say "in reasonable accord" because the term is in some respects rough and must be made precise if it is to be useful.

I shall then turn to the theory of value and shall there divide my attention between a relativistic theory and a simplified form of the theory that I have defended in my *Ethics and Language*.[1] I shall want to show that the latter theory, even in its simplified form, has implications that sharply distinguish it from relativism; and I shall particularly want to show this with regard to the *justification* of value judgments—the topic of justifying reasons being one on which my previous work through faults that are possibly my own, has been seriously misleading.

2

To define "relativism" I must first explain what I mean by a relative term, proceeding by example. My first example, though trivial, will serve to introduce the central points.

The word "tall," when predicated of X, normally relates X to

1. See also Essay II, pp. 10–31.

something else. But the "something else" isn't always the same thing; it may be one thing or another, depending on the circumstances under which "tall" is uttered. A ten-story building is tall in a village, for instance, but not in New York, for with the change in locality there is a change in the sort of building with which it is compared. Or again, a height of five feet eleven inches may or may not make a person tall; it would depend on whether the person is a woman or a man or, for that matter, whether the person, if a man, belongs to this or that race. So "tall" has a meaning that is more than usually a product of its linguistic and factual context, which provides varying answers to the question, "Tall with respect to what else?"

I accordingly wish to say that "tall" is a relative term. It is a relative term not merely, of course, because it stands for a relation, but because in doing so it is not explicit with regard to one of its relata.

Let me restate this in a slightly different way. In its colloquial use "X is tall" means in part, "X is taller than ———." But if we attempt to fill in the blank, in order to specify the rest of what it means, we find that there is no one word or phrase (apart from words that are systematically ambiguous) that we can use in all cases. The blank must be filled in now in one way and now in another, corresponding to the various and implicit meaning that "tall" acquires from the circumstances that attend its use.

The same can be said, *mutatis mutandis*, of all other relative terms; and a blank-containing verbal expansion of them, of the sort I have just suggested, is perhaps the most convenient device by which they can be handled.[2]

Let me turn to a further illustration, concerned with the topic of motion. Popular writers on relativity have made us familiar with such cases as this: A speaker seated in a train may say of Mr. X, who is walking past him, "He is moving at three miles per hour"; but

---

2. When a relative term is expanded into a blank-containing expression, and the blank is appropriately filled in, the resulting term is usually less *vague* than the original one. To that extent the expansions often fail, though harmlessly, to indicate what the relative term, in a given context of utterance, actually means.

a speaker standing near the station, watching Mr. X through the train window as the train goes by, may say of him, "He is moving at much more than three miles per hour." Both statements may be correct, of course, and this is explained by the reminder that the speakers are using different frames of reference. Now we can say much the same thing in this alternative way: Both speakers, in talking about the rate at which Mr. X is moving, are talking about the rate at which he is changing his distance from ———; but they use "is moving" under such different circumstances that we must fill in the blank in different ways—in the one case mentioning some part of the train, say, and in the other case mentioning the station. The term, "is moving," is accordingly a relative term; and the shifts in its implicit, situation-dependent references readily explain why the speakers' seemingly contradictory remarks are actually compatible.

An expansion of "X is moving" into "X is changing its distance from ———" is too simple, of course, to deal with motion of all kinds; but any complication of it would continue to introduce a blank, and one that can't be filled in once and for all. So although the relativity of motion leads to a sophisticated theory, it begins with the simple point that I have made—that "is moving" is a relative term.

My next example is of interest for showing that a term can be relative in one respect but not in another.

In arguing that man is the measure of all things, it will be remembered, Protagoras spoke of the wine that was sweet to Socrates in health but not sweet to Socrates in illness.[3] So perhaps he was saying, in effect, that "is sweet" is a relative term, i.e. that "the wine is sweet" can be expanded into "the wine tastes sweet to ———." Or at any rate, perhaps some neo-Protagorean philosopher might defend the view in this slightly revised form. But in doing so, let me say, our neo-Protagorean philosopher would become a poor ordinary-language philosopher. For in the respect now in question "is sweet" can be considered a relative term only when forcibly stretched from its standard use. I say this for the following reason:

3. Plato, *Theaetetus*, 159.

When "is sweet" is expanded into "tastes sweet to ———," the blank is really unnecessary. It is necessary only when it has to be filled in in various ways, as is here not the case. For if we accept this general style of definition at all, we can more plausibly eliminate the blank in favor of a phrase with constant meaning, taking "is sweet" to be short for "tastes sweet to most people under normal circumstances." There will be no contexts, accordingly, under which we can expand "the wine is sweet" into "the wine tastes sweet to those who are ill." So if in illness we find that it doesn't taste sweet, and conclude on that ground alone that it isn't sweet, our argument will be plainly invalid. A more complicated defintion of "is sweet" would be needed, of course, to preserve the presuppositions and vague suggestions of our language;[4] but there would still, presumably, be no need of a blank. And without the blank, "is sweet" becomes at most a relation-designating and relatum-designating term; it does not become a relative term.

And yet there is another respect—a trivial one, to be sure, having no bearing on the problems of Protagoras or of any other philosopher —in which "is sweet" clearly *is* a relative term. For "is sweet" is often a short way of saying "is sweet comparatively speaking," and in such cases it can readily be expanded into "sweeter than ———." When in Burgundy, for instance, a traveler may say that a certain white wine is sweet, but when in Bordeaux, speaking of a wine of equal sweetness, he may say that it is not sweet. His remarks, though seemingly at variance with one another, may involve no more than a change in his standard of comparison.

Examples of this sort, where the same term is relative in one respect but not in another, are by no means infrequent in our language. They remind us that statements of the form "T is a relative term" are often too general to be of interest in themselves. They may regain their interest, however, once the respect in which T is a relative term is pointed out—as can readily be done by specifying the blank-containing phrase into which T can be expanded.

4. Cf. Nelson Goodman, *The Structure of Appearance* (Cambridge, Mass., 1951), ch. 4, particularly pp. 96 ff.

A relative term, then, stands both for a relation and for this or that relatum, and with regard to the latter it is so inexplicit that its meaning must be grasped from the circumstances under which it is uttered. Let me make clear that it is *more than usually* inexplicit about the relatum. Ever so many terms have this inexplicitness to some degree, but comparatively few of them have it to the degree that my examples have illustrated. There will doubtless be border-line cases but not, I think, troublesome ones. And there are clear cases not only of terms that are relative but also of terms that are not—the latter including "made entirely of iron," for example, or "having a temperature of twenty degrees centigrade." It may be well to note that such expressions as "taller than the Eiffel Tower," and "is changing his distance from the station at Brattleboro, Vermont"—obtained from my expansions of relative terms by filling in the blanks in a particular way—are not themselves relative terms.

Once "relative term" has been defined it becomes a very simple matter to define "relativism." For the sense I want to emphasize, relativism is a type of analysis that takes certain of our terms to be relative terms, its purpose (which it may or may not attain) being to guard our discourse from confusion.

But let me attempt to speak a little more accurately. I suggest that "relativism," with regard to the the general topic Z, can instructively be used to name a meta-theory which claims that the key terms used in discussing Z are relative terms. So relativism with regard to motion takes "moves," "accelerates," etc., to be relative terms; relativism with regard to perception makes the same claim about ever so many adjectives used in describing perceivable objects; relativism with regard to truth makes the same claim about "true" and its near synonyms; and so on. We shall want to exclude, however, those cases in which the key terms are taken to be relative only in some trivial or obvious respect, for the name "relativism" would there be too ponderous to be appropriate. One does not become a relativist about heights, for instance, merely because he accepts my initial example of "tall." And a parallel qualification is needed, of course, for terms that are relative only in atypical contexts.

There are unquestionably other senses that could be given to "relativism,"[5] but this sense seems to me particularly important—important because it stays close to the issues that philosophers (if I may judge by their examples) have wanted to discuss, and because it brings their issues into sharper focus.

Let me now turn to the theory of value, with which the rest of this essay will be concerned. The terms that relativism there takes to be relative terms are "good," "bad," "right," "beautiful," and so on; and although the *respect* in which it takes them to be relative need not be the same for all forms of the view, the one that is usually emphasized, and the only one that I shall here need to discuss, involves a varying reference to these or those people and their differing attitudes.

So in its main form a relativistic theory of value is simply one that expands "X is good," for example, into "X is approved by ———." For certain cases the word "approved" may have to give place to some other attitude-designating term, such as "liked," "favored," or "esteemed"; but in all cases there is some counterpart of the blank. And for varying utterances of "good," relativism maintains, we must fill in the blank now with a reference to the speaker, now with a reference to some group to which the speaker belongs, now with reference merely to most or to many people at many or most times, now with a reference to certain people who are particularly familiar with X, and so on. The only restriction is that the people must be specified by factual terms; for the use of evaluative terms would only renew the question about their meaning and would also fail to ensure that "reduction" of values to facts which relativists, in naturalistic fashion, normally seek to establish.

5. The definition given by Richard Brandt in *Ethical Theory* (New York, 1959) is not far removed from my definition, but there are some differences. See chapter 11 of his book, particularly pp. 272 ff. His section on methodological relativism (pp. 275–78) can profitably be compared with my discussion of that topic in Section 7. An earlier and much discussed account of relativism will be found in W. T. Stace, *The Concept of Morals* (New York, 1937), particularly chs. 1 and 2.

It may easily happen, according to relativism, that the conditions under which "good" is uttered are not sufficient to indicate whose attitudes are in question. We must then ask the speaker to be more explicit. And this should be no more surprising, relativism implies, than the parallel situation in physics. When a man who is talking about motion leaves room for doubt about the frame of reference he is using, we must in that case too ask him to be more explicit.

I think I am correct in suggesting that my definition makes precise a sense of "relativism" that is of philosophical interest. It has no connection, of course, with the view that an action's value depends upon, and thus is "relative to," the circumstances in which it occurs; but that is as it should be, since the latter view tends to be shared by relativists and nonrelativists alike. Socrates, for instance, can scarcely be called a relativist, yet he took it for granted that the value of an act depended on the circumstances, as is evident from his remarks about returning a deposit of arms to a man who is not in his right mind.

My sense is one in which relativism has its forefather in Protagoras; it is close to the professed relativism of Lanz[6] in ethics and of Pottle[7] in aesthetics; and it is sometimes evident, by implication, in the writings of social scientists and historians. Finding that people's evaluations vary with their attitudes and differ from place to place and from time to time, these writers draw or imply a conclusion about what the evaluative terms can be taken to mean. One might expect them to conclude that the terms always describe the attitudes of the speaker or of some group by whom the speaker is influenced, and that is in fact the emphasis in Westermarck's[8] relativism; but perhaps the other relativists consider such uses, though frequent, to be provincial—the provinciality being like that of a physicist who supposes that he must limit himself to frames of reference involving the earth or the sun. For more sophisticated uses of the evaluative terms, these writers seem to say, we need to recognize a potentially

6. Henry Lanz, *In Quest of Morals* (Stanford, Cal., 1936).

7. Frederick Pottle, *The Idiom of Poetry* (Ithaca, N.Y., 1932).

8. Edward Westermarck, *Ethical Relativity* (New York, 1932). For further remarks on the speaker's description of his own attitudes see n. 13, below.

more *varied* reference to people—the people including any of those "for whom" the values may be thought to arise.[9] My blank, it will be noted, simply makes the alleged need of this "for whom" clause (for the sense that I take to be in question) a little more conspicuous.

I have been discussing a relativism that emphasizes attitudes, that being the sort that is usually held; but it is perhaps worth mentioning that relativism could be developed in other ways, and even in ways that take their point of departure from intuitionism. For suppose that a follower of G. E. Moore should come to believe, contrary to Moore himself, that ethical intuitions are attended by individual differences that cannot be altered.[10] He might then wish to expand "X is good" into "X is intuited to have a nonnatural value-property by ————," acknowledging that if something is good relatively to the intuitions of certain people it need not be good relatively to the intuitions of certain other people. So far as I know, however, such a form of intuitionism has never been defended. The intuitionists want to escape relativism, so they render the blank superfluous by tacitly assuming from the start that individual differences, if they attend our intuitions at all, will vanish in the light of careful reflection.

In concluding this part of the essay I want to emphasize a point that I made by implication in the previous section. We must not call a theory of value "relativistic" merely because it acknowledges that our value judgments involve terms that are relative in trivial or

9. The "potentially more varied" reference to people is characteristic of the first part of R. B. Perry's *General Theory of Value*, where one gets the impression that "X is good" can be expanded into "X helps to bring about and satisfy the integrated interests of ————." But in later portions of the book Perry seems to change his view. He there talks as though the blank could be filled in, invariably, by a reference to *all* people. And that, by rendering the blank superfluous, denies relativism in my sense by denying that "good" is a relative term. Let me put it this way: If Perry takes *the* meaning of "X is good" to be the same as that of "X helps to bring about and satisfy the integrated interests of all people," then he may be called, if you like, a "relationa-list" about value; but without any implicit use of a blank he is not, in my sense, a relativist. In his work compare the decidedly relativistic tone of p. 37 with the non-relativistic tone of p. 621.

10. For Moore's views see *Principia Ethica*.

obvious respects. Thus "X is good" is sometimes short for "X is good, comparatively speaking," which in turn can be expanded into "X is better than ———." But we have here only that familiar idiom, previously illustrated for "tall" and for the second of my two uses of "sweet," that permits us to make a grammatically non-comparative adjective do the work of a comparative adjective. The example unquestionably shows that "good" can become a relative term, but it is too inconsequential to establish the "relativity of value," either in my sense or in any useful sense.

5

The aim of this essay, it will be remembered, is to contrast a relativistic theory of value with a simplified version of the view that I have worked out in my *Ethics and Language*. The latter view—i.e. the simplified version, which can conveniently be referred to as "the so-called noncognitive view"—is easily summarized:

It maintains that although a speaker normally uses "X is yellow" to express his belief about X, he normally uses "X is good" to express something else, namely his approval of X. It adds that "good," being a term of praise, usually commends X to others and thus tends to evoke their approval as well. And it makes similar remarks, *mutatis mutandis*, about "right," "duty," and so on.

No one, I suppose, continues to hold this view just as it stands. It was once defended (if not in exactly the above form, then at least in a similar form) by Russell, Carnap, Ayer, and myself;[11] but the need of qualifying it—and always in a direction that takes account of the flexibilities of our language—has since been evident. Essay III of the present volume, which in my *Ethics and Language* was developed into a "second pattern of analysis," made a beginning of these qualifications; and since the war a number of writers, notably Hare, Nowell-Smith and Urmson,[12] have felt the need of further

11. See Bertrand Russell, *Religion and Science* (New York, 1935), ch. 11; Rudolf Carnap, *Philosophy and Logical Syntax* (London, 1935), pp. 22–26; A. J. Ayer, *Language, Truth, and Logic* (London, 1947), ch. 6; and Essay II, pp. 10–31.

12. See R. M. Hare, *The Language of Morals* (Oxford, 1952); P. H. Nowell-Smith, *Ethics* (London, 1954); and J. O. Urmson, "On Grading," *Mind*, 59 (1950), pp. 145–69.

qualifications, some of which I am prepared to accept. It remains the case, however, that the unqualified view has left its imprint on the views that have followed it. Although it has been shown to bear on our discourse only partially, and in ways that are unexpectedly complex, it has not been qualified out of existence. So in spite of its artificial simplicity I want to give it renewed attention.

The view can be contrasted with relativism in a perfectly obvious respect. It does *not* say that the evaluative terms are relative terms, and accordingly it does *not*, in relativistic fashion, expand "this is good" into "this is approved by ————." For note that the expansion maintains by implication that a speaker typically makes a value judgment in the course of expressing his belief. The belief is *about* an attitude, to be sure, and for different ways of filling in the blank will be about the attitude of different people; but it is nevertheless a belief. And the expression of a belief is precisely what the so-called noncognitive theory is rejecting. It holds that a speaker typically makes a value judgment in the course of expressing his *attitude*—his judgment and his attitude being related directly, without the mediation of a belief.[13]

13. It will be asked, perhaps, whether the so-called noncognitive theory objects to relativism even when the blank is filled in by a term referring to the speaker himself— i.e. even when "this is good" is taken to have the meaning of "this is approved by me." The answer must be in the affirmative as long as "this is approved by me" merely expresses the speaker's belief about his approval, and is thus used introspectively. For to introspect an attitude is not to express it. But the answer must be in the negative, of coures, as long as "this is approved by me" is taken, as the idioms of our language readily permit, to lose its introspective function and to serve the purpose of giving direct expression to an attitude. It should be noted, however, that the so-called non-cognitive theory continues to stand apart from relativism. Relativism invariably emphasizes the introspective use of "approved by me" that the so-called noncognitive theory declares irrelevant to the theory of value; for only that use is symmetrical with relativism's general insistence that value judgments, like statements in the social sciences and psychology, express empirically testable *beliefs about* attitudes.

The definition " 'X is good' means the same as 'X is approved by me' " requires special attention in another respect: when it purports to reveal *the* typically evaluative meaning of "X is good" it takes that expression, in spite of the absence of a relativistic expansion, to refer to the approval of different people at different times; for the expression will refer to the approval of the *speaker*, who will not, of course, be always the same person. I hesitate to say, on that account, that the definition takes "good" to be

That there is *a* distinction between the two views, then, is indisputable. But it may at first seem that the distinction depends on a technicality. It may seem that the so-called noncognitive view is *almost* a form of relativism, departing from it only in ways that make no practical difference. I must now show that that is far from being true.

In the first place, the so-called noncognitive view helps us to see that our everyday issues about value are usually genuine and are not likely (apart from possible confusions to which *all* discourse is heir) to turn out to be pseudo-issues.

Relativism can bring with it no such assurance. For—in the form that emphasizes beliefs about attitudes, and the only form I am discussing—relativism is content to purchase its scientific affiliations at a curious price. It provides a scientific solution to those issues in which all parties are talking about the same attitudes, but it leaves us with the disturbing suggestion that many cases will not be of that sort. When Mr. A, for instance, says that socialized medicine is good and Mr. B says that it is bad, there may be only a pseudo-issue—one in which Mr. A is affirming that certain people approve of socialized medicine and Mr. B is affirming that certain *other* people disapprove of it. Neither need be mistaken in that case, and their discussion may continue only because they are confused by their relative terms, each failing to see *whose* attitudes the other is talking about.

The so-called noncognitive view, on the other hand, can easily avoid this paradoxical implication. It can do so simply because it points out that Mr. A and Mr. B, in an example like the above, are

a relative term; for we have here a shift in its reference, dependent on the circumstances of utterance, that is much more systematic than that of the other relative terms that I have illustrated, and one that parallels *any* use of a "token-reflexive" word; so perhaps my definitions of "relative term" and "relativism" could rule out shifts of this sort. But for the moment I need not decide this, since the shift in reference, so far as the theory of value is concerned, raises analytic issues that are *like* those that relativism raises. For present purposes, then, the definition in question can be treated as if it read, " 'X is good' can be expanded into 'X is approved by Mr. ———,' " but with the added proviso that the blank must always be filled in by the proper name (rather than by a pronoun) of the person who utters "X is good."

respectively praising and disparaging the same thing. It thus represents their issue as a disagreement in attitude—one in which the men initially express opposed attitudes rather than opposed beliefs and thus prepare the way for a discussion in which one or the other of their attitudes may come to be altered or redirected. Such an issue is far from any that can be called "pseudo" or "verbal." It is not a purely scientific issue, but it is nevertheless a genuine issue and of a sort whose importance is beyond question.

So much, then, for the first difference between the views. And beyond this there is a second difference, which I consider to be of even greater importance. It is concerned with the *reasons* by which value judgments can be supported, and I can best introduce it in the following way:

When a man expresses a belief—any belief, and hence, a fortiori, any belief about attitudes—his reasons for what he says are intended, of course, to support this belief, showing that it is well grounded, rather than capricious or arbitrary. His reasons are accordingly "reasons for believing," as studied in inductive and deductive logic. Relativism implies that the theory of value need recognize no other reasons than these. But what happens when a man expresses his approval of something? In that case his reasons for what he says are intended to support his approval, showing that *it* is well grounded rather than capricious or arbitrary. His reasons are accordingly "reasons for approving." And the interest of the so-called noncognitive view, I wish to suggest, lies in showing that the theory of value makes very little sense unless it provides for these latter reasons.

Consider once again, for instance, Mr. A's favorable evaluation of socialized medicine. According to relativism his reasons attempt to show that socialized medicine is approved by ———, and are thus reasons for *believing* that it is so approved. For most ways of filling in the blank, then, Mr. A can draw his reasons entirely from that small part of psychology or social science that deals with de facto approvals. Other reasons, I must acknowledge, may sometimes be relevant and will become particularly relevant in cases where

Mr. A happens to be referring, say, to the approval of some hypothetical person who knows all the consequences of socialized medicine. But relativism puts no special emphasis on such references. Value judgments remain value judgments, it implies, and can be fully supported by reasons, even when they describe the approval of those who are factually uninformed.

For the so-called noncognitive view, on the contrary, Mᵣ. A's reasons will be reasons *for approving* of socialized medicine. So we may expect him to speak of the probable effects of socialized medicine on the improvement of public health, for instance, and to add that it frees the poorer classes from worry, that it is less expensive to taxpayers than one may initially suppose, that it doesn't appreciably diminish the number of qualified applicants to medical schools, that its administrative problems are easily solved, and so on. I cannot undertake to say, of course, whether or not these reasons are all of them true; but it will be evident that they are reasons that we shall want to take seriously and are not, like those emphasized by relativism, of the comparatively trivial sort that are used in the course of describing, rather than guiding, approval.

There is nothing new, of course, in the conception of reasons for approving, which simply remind us that the head and the heart can work together. Nor is there anything new in the so-called noncognitive theory's conception of the modus operandi of these reasons. They support an approval by reinforcing it, or in other words, by showing or attempting to show that the object of approval is connected with other objects of approval—the reasons, then, serving as intermediaries that are intended to permit various attitudes to act together. In speaking of the consequences of socialized medicine on the public health, for instance, Mr. A does so on the assumption that these consequences, being themselves approved, will by a familiar psychological principle serve to strengthen an approval of what is taken to be their cause.

What *is* new in the so-called noncognitive theory, however, is its manner of making intelligible the relation between these reasons and the judgment that they support. By taking a (favorable) judgment to express approval, it shows why the *approval* needs to be guided by reasons. Whereas relativism, together with many other views, by taking the judgment to express a *belief about* approval, leads us to suppose that this belief, and only this belief, needs to be guided by reasons.

A moment's thought will show that reasons for approving are extraordinarily complicated. They are as complicated as the causal milieu in which any evaluated object invariably stands. They are of such variety that they fall within *all* the sciences, and thus draw not from some specialized part of what we know or think we know, but draw from the whole of it. They provide the so-called noncognitive view with a cognitive richness that is virtually unlimited. It is of the utmost importance, then, to keep them from being confused with those far simpler reasons—reasons showing that people in fact approve of such and such things—that relativism is content to emphasize.

6

My case, however, is by no means complete. I must take further steps in showing that the methodological aspects of the so-called noncognitive view are its strength. For they may seem, in spite of what I have been saying, to be its weakness. Although they unquestionably run contrary to the relativism that I have been discussing, they may seem to do so only by introducing another and neighboring sort of relativism, and one that is equally open to objections. I think that I can fully disprove this, showing that the neighboring relativism, too, is foreign to the so-called noncognitive view; but I want to discuss the topic as clearly as I can, since (as I remarked at the beginning of the essay) it has often been a source of misconceptions.

To understand the point in question we must remember that the so-called noncognitive view recognizes the possibility of giving factual reasons for evaluative conclusions. My example about socialized medicine repeatedly illustrated these reasons and will be sufficient to show that there is nothing unusual about them. But they cannot, of course, be judged by the rules of deductive or inductive logic.

That is precluded by the very notion of reasons for approving, which fall outside logic simply because they require inferences (if I may call them that) from belief-expressing sentences to attitude-expressing sentences. The truth of the reasons themselves can be tested by logic, but their bearing on the evaluative conclusion is neither logical nor illogical. It is simply nonlogical.

The so-called noncognitive view must accordingly deal with the following question: "When reasons are nonlogical, on what grounds, if any, are we to accept certain reasons and reject others?" And of course the view cannot in sanity maintain that there are no grounds whatsoever. All of us, in common sense discussions, accept certain reasons as *justifying* an evaluative conclusion and reject certain others as *failing to justify* such a conclusion. Consider, for instance, the following example:

A certain state is considering the possibility of introducing a sharply progressive income tax. Mr. Pro claims that the tax would be highly desirable and gives as his reason, "it would for the most part tax the rich, and thus put less burden on the poor." Mr. Con acknowledges that the tax would indeed have that effect, but adds that no such consideration can justify Mr. Pro's favorable judgment. "Actually," he says in reply, "your reason justifies an *un*favorable judgment of the tax, since the rich are already heavily burdened." And so on.

Note that Mr. Con is rejecting Mr. Pro's reason not because he considers it false, but because it fails, he maintains, to justify the conclusion that it is alleged to justify. And regardless of whether Mr. Con is right or wrong in this contention, his remark unquestionably makes good sense. No theorist, whether he is a so-called noncognitivist or something else, could be content to hold that "justify" has no meaning in such a context.

Now it is precisely here that the so-called noncognitive view, in spite of its sharp break with relativism with regard to the meaning of "good", "right," and so on, seems to lead back to relativism by another route. For in providing a nonlogical sense of "justify," and one that allows for individual differences in the way that reasons

guide approval, it seems to have no better alternative than to consider "justify" a relative term. It seems committed, accordingly, to
what may be called a "methodological relativism," or in other words,
to a theory that defends some such principle as this: to say that a
factual reason, R, justifies the evaluation, E, is to say that a belief of
R will in fact cause people of sort ———— to be more inclined to
accept E.

The objections to methodological relativism are much the same,
let me remark, as they are for any other sort of relativism with regard
to values. There will again be the possibility of pseudo-issues; for
when Mr. Pro says that a certain R justifies a certain E, and Mr. Con
denies this, they may neither of them be mistaken, and think they
are disagreeing only because they are confused by their relative
term. And even in cases where the issue is genuine, the evidence
showing that R justifies E will usually involve no more than a psychological or sociological inquiry into the considerations by which such
and such people are influenced. So although methodological relativism stays off stage, as it were, it nevertheless continues to direct
the actors.

But I have been speaking, it will be remembered, about what may
easily *seem* to be the case. I must now make good my claim that it
is not in fact the case.

7

Since the question requires me to explain what "justify" means, I
can best proceed by considering what sort of problem the word is
expected to handle. Suppose, then, that we should attempt to cor-
relate each of a certain set of value judgments with its justifying
reasons—taking care to include only the reasons that really justify
the judgments, and giving warnings about those that, though sometimes forensically effective, really do not justify the judgments.
What would we be doing? Would we be developing only the pro-
legomena to an evaluative inquiry? Or would we be in the midst of
an inquiry that was itself evaluative?

It is tempting to favor the first of these alternatives. "A study of justifying reasons," we are likely to say, "is useful because it permits us to take a nonevaluative first step toward deciding what is right or good—a step that gives us a methodology, with rules for making trustworthy inferences. We can then go on, subsequently, to a second step, where by applying our methodology we can draw our evaluative conclusions with greater security."

But such an answer, as I see it, is entirely incorrect. I suspect that its alleged two steps are two only in appearance, the former being no more than a mirror image of the latter. Or to speak more literally, I suspect that any inquiry of the sort now in question—any attempt to find the factual reasons by which a value judgment can be justified—is itself an evaluative inquiry, and indeed, one that if fully developed would require us to take a stand on each and every evaluative issue that could ever confront us. I have been led to this conclusion by studying examples, of which the following are typical:

Suppose that a theorist should say: "Given any specific judgment of the form, *X is good*, there is one and only one sort of reason that is sufficient to justify it, and that is a reason of the form, *X leads to the general happiness*." Is his claim one that stands a little apart from normative ethics, being concerned only with its methodology, or is it an ordinary ethical claim?

I think there can be no doubt about the matter. Our theorist is more than a methodologist with utilitarian propensities. He simply *is* a utilitarian. His terms "reason" and "justify" must not lead us to suppose that he is making a neutral, methodological claim that is separable from utilitarianism. For how can he hold that *X leads to the general happiness* is the only reason sufficient to justify the conclusion, *X is good*, without holding that anything is good if and only if it leads to the general happiness?

My example is perhaps too general, however, to be wholly instructive, so let me turn to several that are more specific. Suppose that Mr. Asothersdo has accepted a bribe but claims that he has done nothing wrong, since many of his associates did the same thing. Most of us would deny, of course, that his reason does anything at all toward justifying his judgment, whether in this special case or in any similar case. And as I see it, our denial amounts to our saying just this: "Your accepting a bribe is no less wrong when others are doing it than when others aren't doing it." Thus what seems to be our objection to Mr. Asothersdo's logic, in some extended sense of that term, is in practice wholly indistinguishable from an ordinary ethical judgment.

Interesting cases arise when reasons are taken to strengthen a man's position without fully establishing it. Thus Mr. Lowscale says that one of his friends is industrious and therefore a good man. We shall presumably wish to reply that his reason is not *sufficient* to justify his conclusion—thus refusing to make the judgment, "he is good if industrious, regardless of his other qualities." But we shall presumably add that his reason acts as a vectorial force, as it were, in *helping* to justify his conclusion—thus, in effect, making the judgment, "industriousness is a virtue, but a good man must have other virtues as well." So both aspects of our remark about a justifying reason again raise issues that are straightforwardly evaluative.

I could multiply examples endlessly but shall be content to give only one more. Suppose that Mr. Pacifist says, "it is our duty to avoid a war even at the cost of losing our freedom," and gives as his reason, "a war, in this atomic age, would destroy the lives of millions of innocent people, with devastating effects on civilization." This is an argument that most of us are not prepared to handle with the same dispatch as we handle Mr. Asothersodo's argument or Mr. Lowscale's argument. We shall some of us have to deliberate before deciding whether Mr. Pacifist's reason justifies his conclusion or whether it doesn't. And just what will we be trying to decide? Is it some pre-ethical question that bothers us, concerned only with methodology? It seems to me obvious that we are confronted, rather, with a choice between evils—evils that we hope are only hypothetical, but are not so certain to be hypothetical that we can afford to disregard them. Which would be worse: to keep peace at the expense of our freedom or to destroy the lives of millions of innocent people with devastating effects on civilization? When we ask that we are in effect asking over again whether Mr. Pacifist's reason, if true, will justify his conclusion; and the words "reason," "justify," and "conclusion" certainly cannot blind us, in any such living context, to the fact that our question is a genuinely *ethical* question.

So the general situation is this: when we claim that the factual reason, R, if true, would justify or help to justify the evaluative conclusion, E, we are in effect making another value judgment, E', of our own—the latter serving to evaluate the situation that we shall have if the facts of the case include those that R purports to describe.

Once this has been established there is no difficulty in reading off its implications with regard to the topic of my paper. The so-called noncognitive view, in its treatment of justifying reasons, is immediately freed from any suspicion of joining forces with methodological relativism. Indeed we need only review what has been said:

A methodological inquiry, when it attempts to find the R's that will justify a given E, does not stand apart from an evaluative inquiry but simply continues it, yielding ordinary value judgments that are expressed in a different terminology. The so-called noncognitive view, then, which we have seen to be nonrelativistic with regard to ordinary value judgments, is equally so with regard to justifications. Just as it does not take "good" to be a relative term, so it does not take "justify" to be a relative term—for the latter term does no more than extend the issues introduced by the former.

Such is the simple answer to what superficially appears to be a difficult question. But to dispel any sense of perplexity that may attend the answer, let me make the following remark:

If we approach all value judgments with an initial skepticism, supposing that we somehow "must" refuse to make them until we have given a full set of reasons that justify them, then the above reduction of "R justifies E" to the further judgment, E', will indeed perplex us. For we shall never, with this approach, be able to *get started* with our evaluations. We shall withhold judgment about E until we have found the R's that justify it; but in claiming that certain R's justify it we shall, by the reduction in question, be making another judgment, E'; so we must withold judgment about E' until

we have found the R's that justify *it*—and so on. Our initial skepticism will never be dispelled. But that will be true, let me point out,
only if we start with an initial skepticism, and indeed, with an
initial skepticism that infects *all* our value judgments. And why
should we start in any such manner as that? Why cannot we start
as we do in common life? There we have attitudes that we initially
trust and we proceed to express them. Reasons serve not to bring
our attitudes into being but only to redirect them. And if in accepting
or rejecting the reasons we are making new evaluations, and thus
expressing new attitudes, that is only to say that more of our
attitudes, through the mediation of the reasons, are coming into
play. If we initially distrust all our attitudes, in short, our reasons
will not *give* us attitudes; but an initial distrust of all our attitudes is so
fantastic that we need not, surely, take it seriously.

In revealing the scope and variety of justifying reasons, then, the
so-called noncognitive view implies nothing that is paradoxical.
And if it makes no attempt to say which R's will justify a given E,
that is only because, having shown that such an inquiry reduplicates
an evaluative inquiry, it is careful not to go beyond its limited aims.
As a nonnormative meta-theory of norms, its business is not to make
value judgments but only to survey and clarify them.

8

I shall conclude the essay by explaining what a relativistic theory
of value amounts to when seen from the so-called noncognitivist
point of view, for by doing so I can emphasize still further the basic
difference between the two theories—a difference that deserves every
possible emphasis.

Briefly stated my contention is this: when seen from the point of
view in question, relativism is a meta-theory that systematically
forces "good" to have the meaning of "considered good," and
"justifies" to have the meaning of "is considered to justify," and so
on. But let me develop this in more detail.

We have seen that the so-called noncognitive view refuses to
expand "X is good" into "X is approved by ———." But it does

not persist in this refusal, of course, when it deals with "X is *considered* good." For the word "considered" introduces indirect discourse; it yields a sentence that no longer commits the speaker to a value judgment of his own but simply enables him to ascribe value judgments to other people—namely, to the people who are alleged to do the considering. And how will the view handle a sentence of this latter sort?

In the first place, it will take the trivial step of expanding "X is considered good" into "X is considered good by ———," the object being to show, by emphasizing a relative term, that those alleged to do the considering will vary with the circumstances of utterance. (If this were the mark of relativism, by the way, then all theories would be relativistic.) In the second place, it will call attention to the similarity between "considered good by ———" and "approved by ———," a similarity arising from the fact (and for the so-called noncognitive view it is indeed a fact) that X is considered good when and only when it is the object of an actually or potentially expressed approval. And finally, it will go on, roughly but not unacceptably, to its analytic conclusion: it will expand "X is considered good" into "X is approved by ———."

The importance of this observation is evident: it enables us to see that the so-called noncognitive view handles "X is *considered* good" in the same way that relativism attempts to handle "X is good." Accordingly, the so-called noncognitive view not only rejects relativism but also locates its error: it claims that relativism blurs the distinction between the direct discourse of "X is good" and the indirect discourse of "X is considered good," and that it thereafter proceeds to mislead us by handling the former expression as though it were the latter.

If we follow out this criticism we shall find that it is intuitively convincing. All the contentions of relativism, as soon as they are made for "considered good" rather than for "good," become plausible—but also commonplace. It is commonplace, for instance, to maintain that things are often considered good by some people and not by others. For that reminds us, at most, that evaluative problems are often controversial. And it need not even do that: it may show only that a thing is or is not considered good depending on the circumstances that attend it—X being considered good under circumstances C_1, and being considered not good under circumstances C_2. The people who do the considering, in this latter case, need not be engaged in any controversy (cf. p. 77).

Similarly, it is commonplace to maintain that questions about what is considered good can be delegated to the social sciences. The word "considered" pushes *any* question in that direction; for the question then becomes one about what views are *held* by these or those people, and the social sciences can indeed test whether or not they are in fact held.

When a relativist deals with "considered good," then—and the same can be said of "considered right," "considered to be justified," and so on—he tends only to tire our patience. His view becomes surprising only when it is transferred to "good," "right," "justified," and so on; and then, according to the so-called noncognitive view, it is entirely confused.

Indeed, the confusion is such a thorough one that it would be impossible to live by relativism. A consistent relativist, when asked what is good or right, etc., would in effect discuss only what is or was considered good or right, etc., and thus would himself stand committed to no value judgments whatsoever. He would be a nonparticipant on evaluative issues—as no man, in practice, can be.

But we must remember that the relativistic confusion, however curious it may seem to a so-called noncognitivist, is nevertheless very tempting in the social sciences. A social scientist attempts to survey people's evaluations with a temporary detachment—to survey them without as yet taking sides, and thus without as yet participating in the normative issues that they may occasion. So *his* problem is basically different from the problem that he describes. His problem, in short, is concerned with what is *considered* good, whereas the problem that he describes is concerned with what *is* good. By an error parallel to the one that William James called "the psychologist's fallacy," however, he may suppose that his problem is *not* basically different from the one that he describes. And when he yields to this tempting error he may wander from "considered good" to "good" without realizing that he is doing so.

In an important sense of words, then, the so-called noncognitive view defends neither an ordinary relativism nor a methodological relativism. It is an *answer* to relativism; and it can explain, in part at least, why the errors of relativism are tempting ones.

VI. Reflections on John Dewey's Ethics

I

Throughout his ethical writings[1] Dewey has one central purpose—
that of making our moral reflections feel the full force of "the
experimental way of thinking." He belongs, then, to the established
tradition of Hobbes, Hume, Bentham, and Mill: to that extent his
reconstruction of ethics is built on old foundations. But there is also
something new in Dewey's ethics. He insists that empiricism must
explore each and every path that leads from theory to practice and
thus yield an ethics that pragmatically counts for something. And
in telling us how this can be done, Dewey himself summarizes his
views in a single sentence: we must "place *method and means* upon
the level of importance that has, in the past, been imputed exclusively
to ends."[2]

Taken by itself this sentence may seem of modest importance,
recommending merely a change in emphasis. If we dwell on it a
little, however, I think we shall see that it involves much more than
that. For in directing our attention to method and means, Dewey
helps us to see that they must pervade the whole of our ethics. It is
not possible to treat method in a preliminary chapter and means in

1. The following abbreviations are used for books by Dewey: *QC* (*Quest for Certainty*, New York, 1929), *HNC* (*Human Nature and Conduct*, New York, 1922), *RP* (*Reconstruction in Philosophy*, New York, 1950), *DTE* (Dewey and Tufts, *Ethics*, New York, 1908).
2. *QC*, pp. 278, 279.

an appendix. Every aspect of our moral theory, including our very conception of ends, must undergo alteration in the course of his new approach. So Dewey leads us to an ethical empiricism that goes well beyond the older one—an empiricism that, in its future developments, may very well prove to justify his abundant hopes for it.

I shall accordingly devote this essay to tracing the implications of the brief sentence that I have quoted, showing how an increased attention to method and means may be expected to yield important and novel results.

2

Let me begin by looking into Dewey's conception of method—a topic that leads directly into his conception of means, but must first be developed in its own right. In this connection he emphasizes two points: first, that an ethical problem typically arises out of the need of resolving a *conflict in attitudes*, and secondly, that this need can be satisfied, if our problem is to be solved rationally, by an *appeal to consequences*. Taken together, Dewey thinks, these two factors explain the function and nature of ethical deliberation; and he sums up his account of it in an arresting phrase: "Deliberation is a dramatic rehearsal (in imagination) of various competing possible lines of action."[3]

It will be of interest to expand this aspect of Dewey's thought, largely in his own words. His emphasis on a conflict of attitudes is clearly evident when he writes, "The occasion of deliberation is an excess of preferences, not . . . an absence [of them]. . . . We want things that are incompatible with one another; therefore we must make a choice of what we really want." And Dewey adds that our choice of what we really want, which he conceives as tantamount to our reaching an ethical conclusion, is simply "the emergence of a unified preference out of competing preferences."[4]

But a conflict is not resolved, of course, when we yield to some

3. *HNC*, p. 190.   4. *HNC*, p. 193.

preference that, being in the foreground of our attention, makes us forget its relations to our other attitudes. And it is just here that an ethical decision, as Dewey sees it, introduces the second of the two factors that I have mentioned, namely, an appeal to the consequences. By calling the consequences to mind we realize that they too, no less than the action immediately judged, are objects of our attitudes; so we enable our initial attitude to be reinforced or redirected by other ones. Our emerging, unified preference thus takes account of the whole situation that lies before us. This is the function of deliberation in yielding a rational decision. For "rationality," Dewey writes, "is not a force [that works] against impulse and habit, [but is rather] the attainment of a working harmony among diverse desires."[5]

When Dewey discusses his "dramatic rehearsal" he simply presents these two factors—conflict and its resolution by an appeal to consequences—in a manner that emphasizes their interplay. Let me quote him at length:

> We estimate the import or significance of any present desire by forecasting what it would come to . . . if carried out; literally its consequences define its *consequence*, its meaning and importance. But if these consequences were conceived merely as remote . . . their picturing would be as barren of influence on behavior as the mathematical speculations of a disembodied angel. [In actuality] every foreseen result at once stirs our present affections . . . our desires and aversions. [Thus] there is developed a running commentary which stamps values . . . as good or evil. . . . Deliberation is actually an imaginative rehearsal of various courses of conduct. We give way, in our mind, to some impulse; we try, in our mind, some plan. Following its career through various steps, we find ourselves in imagination in the presence of the consequences that would follow; and as we then like and approve, or dislike and disapprove, these consequences, we find the original impulse or plan good or bad[6].

Such is Dewey's conception of method in ethics. He is in part describing, as a psychologist, how we sometimes *do* make ethical decisions. But he is also, as a moralist about method, suggesting

5. *HNC*, p. 196.   6. *DTE*, p. 323.

how we *ought* to proceed; he is advising us to carry out the dramatic rehearsal more frequently, carefully, and systematically than we normally do.

If we look only to the outlines of what Dewey says on this topic, without as yet considering his special manner of developing it, we must acknowledge that it belongs to the *old* part of his empiricism. It italicizes some observations that can be found in Hobbes or Hume. For Hobbes, too, discussed ethical deliberation and pointed out that the "consequences of doing or omitting the thing proposed come successively into our thought, so that we sometimes have an appetite to it, sometimes an aversion to it," and so on.[7] And Hume noted that any initial propensity makes us "cast our view on every side," to "comprehend whatever objects are connected with its original [object] by the relation of cause and effect." Hume added, moreover, that in ethics "it can never the least concern us" to know these relations "if both the causes and effects be indifferent to us."[8]

But if Dewey took his dramatic rehearsal from Hobbes and Hume, he was nevertheless more persistent than they in examining its full complexity, showing that we can profitably take account of its various implications. And if these implications, again, are not always new in the history of ethics, Dewey is nevertheless successful in giving them a fresh vitality and interest.

To substantiate this statement let me turn to a more specific question about ethical method—a question that is discussed quite frequently in Dewey's work and helps to provide the dramatic rehearsal with a corollary.

3

The question that I have in mind is concerned with ethical generalizations—or in other words, with those broad precepts, rules, or principles that are so frequently brought up in the moral discussions of everyday life. How important are these generalizations? To what extent should ethics be concerned with them?

7. Hobbes, *Leviathan*, pt. 1, ch. 6.
8. Hume, *Treatise of Human Nature*, pt. 3, sect. 2.

Here there are three possibilities open to us. The first is that of attempting to dispense with ethical generalizations altogether; but this would represent such an extreme stand that no one, to my knowledge, has ever taken it seriously. The other possibilities make up the two aspects of our not always consistent common sense. One of them defends "action on principle," and indeed, a single-minded devotion to the principle that forbids compromise. The other recommends that a principle be taken only as a tentative guide: it appeals to the maxim "the exception proves the rule"— where "proves," it will be remembered, has its old sense of "tests" rather than its new sense of "establishes."

Now Dewey's stand, with regard to generalizations, may be roughly characterized as one that defends the latter aspect of common sense, opposing it to the former. He wants to give the maxim "the exception proves the rule" a place in our formal ethical theory. In this respect his work reminds us of some views that are now current in England: it reminds us, for instance, of H. L. A. Hart's "defeasible" principles, which make room for a growing set of provisos;[9] or it reminds us of W. D. Ross's prima facie duties, which further consideration may sometimes justify us in leaving undone;[10] or it reminds us of C. D. Broad's right-*tending* characteristics, which may sometimes be offset by wrong-tending ones.[11] Although diverging on points of detail, these writers are alike in their basic aim: they want concepts that will help to free our generalizations from an inflexibility and keep them from overruling the dictates of exceptional cases.

Dewey's procedure, in developing this point, takes the form of comparing ethical generalizations to scientific hypotheses and of insisting that the former, like the latter, stand in a reciprocal relation

9. "Ascription of Responsibility and Rights," *Proceedings of the Aristotelian Society*, 1948–49, pp. 171–94, reprinted in A. G. N. Flew, ed., *Logic and Language*, 1st series (Oxford, 1952). See particularly pp. 174–75 (p. 148).

10. See selections from *The Right and the Good* reprinted in W. Sellers and J. Hospers, eds., *Readings in Ethical Theory* (New York, 1952), particularly p. 183.

11. "Some of the Main Problems of Ethics," reprinted in H. Feigl and W. Sellars, eds., *Readings in Philosophical Analysis* (New York, 1949), particularly p. 552.

to the cases to which we wish to apply them. When a generalization about what is right runs counter to an individual case, we may sometimes wish to conclude, of course, that the individual case is *not* right; but we may also wish to conclude that we need to modify or qualify the generalization. And "it is both astonishing and depressing," Dewey writes, how much of "the energy of mankind" has gone into "fighting for generalizations" and how little of it has gone into revising them "by putting them to the test of action upon them." This view occurs repeatedly in Dewey, being borne out by such a typical passage as the following: "A moral law, like a law of physics, is not something to swear by and stick by at all hazards. . . . Its soundness and pertinence are tested by what happens when it is acted upon. Its claim or authority rests finally upon the imperativeness of the situation that has to be dealt with . . . as any tool achieves dignity in the measure of needs served by it."[12]

There are times, perhaps, when Dewey may seem to exaggerate this point. He speaks of the "supremacy of the individual case" and looks forward to an ethics in which "principles are modified into methods of understanding." This temporarily suggests that he is verging toward the possibility that I have declared too extreme to be taken seriously—the possibility of abandoning generalizations altogether. But taken in their context, these remarks have no such implication. They simply reaffirm the need of testing our generalizations. Dewey speaks of the "supremacy of the individual case" in ethics only as he might speak of the "supremacy of fact" in science— the latter phrase suggesting not that we must banish scientific generalizations, to be sure, but only that we must make our scientific generalization *fit* the facts, progressively revising them to ensure this.

I have suggested that this aspect of Dewey's ethics is closely connected with his dramatic rehearsal, and in particular with the complexities of the dramatic rehearsal, to which he was always sensitive. Let me now briefly trace this connection.

It will be evident that the dramatic rehearsal, potentially at least, requires an appeal to consequences of many sorts—consequences

12. *QC*, pp. 277, 278.

that lie within no *one* special science. The content of our ethical
deliberation, being concerned with the whole course of action that
lies before us, is not exhausted by this or that aspect of psychology,
or biology, or physics, etc., but extends to all the sciences and to the
common sense counterparts of the sciences that we can test in daily
life. For that reason, as Dewey clearly sees, the dramatic rehearsal is
always complicated: it cannot be content with a narrow, specialized
knowledge, but uses the whole man.[13]

And it becomes still more complicated in such ways as this:
Suppose that our deliberation leaves us with a somewhat mingled
attitude toward a certain action. On the whole we approve of it,
but certain of its aspects are not all that we could wish—the action
bringing with it a certain cost, so to speak. We may then appropriately consider various other actions that can attend our proposed
one, hoping that they will remove or reduce its cost. But these
other actions, which in turn may have *their* cost, will require
deliberation as well. Our original dramatic rehearsal, accordingly,
becomes progressively enlarged, generating a family of supple-
mentary ones.[14]

Now in one respect the complexity of the dramatic rehearsal
argues strongly in favour of ethical generalizations. For what are
we to say of the many occasions when, in practice, *we have no time*
to work out individual cases in their own right? To subsume these
cases under a working stock of generalizations, however rough the
generalizations may be, is surely preferable to an invariable policy
of reaching no conclusions about them at all.

But in another respect this same complexity leads us to look
somewhat askance at generalizations. For generalizations, as Dewey

13. *QC*, 273 ff.

14. There are other complexities, of course, that Dewey recognizes. Thus one
may find it pertinent to ask whether a certain desire, which cannot be satisfied directly
without frustrating many other desires, can more easily be satisfied when it is sub-
limated. See *HMC*, pp. 141, 156, 194. The dramatic rehearsal may thus, in its survey
of the total course of action that lies ahead, lead us to consider the causes and effects of
sublimation. It may help us to decide whether or not we (now) "really want" these
sublimations in the kind of person that we are later to *become*.

sees them, do not stand apart from the dramatic rehearsal but are fully subject to it. Our deliberations lead to a generalization when we go through the dramatic rehearsal not for some individual action but rather for a fair statistical sample of a whole *class* of actions. And of course the complexities then become enormous. It will be difficult, for instance, to find any manageable class of actions toward which our attitudes are the same. Each member of the class will have consequences that differ a little from those of the next member; and this difference may, on occasion, make all the difference to our attitudes. So there is every possibility that our generalization will *penalize* certain individual cases—penalize them because of their possibly inessential similarity to the cases on which we have stopped to deliberate. We may easily be mistaken, moreover, in supposing that we have considered a fair statistical sample of the class of actions in question. And in our efforts to deal with a great many cases, we may rehearse each of them quite imperfectly.

The complexities of the dramatic rehearsal, then, reveal at once the advantages and disadvantages of generalizations. And Dewey, wishing to keep the advantages in a way that minimizes the disadvantages, argues for flexible generalizations—ethical generalizations which, like the hypotheses of science, make no pretense of finality and both illuminate and are illuminated by the cases to which we apply them.

Before leaving this topic let me say just a word in criticism of Dewey. Although he grants generalizations an importance, I wonder if he grants them quite enough importance. For if it is sometimes practicable, in judging an individual case, to avoid a *direct* use of generalizations, it is never practicable to avoid an *indirect* use of them. To that extent generalizations are inescapable in ethics. Let me explain this, with attention to the dramatic rehearsal.

Suppose that we should begin our deliberation by giving exclusive attention to an individual case, distrusting any generalization that seems immediately to apply to it. What I am calling a "direct" use of a generalization will then be excluded. But our dramatic rehearsal will lead us to consider the consequences of our individual case; and as these consequences extend on into the future our knowledge of them, unless we are blessed with omniscience, will become less and less specific. We shall know only that such and such a consequence will be likely to fall in class C, another in class C′, and so on, the classes often being quite broad ones. And this immediately introduces the following question:

How can our all too generic knowledge of these consequences have their expected influence—their vectorial force, so to speak—in leading us to decide "what we really want," or in shaping "the emergence of a unified preference out of competing preferences"? It will be "as barren of influence as the mathematical speculations of a disembodied angel," I take it, unless our attitudes are favorable, say, to class C as a whole, and so on; for it is only about these *classes* that we have any knowledge. And it is plainly artificial to suppose that our favor or disfavor of these classes will not be guided by ethical generalizations that we have made in the past. Here we shall be making an "indirect" use of generalizations—a use that does not spare us a rehearsal of our individual case, but enters into that very rehearsal as a *part* of it. We may, to be sure, feel that these generalizations too are flexible and modifiable; but all the same we temporarily use and abide by them—having, indeed, no alternative but to do so, save that of refusing to let our present deliberation be guided by our past ones.

By its very nature, then, the dramatic rehearsal makes generalizations inescapable in ethics, if not directly, then indirectly. Dewey says nothing that denies this, and perhaps he half imqlies it by comparing ethical generalizations to scientific hypotheses—the latter, obviously, being inescapable in science. But the comparison between ethics and science can only be a rough one (in *my* opinion, though *not* in Dewey's) since the dramatic rehearsal, with its preferences and aversions that "stamp values," has no *exact* counterpart in science. Where in science proper does this "stamping" occur? So I could wish that Dewey had worked out this particular part of the comparison in more detail.

It remains possible, of course, to advocate that we test any given generalization by deliberating about a special case of it; for our deliberation about the special case will not lead us to ethical generalizations exclusively, and the generalizations to which it does lead us will in any event be other than the one we are testing. So my criticism in no way questions Dewey's central contention—his contention that our ethical generalizations must often be revised in the course of being applied, and thus guarded from an inflexibility.

4

Let me remind the reader that this essay is developing a single sentence from Dewey—a sentence recommending that we "place *method and means* upon the level of importance that has, in the past, been imputed exclusively to ends." Having spoken of method, let me turn to the related topic of means, and more generally to the "continuity of means and ends" to which Dewey has given so much emphasis.

I find this the most original and important part of Dewey's ethics, but I also find it the part that is least clear. Its unclarity arises, I suspect, from the fact that Dewey cannot control his excitement about it and is tempted to pile one idea upon another without attention to the needed distinctions. So in interpreting his views I must prepare the way by making some observations of my own.

We can readily observe that our colloquial manner of speaking about means and ends is very rough. Both of the words have a meaning that is colored by their context, and only a very persistent study could do justice to their rich ambiguity. But remembering the central position of desires in Dewey's dramatic rehearsal and their function in "stamping values," let us be content to examine "means" and "ends" in the contexts, "desired as a means" and "desired as an end"—our purposes requiring no more than that.

Now in one sense of the words, to desire something as an end is to desire it for its own sake, and to desire it as a means is to desire it for the sake of its consequences. So let me illustrate these notions, taking a very simple example. Suppose that Mr. Smith is planning to make a wooden box to be used for sending a fragile article through the mail. Does he desire the box for its own sake, or for the sake of its consequences? Or rather, let us split up this question into two smaller ones, asking first whether he desires the box *wholly* for its own sake, and secondly whether he desires it *partly* for its own sake; for the words "wholly" and "partly" will make a great difference to our answer.

If we ask whether Smith desires the box wholly for its own sake, we must answer, of course, that he does not. He desires it, partly at least, because it will help him to satisfy another of his desires— namely, his desire to send an article through the mail.

But if we ask whether Smith desires the box *partly* for its own sake, we may quite possibly (though not necessarily, of course) have to answer that he does. He may be an amateur carpenter who takes pleasure in making boxes, finding the product of his handiwork immediately rewarding. Although he wants the box largely in order to use it, he may also want it in some measure for itself. As Smith himself may put it, he is glad that his need of sending something through the mail gave him an "excuse" for making it. In part, then, he may desire it not for its consequences but for its own sake.[15]

Let me now explain how the notion of desiring something for its own sake, wholly or partly, is related to Dewey's ethics. I must immediately make clear that the notion is *not* one that Dewey himself, in the constructive part of his work, wishes to associate with the word "end." Indeed, his own use of "end," for most of his contexts, becomes intelligible only when understood in a quite different sense. But I shall come to this further, typically Deweyan sense of "end" presently, and shall meanwhile continue to discuss the sense that I have been illustrating. My reason for doing so is that Dewey's contexts *sometimes* suggest the sense now in question. That

15. I speak of a man's desiring some *object* for its own sake and not of his desiring certain of his *experiences of* this object for their own sake. If I should extend my analysis to include *experiences of* an object (and the matter is too complicated to permit my developing it here) I should need a distinction parallel to that between "inherent" and "intrinsic" value, as discussed (though always with reference to satisfactions rather than to desires) by C. I. Lewis in his *Knowledge and Valuation* (Chicago, 1946), ch. 14.

is true particularly in the destructive part of his work, where he laments the exaggerated importance that has been given to ends, insisting that writers on ethics have been "curiously hypnotized"[16] by them. I must explain, then, why this familiar, desired-for-its-own-sake sense of "end" fails to impress Dewey—why he deliberately plays down the notion. The explanation is implied, I think, by Dewey's description of the dramatic rehearsal.

5

Let me ask, first, about the status of things desired *wholly* for their own sake. If I interpret Dewey correctly, he takes it for granted that nothing of importance is likely to answer to this description. Or more specifically: he is content with the hypothesis that we *very rarely* desire anything wholly for its own sake, and that in the few cases that we do, we do not do so for very long; for even a brief, imperfect dramatic rehearsal will be sufficient to change our desire into one that is more complicated. Let me explain this by example.

If we are interested in music, do we desire to hear music wholly for its own sake? At first, just possibly, we may; but we must remember that hearing music *has* consequences—if not those of inspiring us, and so on, as some have thought, then at least those of relaxing us and of enabling us to get through life without the inefficiency that attends boredom. Now if on some special occasion we are deliberating on whether or not we should listen to music, our dramatic rehearsal will be likely to reveal some such consequence as the one I have mentioned—a consequence, presumably, that we also desire. So our initial desire to hear the music wholly for its own sake will be transformed to a more complex desire. We may still, of course, desire the music *largely* for its own sake, but we shall also desire it for the sake of the consequences in question. We shall no longer, then, be desiring music *wholly* for its own sake.

The case is even clearer when we consider the large "ends" that have been recommended in traditional ethics. If we are prepared to call these ends at all, we must certainly deny that they are ends in

16. *RP*, p. 131.

the sense of being desired wholly for their own sake. In fact, it may be doubted whether they can, as a psychological possibility, be desired wholly for their own sake; and it may be equally doubted, in consequence, whether there is any point in saying that they *ought* to be so desired. Take, for instance, the greatest happiness of the greatest number. I have no doubt that many people desire this, in altruism, *partly* for its own sake; but I suspect that they also desire it partly for its consequences—its consequences, say, in promoting a social cooperation that will affect (given the dependence of one group of people on another) the happiness of their family and their friends. And the happiness of their family and their friends pretty certainly counts for more, in any dramatic rehearsal that constitutes their deliberations, than the happiness of those whom they have never met or want to meet. They desire the happiness of all, in short, *in part as a means* to the happiness of a very small group. And in general, if we ask whether anyone can desire the greatest happiness of the greatest number *wholly* for its own sake, I think we must answer that the probability of it is close to zero.

Perhaps that is why Dewey speaks of the utilitarians with qualified admiration. "Upon the whole," he writes, "utilitarianism has marked the best in the transition from the classic theory . . . to what is now possible. . . . It made moral good natural, humane, in touch with the natural goods of life . . . but it was still profoundly affected in fundamental points by old ways of thinking. It never questioned the idea of a fixed, final and supreme end."[17] Just what "fixed, final, and supreme end" means here requires interpretation; but if Dewey took it to imply something that we were expected to desire wholly for its own sake—and perhaps even the *only* thing we were expected to desire (whether wholly or partly) for its own sake—then we can readily see, from what I have said above, why his emphasis on the dramatic rehearsal, together with a psychology respectful of common sense, would have led him to reject any such end as foreign to human nature.

17. *RP*, p. 143.

6

I have so far been speaking only of things desired *wholly* for their own sake and have tried to show why Dewey might understandably have felt that they are too rare and transient to be of interest. But I have still to discuss things desired *partly* for their own sake. Why does Dewey not make *these* central to his ethics? Why does he not suggest that they are to be considered a man's ends, and thus acknowledge that the dramatic rehearsal is merely a way of discovering the means to these ends?

The answer, of course, cannot take the form of saying that things desired in part for their own sake are too rare and transient to be of interest. Quite evidently, they are not rare. We have found instances of them in Mr. Smith's box, and in music, and (for altruists) in the greatest happiness of the greatest number. And examples can easily be multiplied. A patron of a French restaurant, for instance, normally likes eating partly for its own sake and not just as a means of surviving. A man who takes his daily walk normally likes walking partly for its own sake and not just as a means of getting somewhere, or as a means of improving his health. And so on. In each of these cases, moreover, the desire in question may *continue* to be of a partly-for-its-own-sake kind; it need not be only transiently of that kind.

But we can still explain why Dewey did not emphasize things desired partly for their own sake—or why, rather, he did not discuss them in the way moralists have traditionally discussed "ends." His procedure is guided, I think, by the realization that things desired partly for their own sake are altogether *too numerous* to be discussed in such a manner. They include a large percentage of the things that we desire in any way whatsoever. Such a view can readily be ascribed to Dewey. He thinks that each successive consequence, as it is brought to our attention by the dramatic rehearsal, is likely to introduce a new force in shaping our "emerging, unified preference"; and to whatever extent a consequence can do this, even before *its* consequences are envisaged in their turn, it will be moving us with immediacy.[18] Things partly desired for their own sake, then, are so ubiquitous that they require little discussion beyond that given to objects of desire in general. This holds true, of course, not only of desires but of all attitudes, whether favorable or unfavorable.[19]

We must especially notice, in this connection, that the degree to which we desire something for its own sake is not at all a measure of the degree to which we desire it "all things considered." Our desire for it may grow stronger, or grow weaker, or become nullified, as we take into account the total situation in which its object arises. A man who likes skiing for its own sake, for instance, may like it all the more if he thinks it is good for his health. Or alternatively, he may like it rather less, or not at all, if he thinks it takes so much time that it keeps him from doing his work. And the same is true even for much stronger desires. A man who wants to survive partly for its own sake, no matter how strong this impulse may be, will normally want to survive all the more if he thinks that his children need his support. And alternatively, he may be less moved by his survival, knowingly risking it, if he thinks it can be purchased only at the expense (say) of his patriotism.

Evidently, then, our ethical deliberation will be decidedly incomplete if we select some one thing that we desire partly for its own sake—even if we desire it very strongly in that way—and limit our deliberation to a discovery of the means of obtaining it. That would represent a "one-way logic," which Dewey finds tolerable only when it is fully recognized as a temporary oversimplification.

18. *HNC*, p. 192.

19. For simplicity, I tend throughout the paper to deal only with favorable attitudes, treating unfavorable ones by implication. A full account would point out that (1) we may favor something partly for its own sake and partly for the sake of its consequences, or (2) we may favor something partly for its own sake, and favor it on the whole, *in spite of* our disfavor of some of its consequences, or (3) we may favor something partly for its own sake but disfavor it on the whole because of our disfavor of its consequences, and so on for other possibilities, in all of which the consequences make a difference to our emerging favor or disfavor. My discussion is schematized, then, in that it attends only to (1) above.

For no matter what we select, it will be likely to have its cost of maintenance, so to speak, and also its purchase cost; and for all we know, these costs, when examined, will impress us as too high. Indeed, when deliberation is conceived as a dramatic rehearsal it is never just a way of finding how to satisfy some specially privileged desire. It is rather a way of deciding whether or not to yield to this desire—a matter that depends on the way in which it fits in with our other attitudes.

This observation, which I read off as it were from Dewey's account of the dramatic rehearsal, helps us to see why Dewey was so insistent on cause-and-effect relationships. It is psychologically unsound, he thinks, to say of any one thing desired partly for its own sake, "that is all that really matters, as I can fully realize even before examining the causal milieu in which it stands." For any such thing will at most simply be *one* of the *many* things that really matter. And we are not in a position to say even that about it until we have seen it in its causal milieu—in the total course of action of which it constitutes only one aspect, and an aspect toward which our initial desire may change, once the other aspects of the total course of action have been taken into account.

For a Deweyan conception of ethics, in short, an appeal to the consequences must be introduced at the very beginning of ethics. For if we are to leave them until later, what are we to discuss before then? Clearly, we can only go on in the old, impractical way, discussing purportedly privileged objects of desire, such as survival, social happiness, etc.—objects that we shall attempt to privilege without as yet having fresh knowledge of the causal milieu which, through a dramatic rehearsal, is essential in helping us to decide whether or not we really *want* to privilege them.

7

I have so far been discussing "ends" only in a sense that connects the term with things desired for their own sake; and I have been explaining why Dewey, in the passages where he seems to be using this familiar sense, insists that traditional ethics has made too much of ends. For if the ends are expected to be desired wholly for their own sake, then there virtually *cannot* be such ends—not, at least, for long. And if they are expected, merely, to be desired in part for their own sake, then they will be too numerous to require special attention; nor will it be feasible, in deciding whether or not to pursue some one of these (partial) ends, to begin by abstracting it (as has so often been done in traditional ethics) from the causal milieu in which it stands.

And yet it is a pity to allow a familiar word like "end" to have a sense for which one has little use. So in the constructive parts of his work Dewey proceeds to divert the term to quite another sense. He gives us very little notice, unfortunately, of having done so; and his work becomes confusing on that account. But I think it is possible from his contexts to see what sense he has in mind. It is a sense not at variance with *one* of the many senses that are in common use; but to distinguish it from other senses I shall use the longer term, "end in view."[20]

An end in view is often desired partly for its own sake, but that is not at all an essential feature of it. If it should happen to be desired entirely for the sake of its consequences, it could (for this sense) still be called an end. Its essential features are these: In the first place it is taken, quite temporarily and tentatively and in a special set of circumstances, to be a privileged object of desire—or in other words, an object of desire that is not likely, so one suspects, to be redirected or outweighed by various other desires that deliberation may have as yet left out of account. In the second place, it tends to have a prominent place in one's conscious attention—the sort of place that makes one ask, "how can I obtain this?" as distinct from the question, "will I be likely, when I have deliberated further, to find that I really want to obtain it?"

We can find a simple example of an end in view, then, by returning to Mr. Smith, who it will be remembered wanted a wooden box suitable for sending something through the mail.

20. *HNC*, p. 225.

Initially, Mr. Smith presumably did not take the box as his end in view. But after he had designed it and was left with the task of making it, he presumably did. That is to say, he presumably assumed that his desire for the box would be unlikely to need reconsideration; and he let it predominate in his attention in a way that guided his selection of means—means that included buying the necessary wood, sharpening his tools, and so on.

Any such end, of course, soon gives place to another; so, as Dewey puts it, "ends are endless."[21] Once Mr. Smith finished making his box, for instance, he doubtless considered it as a means to another end in view—namely, that of getting an article into the hands of a friend. And once the latter end in view had been obtained, Smith doubtless became concerned about still another, wanting (say) to have his friend use the article in a special way. And so on.

I think my remarks are quite faithful to Dewey's own discussion of ends in view. Thus he writes: "Means and ends are two names for the same reality. The terms denote not a division in reality but a distinction in judgment."[22] And we have just seen this by example, where the same reality, Smith's box, was taken now as an end and now as a means. Again, Dewey writes that we must "advance to a belief in a plurality of changing, moving, individualized . . . ends."[23] And from the same example it will be evident that ends in view, as above defined, can readily be described in this way.

Dewey's ends in view are important, in my opinion, chiefly for showing how we can safely attempt to escape, temporarily, from the *complexities* of the dramatic rehearsal. We cannot go on, indefinitely, with our deliberations about whether or not to yield to certain desires, but must often, in practice, let them freely move us, and set about finding the means of satisfying them. So we temporarily privilege their objects, taking them as ends in view. Yet we need not privilege them once and for all. That would be typical of the old procedure in ethics, involving a conception of an end to which Dewey is hostile. Rather, we can privilege them for the moment, and tentatively, permitting a renewed dramatic

21. *HNC*, p. 232.   22. *HNC*, p. 36.   23. *RP*, p. 132.

rehearsal to correct our procedure whenever occasion for further deliberation arises.

What I have been saying about ends serves by implication, of course, to show why Dewey places so much emphasis on means. The implications are not quite so straightforward as they may at first seem, however, so let me make them more explicit.

Evidently, an attention to means is always important if we are actually to *reach* an end in view. Mr. Smith will never make his box if he does not think about how to make it, and quite similarly, but on a larger scale, a man will never make the world safe for democracy unless he thinks about how to do *that*. But however important these means to ends in view may be, it is not they alone that Dewey wants to emphasize. They are not, in his opinion, the sort of means that are most central to ethics. Nor must Dewey's varying uses of the word "means" be allowed to conceal this from us.

We have a more important and typical concern with means, in ethics, when instead of merely *implementing* some end in view, we are considering whether or not we need to *revise* the end in view. I am not speaking of cases where we have secured one of our ends and are simply going on to another. I am speaking of cases that are similar to those I have mentioned earlier, in discussing costs of purchase and of maintenance—cases, where having for some time sought means to an end in view, we pause to deliberate about the means, to decide how much we like *them*, and to consider whether our end in view really justifies them—or again, cases when we pause to see our end in view in the light of *still further consequences*, and consider whether the latter call our old end in view into question. Such a case arises, trivially, when Mr. Smith begins to wonder whether or not to make his box—either because he finds it unexpectedly hard to obtain the needed sort of wood or because he learns that his friend does not want the article that he is planning to send him. It arises, nontrivially, in any college where an instructor's end in view of keeping his job can be secured only by means of concealing his opinions from his colleagues, and where keeping his job will have the further result of forcing him to teach only half-truths to his students.

You will note that the "means" in these latter examples are much more than means to some temporarily unquestioned end in view. They deal with the full causal milieu in which *any* object of desire *always* stands. And Dewey's insistence on the importance of means, so conceived, is simply his reiteration of our need to guide our desires in the light of all possible knowledge—a procedure that, as we have seen, requires us to reckon with consequences from the very start. There can be no thought, in a Deweyan ethics, of leaving means, in this broad sense, to be considered "later," and "by others."

8

I have been discussing, let me say once more, Dewey's recommendation that we "place *method and means* upon the level of importance that has, in the past, been imputed exclusively to ends." I want now briefly to point out, with a dogmatism imposed by the necessity for brevity, in what respects Dewey's views lead to a more *practical* ethics.

The practicability of his modifiable, flexible generalizations is too obvious, I trust, to need further mention. The practicability of his work on means, which needs italicizing, springs largely from the fact that it helps us to realize, in ethics, that we need not be pre-occupied with vast generalities—generalities that deal with survival, say, or with the greatest happiness of the greatest number. No such thing, we have seen, can be desired wholly for its own sake, with everything else desired wholly as a means to it; so there is no point in saying that it ought to be so desired. It can be desired only in part for its own sake, and at most, then, can be taken only as a particularly strong end in view. But why, in that case, need we be so preoccupied with it? For it would be such a vast, remote end in view that we should be likely to get thoroughly lost in our efforts to implement it with means. And besides, in deciding whether we really wanted to accept it as an end in view, we should have to examine *its* consequences—again an undertaking where we should be likely to get lost.

Meanwhile we have far more practical alternatives. One is that of developing a meta-ethics—or, in other words, that of clarifying what ethical judgments mean and of seeing what methods can be used in establishing them. A great part of Dewey's ethics is just that. It says, in effect: "Draw such ethical conclusions as you will, but at least consider whether the *methods* here proposed—methods that make use of the whole of one's empirical knowledge of guiding desires—are not really the ones that you will find most useful."

The other practical alternative is that of favoring generalizations that are at most middle-sized—generalizations dealing not with anything of the magnitude of the greatest happiness of the greatest number, but rather with such issues, for instance, as how we ought to educate children, or how we ought to revise our conceptions of democracy, or what stand we ought to take on freedom of speech. On this level of generality the difficulties of handling any substantial part of the course of action before us are still great; but they are no longer so difficult that they need cause us to become lost. You will realize that Dewey himself has written much on these topics; and by his conceptions it is they, rather than vast, allegedly ultimate ones, that moral philosophy has to be concerned with. Else philosophy's proposed ideals will do no more than "serve vaguely to arouse 'aspiration,' "[24] without providing our aspiration with any ascertained direction.

Since the second World War we have had much work on meta-ethics; but we have had, quite regrettably in my opinion, very little work by philosophers that resembles Dewey's work within ethics proper. Perhaps that is because, on these relatively specific topics, one so *obviously* has to know so much about cause and effect relationships. Most philosophers still like to feel that they have a special subject matter, well insulated from anything that the social

24. *QC*, p. 279.

scientists, and scientists in general, have to tell them. That is not healthy for philosophy; and it is all too likely to lead to an ethics that continues, as of old, to plead for its ultimates—the fact that one is totally ineffectual being decently concealed by an impressive terminology. Let us hope that Dewey's influence will help to counteract this.

9

In concluding this essay, I should like to point out that I have invariably related my remarks on method and means to the dramatic rehearsal—doing so, of course, simply because Dewey does. Had I time to develop this further, I should want to become more critical, discussing whether or not the dramatic rehearsal is as important as Dewey supposes. In particular, I should like to question Dewey's wisdom in emphasizing "personal problems" in ethics (or problems that arise when a man is simply making up his own mind about what he "really wants") as distinct from "interpersonal problems" (or problems that arise when one man "really wants" something and another man "really wants" something else, the two things being incompatible). For suppose one man's dramatic rehearsal leads him to act in favor of racial discrimination, say, and another man's dramatic rehearsal leads him to act against it. This certainly involves an ethical issue; and Dewey's methodology for ethics, though it may have implications with regard to such an issue, never works them out explicitly.

But in developing this latter part of meta-ethics I should have to introduce many topics that I have discussed elsewhere. I should have to discuss disagreement in attitude, for instance, which is reminiscent of a Deweyan conflict writ large. And I should have to discuss the aspects of our language that permit us to express and evoke attitudes—those same attitudes which Dewey quite properly reckons with in his account of the dramatic rehearsal, and yet somehow forgets, in his emphasis on prediction, in explaining what ethical judgments can be taken to mean. But these topics make up far too long a story, so let me add no more than this remark:

If Dewey's conception of method in ethics is curiously incomplete, it nevertheless impresses me, so far as it goes, as genuinely insightful. Its implications with regard to the flexibility of generalizations and with regard to the importance of refusing, from the very start, to consider ends independently of means, are likely to demand attention in any ethics that is respectful of an empirical psychology. And if we may hope that Dewey's work will eventually take its established place in the ethical tradition, we may also hope, and with confidence, that ethics will eventually cease to be confined to the classroom and the library and will take on an active role in guiding our practical life.

VII. Moore's Arguments against Certain Forms of Ethical Naturalism

In the third chapter of his *Ethics*,[1] G. E. Moore gave several arguments to show that "right" and "wrong" do not refer merely to the feelings or attitudes of the person who uses them. During later years he has become more and more sensitive to the flexibilities of ordinary language, and I doubt whether he would still maintain that "right" and "wrong" are *never* so used. But perhaps he would still take seriously the view that *if* a man uses these terms in that way, he is not using them in any sense that is relevant to the issues with which moralists usually deal. Interpreting some of his arguments in a way that makes them support this latter contention, I wish to determine how much they prove.

2

The contention of the arguments, stated more formally, is that the definitions,

D1: "X is right" has the same meaning as "I approve of X," and,

D2: "X is wrong" has the same meaning as "I disapprove of X,"[2] where "I" in the definiens is to be taken to refer to whoever uses the

1. New York, 1912. (The present essay was written before Moore's death in 1958).

2. The words "approve" and "disapprove" may be taken to designate feelings which the speaker *tends* to have, thereby permitting him to speak truthfully about his present approval or disapproval even though he has no strong immediate feelings at the time. Moore has mentioned this in connection with Westermarck, in *Philosophical Studies*, p. 332.

terms defined, are definitions that distort or ignore the senses that are of most importance to normative ethics.

If Moore's arguments were successful in proving this contention, they would undoubtedly be of interest. There is presumably some roughly intelligible sense, or set of senses, in which not only professional writers on normative ethics, but also "amateur moralists" of all sorts, are earnestly trying to decide what is right or wrong and to argue such matters with others. These people would be helped by definitions that freed their usage of "right" and "wrong" from confusions. They would not be helped, however, by definitions that made these terms refer to something quite foreign to the issues which, confusedly envisaged though these may be, are troublesome to them. If D1 and D2, above, did this and if they were insistently introduced into any ordinary ethical argument, they might only lead people to "change the subject" of their argument, and might do so in a way that would escape attention, because the old words would still be used. They might be "issue-begging" definitions.

This consideration is not, of course, unanswerable. A theorist might reply that the way in which people usually use "right" and "wrong" is *totally* confused—that no clear issue could ever be salvaged from the ordinary sort of ethical argument. He might then wish to *give* the terms a meaning in accordance with D1 and D2, not hoping to remain "faithful" to the confusions of common usage, but hoping rather to shock people into realizing that if they do not use his sense, or naturalistic ones like it, they will be dealing with pseudo-problems. In the same way a behaviorist might define "soul" in terms of processes in the higher nervous system. His purpose (whatever one may think of it) would presumably be to shock people into believing, with him, that "soul" must either mean something like this or else be a label for a confusion.

One *might* proceed in that way, but I for one do not wish to do so. Although ethical terms are used in a manifestly confused way, it is certainly ill-advised to cry "total confusion" until all alternatives are carefully tested. It is well, in beginning, to assume that the ethical terms, as usually used, are *not* totally confused. This assumption will lead us to *look for* some salvageable element in their usage. Unless we look for it, we cannot be sure whether or not it exists, and whether or not that very element is the one which presents normative ethics with its most characteristic difficulties. So let us assume, at least for the present, that ethical terms are not totally confused; and let us further assume that *if* Moore's arguments correctly prove his contention—if D1 and D2 distort or ignore the senses that are most interesting to writers on moral matters—then these definitions are question-begging and productive of even greater confusions, rather than of more clearly envisaged issues.

3

The first argument may be formulated, without significantly altering the force of Moore's own words,[3] as follows:

(1) It may happen that one man, A, approves of X, and another man, B, disapproves of X.

(2) Thus according to D1 and D2, above, A may say "X is right," and B, "X is wrong," and both be telling the truth.[4]

3. *Ethics*, p. 91: "If, whenever I judge an action to be right, I am merely judging that I myself have a particular feeling towards it, then it plainly follows that, provided I really have the feeling in question, my judgment is true, and therefore the action really is right. And what is true of me, in this respect, will also be true of any other man. . . . It strictly follows, therefore, from this theory that whenever *any man whatever* really has a particular feeling towards an action, the action really is right; and whenever *any man whatever* really has another particular feeling towards an action, the action really is wrong." And, p. 93: "If we take into account a second fact, it seems plainly to follow that . . . the same action must be quite often both right and wrong. This second fact is merely the observed fact, that it seems difficult to deny, that, whatever pair of feelings or single feeling we take, cases do occur in which two different men have opposite feelings towards the same action."

4. According to the usual conventions of logic, an "X" may not undergo substitution when it occurs between quotation marks. For the present, however, I wish "X" to be used in a different way. If the reader should erase the mark "X," whether it occurs between quotation marks or not, and replace it, *throughout*, by some one name of a particular action, with the assumption that that name is perfectly unambiguous, he would then have the sort of argument that I intend. This explanation will serve to indicate what I mean in saying that "X is right" may tell the truth. I simply mean that that expression, when the first letter of it is replaced by a name, may tell the truth.

(3) Hence if "right" and "wrong" are used in accordance with D1 and D2, X may be both right and wrong.

(4) But if "right" and "wrong" are used in any typical ethical sense, then X cannot be both right and wrong. (This is evident to "inspection."[5])

(5) Therefore the sense ascribed to "right" and "wrong" by D1 and D2 is not any typical ethical sense.

Criticism of the first argument must be concerned with the way in which Moore can get to step (3). Is it possible, using innocent premises and valid logic, to prove that if "right" and "wrong" are used in accordance with D1 and D2, X may be both right and wrong? We may properly suspect that it is not possible, simply because a quite different conclusion may be derived from D1 and D2. The last part of (3), namely,

(a) X may be both right and wrong,

becomes equivalent by D1 and D2 (as can be seen by simple substitution, with only trivial grammatical changes) to

(b) I may both approve and disapprove of X.

This latter statement can, within the limits of linguistic propriety, be taken as a contradiction. Hence D1 and D2 imply that (a) may be taken as a contradiction. One may accordingly urge that

(3x) If "right" and "wrong" are used in accordance with D1 and D2, X cannot possibly be both right and wrong.

Note that this conclusion, so far from pointing to a way in which D1 and D2 distort ordinary usage, points to a way in which they are faithful to it. Note further that if we should accept both (3x) and also Moore's (3), we should have to conclude that D1 and D2 imply the contradiction that X may and also cannot possibly be both right and wrong. Now whether or not D1 and D2 distort ordinary usage, it is scarcely plausible that such innocent definitions should imply so flagrant a contradiction. Hence, if we accept the derivation of (3x), we may properly suspect some error in Moore's derivation of (3).

5. *Ethics*, pp. 86 ff.

One *need* not, of course, maintain that (b) above is a contradiction; and since we habitually try to make consistent sense out of any utterance, we might be led to more charitable interpretations. We might take it as a paradoxical way of saying, "I may approve of certain aspects of X, and also may disapprove of other aspects of it"; or we might take it as testifying to a possible conflict of attitudes—a paradoxical way of saying, "certain of my impulses may lead me to approve of X, but others may lead me to disapprove of it." But if we are content to make these more charitable interpretations of (b), may we not make similarly charitable interpretations of (a), and so proceed to question (4) in the argument? If there is any reason against this Moore certainly leaves it unmentioned. And in any case there is certainly one way, and a linguistically appropriate way, of interpreting (b) as a contradiction; hence for one use of the definiens, D1 and D2 have not been shown to distort ordinary usage. The definitions may still be objectionable, but Moore's first argument has by no means shown that they are.

It is interesting to see just where Moore's derivation of (3)—in my own, but I think faithful, statement of his first argument—is invalid. This step seems to follow from (2), which in turn is perfectly correct; but it seems to follow only because of a confusion about pronouns.[6] In (2), which reads, "according to D1 and D2, A may say, 'X is right,' and B may say, 'X is wrong,' and both be telling the truth," the words "right" and "wrong" occur in direct quotations. Hence the word "I," which by D1 and D2 is implicit in the use of the ethical terms, is appropriately taken as referring not to Moore, or any one speaker, but rather to the people quoted as having judged that X was right or wrong. The "I" implicit in "right" refers to A, and the "I" implicit in "wrong" refers to B. But in (3), which may be abridged as, "according to D1 and D2, X may be both right and wrong," the words "right" and "wrong" are not quoted

6. The confusion is one which often attends the use of what Nelson Goodman has called "indicator words." My criticism of Moore's first argument is largely a matter of applying Goodman's work to a special case. See chapter XI of his *The Structure of Appearance*.

by Moore as having been used by somebody else. Hence by D1 and D2 themselves, which are to the effect that ethical terms refer to the speaker who uses them (as distinct from a speaker who quotes how others used them), the implicit "I" in (3) refers not first to A and then to B, but rather to Moore, or whoever it is that says "X may be both right and wrong." Briefly, the implicitly quoted "I's" in (2) do not refer to the same person as the implicit and unquoted "I's" refer to in (3). By assuming that they do Moore makes an invalid step in his argument appear valid.

This point can helpfully be put in another way. It would seem that

(a1) If "X is right," said by A, is true, then X is right.

And that

(a2) If "X is wrong," said by B, is true, then X is wrong.

And it is certainly true that *if* (a1) and (a2) were both true, and *if* their antecedents could both be true, then their consequents could both be true. Thus if D1 and D2 entitled one to accept (a1) and (a2) and also entitled one to accept as possible the conjunction of their antecedents, it would entitle one to accept as possible the conjunction of their consequents, or in other words, to assert that X might be both right and wrong. This is what Moore, by (3), seems to maintain, in part. But unfortunately for Moore's argument, D1 and D2 entitle one to accept *neither* (a1) *nor* (a2). For by D1, (a1) is like:

If "I approve of X," said by A, is true, then I approve of X.

And by D2, (a2) is like:

If "I disapprove of X," said by B, is true, then I disapprove of X.

And neither of these statements is true, so long as the quoted 'I's" in the antecedents each have a different referent from that of the unquoted "I's" in the consequents. It will thus appear that Moore, who tacitly presupposes (a1) and (a2) in getting from step (2) to step (3) in his argument, fails to show that D1 and D2 lead to what, for ordinary usage, would be an absurdity. In the course of showing the alleged absurdity, he unknowingly rejects an implication of these definitions with regard to the falsity of (a1) and (a2), and so, in effect, *rejects* the definitions in the very course of an argument that tries to show the absurdity of what their *acceptance* would imply.

If D1 and D2 had read, respectively,

"X is right" has the same meaning as "*Somebody* approves of X," and

"X is wrong" has the same meaning as "*Somebody* disapproves of X,"

where the "somebody" could be a different person in each case, then Moore would be entitled to step (3), and his argument would be correct in showing that *these* naturalistic definitions distort ordinary usage, so long as (4) is granted. But in showing merely that, he would leave untouched the far more interesting definitions that D1 and D2 actually provide.

Moore must be granted step (2) in his argument. By D1 and D2, A may say, "X is right," and B, "X is wrong," and both be telling the truth. And it may be that Moore could proceed *in another* way from that point on to show that these definitions violate ordinary ethical usage. But the only other plausible way, I think, is that which Moore himself develops in his third argument, as here listed; and that must be discussed in its proper place.

4

The second argument may be formulated, again not in Moore's own words,[7] but in words which are faithful, no doubt, to their import, as follows:

7. *Ethics*, p. 97: "An action [which a man] formerly regarded with . . . disapproval, he may now regard with . . . approval, and *vice versa*. So that, for this reason alone, and quite apart from differences of feeling between different men, we shall have to admit, according to our theory [i.e. the definitions criticized in the argument in question] that it is often *now* true of an action that it *was* right, although it was formerly true of the same action that it *was* wrong."

I have tried to preserve the force of these words in steps (1) and (2) of my formulation of the argument. It will be obvious that I have taken liberties; but Moore's words become so entangled with the tense of verbs, as well as with "now" and "formerly," and the notion of "truth at one time but not another," that a more complete investigation into what he actually may have meant would be impossible in limited space. The notion of "truth at a time" and the other sources of confusion are exhaustively

(1) A may be telling the truth if he says, "I now approve of X, but I formerly disapproved of X."

(2) Hence, by D1 and D2, A may be telling the truth if he says, "X is now right, but X was formerly wrong."

(3) But in any sense of "right" and "wrong" that is typically ethical, A may *not* tell the truth in saying "X is now right but X was formerly wrong." This could truthfully be said, perhaps, if each "X" in the statement referred to a *different* action of the *same kind*, for a present and former X could have different consequences; but it would be contradictory, in any ordinary sense of the terms, if "X" referred throughout, as is here intended, to the very same action. (This is evident to "inspection.")

(4) Therefore the sense ascribed to "right" and "wrong" by D1 and D2 is not any typical ethical sense.

Criticism of the second argument must be concerned with the derivation of step (2). This seems to follow directly from (1) by substitution in accordance with D1 and D2; but in fact it also requires "corollaries," so to speak, of D1 and D2, namely:

D1c: "X was (formerly) right" has the same meaning as "I (formerly) approved of X,"

and

D2c: "X was (formerly) wrong" has the same meaning as "I (formerly) disapproved of X."

These definitions differ from D1 and D2 only in that the temporal reference, in both definiendum and definiens, is shifted from present to past.[8] It is readily obvious that (2) follows from (1), granted that

analyzed by Goodman, though without any specific reference to Moore, in *The Structure of Appearance*; the reader interested in pursuing these matters will do well to refer to that work. Meanwhile I can only dogmatize in saying that if I had been more faithful to Moore's words I should have had more fallacies to untangle than my present formulation of the argument involves.

Steps (3) and (4) in my formulation are parallels to the remarks in *Ethics*, pp. 86 and 81 ff.

8. In point of fact, only D2c is needed for the inference from (1) to (2), together with D1; but I list D1c as well simply because the argument could so easily be recast in a way that would require it.

D1 and D2 are taken to have the above "corollaries," and since I accept the remainder of the argument—though not without hesitations about (3)—I accept the argument. But I do so *only* with the proviso that D1c and D2c are understood to be implied by D1 and D2.

Now it is certainly a natural thing to assume that D1 and D2 *do* imply D1c and D2c. But there is another possibility which is of no little interest. One might insist that "right" and "wrong" always refer to the attitudes that the speaker has *at the time that he uses the words*. Any temporal reference in a sentence that includes these words might always be taken as referring to the time at which the action said to be "right" or "wrong" *occurred*, rather than to the time at which it was *approved*. Such a view is provided by the following definitions, which are revised versions of D1 and D2:

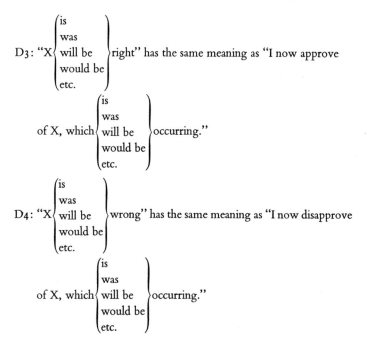

D3: "X $\begin{cases} \text{is} \\ \text{was} \\ \text{will be} \\ \text{would be} \\ \text{etc.} \end{cases}$ right" has the same meaning as "I now approve

of X, which $\begin{cases} \text{is} \\ \text{was} \\ \text{will be} \\ \text{would be} \\ \text{etc.} \end{cases}$ occurring."

D4: "X $\begin{cases} \text{is} \\ \text{was} \\ \text{will be} \\ \text{would be} \\ \text{etc.} \end{cases}$ wrong" has the same meaning as "I now disapprove

of X, which $\begin{cases} \text{is} \\ \text{was} \\ \text{will be} \\ \text{would be} \\ \text{etc.} \end{cases}$ occurring."

Note that by these definitions one cannot say anything equivalent to "I approv*ed* of X" by using "right," unless, perhaps, in such an idiom as "I used to feel X to be right."

It is easy to see that if the second argument were rewritten with references to D1 and D2 replaced by references to D3 and D4, the argument would not be valid. (2) would then not follow from (1). For the statement,

X is (now) right, but X was formerly wrong,

would be equivalent, according to D3 and D4, with direct substitution, to,

I now approve of X, which is occurring (now), but I now disapprove of X, which was occurring formerly.

This latter statement could not be true, either on account of the incompatible attitudes asserted or because of the impossibility of making X refer to the same action.[9] Hence the former statement, being equivalent to the latter, could not be true. But according to (2), in the rewritten argument, the former statement *might* be true; for (2) would read:

By D3 and D4, A may be telling the truth if he says, "X is now right but X was formerly wrong."

Hence (2), being false, could not follow from the innocent premise, (1); and with the collapse of (2) comes the collapse of the remainder of the argument.

Accordingly, although Moore's second argument holds against D1 and D2, provided that certain rather natural assumptions are made about the temporal references involved, it does not hold against D3 and D4, which specifically rule out such assumptions. Since Moore thinks that his argument holds against *any* definition that makes "right" and "wrong" refer solely to the attitudes of the speaker, it is clear that he presses the argument for more than it is worth.

9. I am assuming (as one common idiom, at least, permits me to) that the time taken in uttering this sentence is not sufficient to prevent the "nows" from referring all to the same time, and is not sufficient to justify the change in tense from "is" to "was."

I do not wish to defend D3 and D4 as they stand; for on grounds different from Moore's I consider them misleading, and likely to make people overlook the central issues of ethics. But I do wish to defend these definitions from *Moore's* objections. By so doing I shall be free, as I otherwise should not, to amend the definitions in a very simple way, quite without mention of nonnatural qualities, and thereby make them give (as closely as the vagueness of ordinary usage will allow) *one* sense, at least, that I consider to be typically ethical. This will be explained later.

There is one curious consequence of D3 and D4, suggested by Moore's second argument, which may more plausibly cast doubt on the conventionality of these definitions. If A, speaking at a time, t1, should say,

(a) X is right,

and speaking at a later time, t2, should say,

(b) X was wrong,

then his second statement *would not contradict* the first. For by D3 and D4, (a) and (b) would become,

(aa) I now approve of X, which is occurring,

and

(bb) I now disapprove of X, which was occurring.

These statements, if A makes them, respectively, at t1 and t2, are compatible: for the "now" in (aa) would not refer to the same time as the "now" in (bb). And "X" might designate (as it must to make these considerations of interest) the very same action in both statements; since the change from "is occurring" in (aa) to "was occurring" in (bb) would testify to nothing more than that t1, at which (aa) was said, was earlier than t2, at which (bb) was said. Hence, since (aa), said by A at t1, would be compatible with (bb), said by A at t2, it follows, by D3 and D4, that (a), said by A at t1, is compatible with (b), said by A at t2. And *if* (a) and (b) are not compatible, under any circumstances of utterance, so long as "right" and "wrong" are used in any typical ethical sense, then it *would* follow that D3 and D4 do not preserve any typical ethical sense. But is it so obvious that (a) and (b), uttered in the way mentioned, are not compatible? My "inspection" is not so final on this matter as Moore's might be; but further discussion of this point will be easier after we deal with the third argument, to which we must now turn.

5

The third argument[10] may be formulated as follows:

(1) If A says, "I approve of X," and B says, "I do not approve of X," their statements are logically compatible.

(2) Hence, by D3 and D4,[11] if A says, "X is right," and B says, "X is not right," their statements are logically compatible.

(3) Thus, according to D3 and D4, if A says, "X is right," and B says, "X is not right," A and B, so far as these statements show, do *not* differ in opinion.

(4) But if A says, "X is right," and B says, "X is not right," then, in any typical sense of the terms, they *do* differ in opinion, so far as these statements show.

(5) Therefore D3 and D4 do not give any typical ethical sense of the terms they define.

Criticism of the third argument must be concerned with the inference from (2) to (3), and with the truth of (4). The inference from (2) to (3) is one that Moore would justify, no doubt, by the assumption:

10. *Ethics*, pp. 100 ff.: "If, when one man says, 'This action is right,' and another answers, 'No, it is not right,' each of them is always merely making an assertion about *his own* feelings, it plainly follows that there is never really any difference of opinion between them: the one of them is never really contradicting what the other is asserting. They are no more contradicting one another than if, when one had said, 'I like sugar,' the other had answered, 'I *don't* like sugar'. . . . And surely the fact that it [the type of analysis under consideration] involves this consequence is sufficient to condemn it."

11. In point of fact, only D3 should be mentioned, since the argument does not use the word "wrong" which D4 defines. But I mention D4 simply because the argument could so easily be rewritten, using "wrong" instead of "right," with no effect on its validity or invalidity. D1 and D2 might also have been referred to, since the argument, if it holds at all, would hold against any definition that made ethical terms refer solely to the speaker's own attitudes.

(a) When A and B each make an ethical statement, they differ in opinion, so far as these statements show, only if their statements are logically incompatible.

Now clearly, if "A and B differ in opinion" is taken as just another way of saying "A and B have beliefs which, if they expressed them verbally, would lead them to make incompatible statements," then (a) above is true. Let us assume that Moore intends "differ in opinion" to be understood in this sense, and that he is therefore entitled to go from (2) to (3) in the argument, via (a). In that case we must, in order to make the argument valid, assume that (4) in the argument uses "differ in opinion" in this same sense. And the force of my criticism is that (4), so interpreted, is by no means obvious.

It *is* obvious, I grant, that in any typical ethical sense, when A and B assert "X is right" and "X is not right," respectively, they are in *some* sense differing or disagreeing. But I do not grant that A and B must, in that case, be "differing in opinion" in the sense of that phrase that we are assuming Moore to intend. I think Moore was led falsely to affirm (4) simply because, due to an exaggerated emphasis on the purely cognitive aspects of ethical language, he could not understand how people could differ or disagree in any sense without differing in opinion in the narrow sense above defined.

The sense in which A and B, asserting "X is right" and "X is not right," respectively, clearly do "disagree," is a sense that I shall preserve by the phrase, "disagree in attitude." A and B will be said to disagree in attitude when they have opposed attitudes to something, and when at least one of them is trying to alter the attitude of the other. I have elsewhere argued that disagreement in this sense is very typical of ethical discussion, hence I shall not elaborate that point here.[12] It will be enough to point out that disagreement in attitude often leads to *argument*, where each person expresses such beliefs as may, if accepted by his opponent, lead the opponent to

12. Essay II, pp. 26 f., and Essay I, passim.

have a different attitude at the end of the argument. Attitudes are often functions of beliefs, and so we often express beliefs in the hope of altering attitudes. Perhaps Moore confused disagreement in attitude with "difference of opinion," and this confusion led him to assert (4).

Of course "difference of opinion" *might* be understood to mean the same as "disagreement in attitude"; but if Moore intended that, he would not be entitled to go from (2) to (3), and the third argument would still fail, even though (4) would then be true.

Note that when people disagree in attitude, neither need have any false belief about his own or the other's attitude. If A says, "X is right," and B says, "X is not right," and both accept D3, then it is quite possible that A and B should *both* know that A approves of X and that B does not. They may disagree in attitude none the less. They are not describing attitudes to one another—not, in Frank Ramsey's phrase, "comparing introspective notes." Neither is exclusively interested in knowing the *truth* about the other's *present* attitudes. Rather, they are trying to *change* each other's attitudes, hoping that later on their attitudes will be of the same sort. It is not necessary for their ethical judgments to be logically incompatible if they are to indicate disagreement in attitude.

Granted, then, that one has an introspective feeling that verbally-seeming incompatible judgments about right and wrong are actually incompatible, this feeling might testify only to the presence of disagreement in attitude, rather than to logical incompatibility. Or perhaps the fact that people who disagree in attitude often do, as well, make incompatible assertions about the consequences of the object of attitude, etc., in the course of their argument, may lead one to feel, without warrant, that the ethical judgments themselves, in any typical sense, must be incompatible. In my opinion the ethical terms are in fact used so vaguely that people *have not decided* whether "X is right," said by A, and "X is not right," said by B, are to be taken as incompatible or not; nor will Messrs. A and B be likely to have decided it. So *we* may decide it either way we like, so long as we are faithful to the issues which ethical arguments usually raise. We may, under certain circumstances of utterance, though not all, make the judgments incompatible. I have dealt with this in the essay, "Persuasive Definitions"[13] and have here only time to say that such a procedure can be developed in a way that avoids Moore's objections. On the other hand, we may make the judgments, uttered by A and B respectively, logically compatible, as is done by D3 and D4. Either alternative, so far as I can see, will permit the ethical terms to raise the issues which ethical arguments usually raise in common life, though of course they do not permit the terms to be used in the way that some philosophers, in their confusion, may want to use them. I can pretend to no superhuman certainty on this last point, of course, nor can I here expatiate as I should like; but I hope I have said enough to show that D3 and D4 present serious alternatives to Moore's nonnatural quality.

I must add, however, that D3 and D4 are misleading in that they do not properly suggest disagreement in attitude. They suggest too strongly a mere "comparing of introspective notes." But this can be remedied by qualifying D3 and D4, as promised on page 127, in a very simple way. "Right," "wrong," and the other ethical terms all have a stronger emotive meaning than any purely psychological terms. This emotive meaning is not preserved by D3 and D4 and must be separately mentioned. It has the effect of enabling ethical judgments to be used to alter the attitudes of the hearer and so lends itself to arguments that involve disagreement in attitude. So qualified, D3 and D4 seem to me to be immune from all of Moore's objections.

The consideration that was perplexing on pages 127 f.—namely, that "X is right," said by A at t1, is logically compatible according to D3 and D4 with "X was wrong," said by A at t2—can now be explained. It is clear that in any typical sense these statements are "opposed" in some way; but I think it is well within the limits of vague common usage to say that the statements, under the circumstances of utterance mentioned, may be taken as logically compatible, just as D3 and D4, qualified by reference to emotive meaning, would

13. Essay III, Sect. 5.

imply. Their *seeming* incompatibility springs from the fact that the judgments exert a different sort of emotive *influence*—that the judgment at t2 undoes the work of the judgment at t1. For instance, if B was led by A's judgment at t1 to agree in attitude with A, he may, if he has not subsequently changed his attitude, find himself disagreeing in attitude with A at t2. So in a rough but intelligible way of speaking, B may properly charge A with "going back on" his former "opinion." But we need not insist that this ready way of speaking maintains that A's statement at t1 was logically incompatible with his statement at t2. May it not be taken to mean that A has come to have an attitude and to exert an influence which oppose his former attitude and influence?

6

It will now be clear that none of the arguments I have criticized is conclusive. 'Moore's *method* of argument, as I have freely interpreted it, is very useful. It consists of drawing consequences from a proposed definition and then showing that these consequences are "odd" according to any *usual* sense of the word defined. This "oddness" may suggestively raise the question as to whether the proposed definition is issue-begging. But although the method is useful it may be misapplied, either in drawing the consequences of the proposed definition or in judging whether these consequences show that the proposed definition is likely to beg issues. I think that Moore has misapplied the method throughout, in one or another of these ways.

Although Moore's arguments do not prove as much as he thinks (or at least, as much as he thought when writing the *Ethics*), they are by no means useless. I hope that his repudiation of much of *Principia Ethica*[14] will not be interpreted by careless critics as implying that his work in ethics has gone for nothing. However much Moore himself may have been misled by language, he is much more sensitive to its pitfalls than many of his naturalistic opponents, and some of his arguments help one to realize this. In the second and

14. See "Is Goodness a Quality," in *Philosophical Papers* (New York, 1959).

third arguments we have found that D1 and D2 cannot be accepted without qualification. Explicit recognition must be added about the confusing character of tense in ethical judgments, of disagreement in attitude, and of emotive meaning. Naturalistic analyses which are content to ignore these matters—which indeed they all were at the time that Moore wrote—are insensitive in a way that the second and third arguments help to point out.

Lest I myself be accused of linguistic insensitivity, I wish to emphasize that D3 and D4 require further qualifications than those which I have here given. "Right" and "wrong," being particularly vague and flexible, may be defined in any number of ways, quite within the limits of that muddy continuum which we call "ordinary usage." No *one* definition can possibly deal with their varied usage; and perhaps no *list* of definitions, however long, would be adequate. All that one can do is give "sample" definitions and then hope to avoid confusion by coming more adequately to understand (as I. A. Richards has so often urged) the flexibility of ordinary language.

In particular, "right" and "wrong" are subject to changes in meaning with different contexts. For instance, when we ask someone the *question* "is X right?" we do not usually want the hearer to tell us whether *we* now approve of X, as D3 and D4 might readily suggest. We should be more likely to want the hearer to say whether *he* approves of X and to influence us with regard to our subsequent approval. Or we might want to know what attitudes others have to X, and so on. Or, if we know to begin with that the hearer approves of X, we may use the question "is X right?" to insinuate that it is not, and so to indicate that we disagree with the hearer in attitude—a disagreement that may later lead to an argument in which many beliefs would be expressed of a sort that might lead, as a matter of psychological fact, to the alteration of our own or of our opponent's attitude. And again: if a man is "trying to decide" whether X is right, he is usually not merely trying to characterize his present attitudes. Such a decision would usually be forced upon him by a conflict of attitudes and would arise in the course of his efforts to resolve the conflict. It would introduce factual considerations of precedent, the attitude of society, the nature and consequences of X, etc., that may determine whether or not he will subsequently attain a state of mind in which he approves of X, with all impulses to the contrary being repressed or redirected. These are cases in which "right" is used in a way that varies, greatly or slightly, from the way in which D3 would suggest. They are a few instances among the many which show that D3 and D4 must be taken only as "sample" definitions.

7

But although only "sample" definitions, D3 and D4, qualified by reference to emotive meaning, are for many purposes very interesting samples. In this last section of my paper I wish to show that they have consequences which may account for certain of Moore's own conclusions:

It seems quite likely, judging from parallel remarks in *Principia Ethica* (p. 7) that Moore would deny that

"If I now approve of X, X is right"

is an analytic statement, in any usual sense of words. By D3 this is analytic; and I am prepared to accept that consequence, and at the same time to insist that D3 is as conventional as any precise definition of a vague common term can be, *if* D3 is qualified with reference to emotive meaning. What I do not admit, however, is that the statement is *trivial*, in the way most analytic statements are. The emotive meaning of "right," in the above statement, might serve to induce the *hearer* to approve of X, provided the speaker does. Any hearer who does not want to be so influenced may accordingly object to the statement, even though it is analytic. Although trivial in regard to its cognitive aspects, the statement is not trivial in regard to its repercussions on attitudes; and one may refuse to make it, as I should, very often, for that reason. There are times when I, and all others, wish to induce others to share our attitudes; but few of us want to do so for every case, or to act as though the hearer is expected to agree with us in attitude even before we assert more than hypothetically what attitude we ourselves have. For that reason the above statement would rarely be made. That is far from what Moore would conclude, but I think it may explain why Moore, consciously sensitive only to the cognitive aspects of language, should insist that the judgment in question, not being trivial, could not be analytic.

In the *Ethics* (p. 131) Moore makes some penetrating remarks. He mentions, with apparent agreement, certain theorists who "have assumed that the question whether an action *is* right cannot be completely settled by showing that any man or set of men have certain feelings . . . about it. They would admit that the feelings . . . of men may, in various ways, have a bearing on the question; but the mere fact that a given man or set of men has a given feeling . . . can, they would say, never be sufficient, *by itself*, to show that an action is right or wrong." With this I entirely agree, and in fact it is implied by D3 and D4, provided these definitions are qualified by reference to disagreement in attitude and emotive meaning. To settle a question about "what is right" is presumably (for this context) to settle a disagreement that may exist between A and B, when the former maintains "X is right" and the latter maintains "X is not right." This disagreement is a disagreement in *attitude* and will be settled only when A and B come to have similar attitudes. Should any other people take sides with A or B, the settlement of the argument would require these people as well to end by having similar attitudes. Now one cannot hope to bring about such a uniformity of attitudes merely by pointing out what any one man or set of men actually do approve of. Such a procedure may, as Moore says, "in various ways have a bearing on the question," but a knowledge of what any man approves of *may* totally fail to alter the approval of some other man. If approval is to be altered by means of beliefs, all manner of beliefs may have to be utilized. One may, in fact, have to make use of all the sciences; for the beliefs that will collectively serve to alter attitudes may be of all different sorts; and even so, one cannot be guaranteed success in altering them by this means. It is for that reason that the support of an ethical judgment is so very difficult. To support ethical judgments is not merely to prove their truth; it is to further, via changes in beliefs, for instance, the influence which they exert. I accept the above quotation from Moore, then, but it will be obvious how very different my own reasons are.

I wish to make clear that although an analysis along the lines of D3 and D4, with reference to emotive meaning and disagreement in attitude, stands as an alternative to Moore's nonnaturalistic views, it does not positively disprove the view that "right," whether directly or indirectly, has to do with a nonnatural quality. What Moore would now say about "right" I do not know, but he *could* say, without rejecting emotive meaning or disagreement in attitude, that "X is right" sometimes means that X has some quality, or is related to something else that has some quality, which is wholly inaccessible to discovery by scientific means. "Right" could then be granted an emotive meaning, but only because it designates such a quality. If the quality is assumed to be one that arouses approval, its name would acquire a laudatory aura. And people could be acknowledged to disagree in attitude about what is right, but only because they approve or do not approve of something, depending on whether or not they believe that this quality is in some way connected with it. If Moore wishes to maintain this, and if he actually is confident that he encounters this quality in his experience or "intuition," and if he is sure that the quality is nonnatural, then I cannot pretend to have said anything here which is likely to convince him to the contrary— even though I should privately suspect him of building up elaborately sophisticated fictions in the name of common sense. I do contend, however, that if Moore is to support such a view, he must argue for it in a more positive way. He cannot hold it up as the only alternative to manifest weaknesses of naturalism. The kind of naturalism which he was combatting, which ignores disagreement in attitude and emotive meaning, does indeed require an alternative; but unless new arguments can be found to the contrary, such an alternative can be developed along the lines I have here suggested.[15]

15. For analyses which closely resemble the one I defend here, see: A. J. Ayer, *Language, Truth, and Logic*, ch. 6; Bertrand Russell, *Religion and Science*, ch. 9; W. H. F.

The present alternative, I must add, is far from crying that ethical judgments represent a "total confusion." To ascribe to a judgment a meaning that is partly emotive is by no means to insist that it is confused. Should emotive meaning be taken for something that it is not, that would indeed be a confusion; but if emotive meaning is taken for what it is, it remains as an unconfused part of the meaning that ethical judgments manifestly do have. Nor does this type of analysis imply the curious view that ethical issues are "artificial." Issues that spring from disagreement in attitude, so far from being artificial, are the very issues which we all have overwhelmingly compelling motives for resolving. None of us is so remote from society that he can survey the divergent attitudes of others without feeling insurmountable urges to take sides, hoping to make some attitudes preponderate over others. We are none of us "isolationists" on *all* matters, simply because what others do and approve of doing is so often of near concern to us. I have here, temporarily, suspended any taking of sides on moral matters; but that is only to keep my *analysis* of moral judgments distinct from any efforts of mine to exert a moral influence. This temporary detachment in no way implies—as it is scarcely necessary to insist—that I consider ethical issues to be artificial, or that I maintain, with gross paradox, that it is wrong to discuss what is right or wrong.

Barnes, "A Suggestion about Values," *Analysis*, *1* (March 1934), 45–46; C. D. Broad, "Is 'Goodness' a Name of a Simple, Non-natural Quality?" *Proceedings of the Aristotelian Society*, 1933–34 (where acknowledgment is given to Duncan-Jones); and Rudolf Carnap, *Philosophy and Logical Syntax*, sect. 4.

VIII. Ethical Judgments and Avoidability

In the essay entitled "The Emotive Meaning of Ethical Terms" [1] I have pointed out that ethical statements are used to influence people, that they change or intensify people's attitudes, rather than describe what these attitudes already are. The influence is mediated not by some occult property which the ethical terms mean, but simply by their *emotive* meaning, which fits them for use in suggestion.

In the present essay we must put this analysis to an important test. We must see whether it permits us to make intelligible the relationship between ethical judgments and the "freedom" of the will.

Our question arises from such commonplace instances as the following: A. "You ought not to have done that." B. "But I simply couldn't help it!" It is clear that if A believes B, he will immediately withdraw his ethical judgment. No one feels comfortable about judging a man for actions which he "couldn't help," or which, in other words, he was not "free" to alter. But why? What relation is there between "you ought not to have done it" and "I couldn't help it" which permits the one to be a generally accepted *reason* for rejecting the other? This is our central question. A great part of our attention, however, will be devoted to a

---

1. Essay II, pp. 10–31.

preliminary question: What does "I couldn't help it" *mean*, when used to oppose an ethical judgment?

2

Instead of the awkward expressions, "I couldn't help it" and "I was not free to do otherwise," it will be more convenient to use the expression "my action was not avoidable." Our preliminary task, then, will be to define the word "avoidable."

Since the main difficulties about avoidability arise when we speak of actions which occurred in the past, we can simplify matters by defining the word for such contexts only. The definition is as follows:

"A's action was avoidable" means *if A had made a certain choice, which in fact he did not make, then his action would not have occurred.*

We shall see that this definition is acceptable, at least in general outline. It is by no means surprising or novel. Hobbes gave the same definition and was partly anticipated by Aristotle.[2] But modern theorists, even though well acquainted with the definition, frequently reject it. It is thought to be relevant and important elsewhere, of course, but of no importance in making clear what sort of avoidability is presupposed by an ethical judgment. Since we shall accept a definition which is often deliberately rejected, we must carefully test it for the ethical contexts here in question to make sure that our departure from current trends of thought is not mistaken.

For example: An army officer has failed to win a battle. His commander tells him that he ought not to have failed. He replies that his failure was unavoidable. We must determine whether the circumstances under which the commander would accept this reply would be the same, regardless of whether he understood "avoidable" in a common sense way or in accordance with the definition.

Suppose that the officer had been confronted with overwhelming

2. *Leviathan*, pt. 2, ch. 21 (a more detailed discussion will be found in Hobbes' *The Questions Concerning Liberty, Necessity, and Chance*); *Nicomachean Ethics*, bk. 3, ch. 1.

odds. The commander would then acknowledge, in common sense fashion, that the officer's failure was not avoidable. Nor would it be, according to the definition. It is not true, as "avoidability" in the defined sense would require, that if the officer had chosen differently the failure would have been prevented. It would have occurred no matter what the officer had chosen.

Suppose that the failure was due not to overwhelming odds but only to the officer's leading his men into a needlessly exposed position. The commander would then say that the failure was avoidable. And so it would be, according to the definition. For if the officer had chosen differently—if he had chosen to keep his men in a less exposed position—the failure would have been prevented.

Suppose, as before, that the failure was due to the officer's leading his men to a needlessly exposed position. And suppose that the officer insisted, contrary to the commander's contention, that the failure was *not* avoidable, giving the following argument: "I acknowledge that if I had chosen to keep my men away from the exposed position I should have prevented the failure. But I *couldn't choose* to do so. There were causes operating that made me choose just as I did. My choice, my actions, and the resulting failure were an inevitable outcome of natural law. Hence the failure was unavoidable." The commander would not listen for a moment but would dismiss the argument as ridiculous. And so he would be entitled to do, if he used "avoidable" in the defined sense. An "avoidable" action, according to the definition, is one that would not have resulted *if* (contrary to fact) a different choice had been made. Now clearly, what would have resulted if a man had chosen differently has nothing to do with whether or not his actual choice was determined. Similarly, the fact that rivers would have been lower if there had been less rain has nothing to do with whether or not the actual amount of rainfall was determined. According to the definition, then, arguments that seek to prove unavoidability by reference to determinism are to be dismissed as ridiculous, just as the commander would dismiss them.

In these three cases the proposed definition has proved consonant with common usage. There are other examples which will require us to revise the definition, but since these bring in nothing that will invalidate what is immediately to follow, they can be neglected until later on (Section 5).

A more important point now arises. The definition must do more than retain the customary denotation of "avoidable." It must also permit us to answer our central question. It must enable us to explain why avoidable acts alone are open to ethical judgment.

We shall soon see that the definition permits an extremely simple answer to this question. And yet this is generally denied. Theorists have repeatedly objected to the definition on the ground that it makes impossible any answer whatsoever. The objection has in part been anticipated by our army officer, in the last of the above cases, but in order to be safely rid of it, let us summarize it more fully:

"It is utterly beside the point," the objection proceeds, "to speculate about impossibilities. The proposed definition leads us to do this; but if avoidability is to be related to ethical judgments, it must deal only with the results of choices that were *possible*, granted the actual laws and causes that were operating. Suppose that a man's choice and his consequent actions were rigidly determined. He would then be a victim of circumstances, a victim of whatever hereditary and environmental factors produced the choice. It would be absurd to hold him responsible. It would be doubly absurd to "prove" him responsible by pointing out that his action was "avoidable" in the defined sense—by pointing out, in effect, that *if* his heredity and environment had yielded a different choice, his action would not have occurred. This conditional assertion, however true, leaves him no less a victim of circumstances in the *actual* case, hence not responsible, not open to judgment. The definition fails to make the relationship between avoidability and ethical judgments in any way intelligible. Indeed, no definition will succeed in this respect unless it refers to indeterminism; for only acts proceeding from choices that were not causally inevitable can sanely be considered open to judgment."

The last part of this objection is easily refuted. Reference to indeterminism, which the objection considers salutary, will throw no light on the difficulty. If a man's choice was not determined, it was theoretically unpredictable. The man himself could not have foreseen his choice nor taken any steps to prevent it. It would not have sprung from his personality but from nothing at all. He would still be a victim, not of natural forces, but of chance. What room is there here for an ethical judgment?[3]

The more destructive part of the objection is equally at fault. The contrary-to-fact conditions which occur in the definition of "avoidable" are by no means irrelevant. If they seem to be it is because of the confusion that Essay II sought to correct—a confusion about the meaning of ethical terms. The paradox which the objection attributes to the definition of "avoidable" is in fact due to a faulty analysis, tacitly presupposed, of the meanings of "right," "wrong," and "ought." If we dispel this confusion the plausibility of the objection will vanish.

3

Let us recall, then, that ethical judgments have a quasi-imperative force because of their emotive meaning. They influence people's attitudes, rather than describe what these attitudes already are.

Our chief purpose in influencing people's attitudes, obviously enough, is to lead them to *act* in a way which they otherwise would not. We tell a boy that he ought not to eat a green apple in order to keep him from eating it. Our purpose is much the same when we make ethical judgments of something which has already been done. If the boy has eaten the green apple, we tell him that he ought not have done so. We are not, to be sure, trying to do anything about that particular action, which is past and gone. But we are trying to prevent similar actions in the future. The emotive meaning of "ought" greatly assists us. It enables us to build up in the boy an adverse attitude to his act, making him recall it, say, with an

3. It is not necessary to develop this point, since it has been made time and again by others. For a particularly clear treatment see C. D. Broad, *Determinism, Indeterminism and Libertorianism* (Cambridge, 1934).

unpleasant feeling of guilt. The feeling becomes associated not with the past act alone but with all others like it. It deters the boy from eating any more green apples. (We usually add to our ethical judgment the remark, "see that you don't do it again," and repeat our ethical judgment after the apple has made the boy ill, when his pain makes it easier to build up unpleasant associations with the action. These subsidiary devices, to say nothing of all forms of punishment, serve the same purpose as ethical judgments, although they operate in a different way.)

Other cases are only slightly more complicated. We often make ethical judgments of characters from a novel. By building up in the hearer, through ethical judgments, an adverse attitude to an imaginary character, we prevent the hearer from taking this character as a model for his own subsequent conduct.

When the purpose of modifying actions is not consciously present, it is latent. In other words, if a person is reminded that such a purpose will not be served by the ethical judgment he is making, he will acknowledge that he is wasting his time in making it. (This is not true for certain uses of the ethical terms; but since these have no relation to avoidability, we need not consider them.)

It will be clear, then, that *ethical judgments look mainly to the future.* Even when they are made of past or imaginary acts, they still serve a dynamic purpose—that of discouraging (or encouraging) similar acts later on.

It is precisely here that ethical judgments become related to avoidability. Ethical judgments are used to modify actions of the kind judged. But the kind of action which can be modified in this way is limited. Judgments often induce men to give money to charity but never make men add a cubit to their stature. If we tell a man that he ought to give to charity, our judgment may serve its purpose. If we tell him that he ought to add to his stature, our judgment will not serve its purpose. Since we are unwilling to talk aimlessly we confine our ethical judgments to actions of the first sort, to those which ethical judgments are likely to modify. But only avoidable acts, in the sense defined, are likely to be modified by ethical judgment. Hence only they are judged. Such, in brief, is the answer to our central question.

We must consider more carefully, however, why ethical judgments control avoidable acts alone. Let us return to the example about the army officer:

Suppose that the officer's failure was avoidable—that a different choice of his would have prevented it. From this it follows, granted uniformity of nature, that failure will in fact be prevented, in any future cases of the same sort, if the officer then makes the requisite choice. Of course no future cases will be of exactly the same sort as the past one, but some may be roughly so. It is *probable* that the officer will not fail if he is led to choose differently in these cases. The officer will be led to choose differently, quite possibly, by the quasi-imperative force of the commander's ethical judgment. A judgment of his past failure will make him ashamed of himself and induce him to choose differently in any roughly similar case that may arise. In this way the ethical judgment will diminish the probability of future failures. To generalize: a judgment of an avoidable act is likely to control actions of the kind judged.

Suppose, however, that the failure was unavoidable. By steps of reasoning like those above it follows that failure will probably occur, in future cases of roughly the same sort, even if the officer chooses differently. An ethical judgment will not serve, therefore, to prevent failures. It will exert its influence only through the mediating step of controlling the officer's choice, and this will not be enough. To generalize: a judgment of an unavoidable act will not control actions of the kind judged.

The relation between "you ought not to have done that" and "it was unavoidable" now loses its aura of mystery. The latter statement is recognized as a *reason* for giving up the former because it shows, if true, that the former will not serve its purpose. The relationship is not logical but psychological. It is a psychological fact that people are unwilling to make purposeless ethical judgments.

The following analogy may be helpful: A says, "please open the window." B replies, "I can't; it is built into the window frame."

B's statement may properly be called a "reason" which is psychologically related to A's imperative. It leads A to withdraw the imperative as useless in serving any purpose. In a similar way the statement "it was unavoidable" leads a person to stop making an ethical judgment.

These considerations introduce no unusual features into ethical methodology. In Essay II we saw that empirically verifiable reasons, when used to support or oppose an ethical judgment, are always related to the judgment psychologically.[4] This is to be expected. A man uses an ethical judgment in order to exert an influence. He can be "refuted" only by being led to exert a different kind of influence or else to exert no influence at all. Empirical reasons change his beliefs about the consequences or effectiveness of his influence, and in this manner *may* change the kind of influence which he afterwards exerts. Whether or not the reasons will effect this change depends upon the man's temperament. It so happens that men are temperamentally much alike in being unwilling to judge unavoidable actions. The close relationship between avoidability and ethical judgments depends upon this psychological fact.

The answer to our central question has now been given, at least in outline. Very little of it is new. The definition of "avoidable" is a familiar one, and even the explanation of how avoidability is related to ethical judgments is familiar, not in connection with the present problem, but in analogous cases presented by theories of punishment. Preventive and reformatory theories have long made clear that punishment of unavoidable acts serves no purpose. All that has been overlooked is that ethical judgments, being used dynamically, have also a preventive and reformatory function.

4. This generalization may at first seem too broad. If a man said "go away and stay here" we should object to his imperative for a logical reason. May we not object to ethical judgments, then, for a logical reason? Yes, but our reason *would* be logical, not an *empirically verifiable* one logically related to the judgment. It would therefore constitute no exception to the generalization.

There are exceptions, but quite trivial ones. Should a man make some very curious ethical judgment, we might reply, "come, you don't feel so yourself." According to Essay II this would be an empirical reason logically related to the judgment.

Theorists have been blinded to this obvious fact by their neglect of emotive meanings.

Let us now digress a little and decide whether ethics need concern itself about the indeterminism of the will.

It is clear that ethical judgments do not presuppose indeterminism. They presuppose only avoidability, which depends solely upon the results of choice not upon the absence of its causes.

It would seem, rather, that ethics presupposes determinism. Ethical judgments must control actions through the mediating step of controlling a man's choice. If the man's choice were not determined it would not be controlled in this manner, or in any manner. Ethical judgments would be powerless to influence people's conduct. Is not determinism necessary to provide ethical judgments with any function?

A moment's reflection will show that this is not strictly the case. We must presuppose at least a "partial" determinism but need not necessarily presuppose a "complete" determinism. The meaning of these terms will be clear from the following example: The motion of the sun would be called "partially" determined if, from an exhaustive knowledge of laws and circumstances, we could predict that it would rise tomorrow at some time between five and six o'clock, say, but could not predict more specifically than this. It would be "completely" determined if we could predict that it would rise, say, at exactly five fifteen. Now ethics presupposes only the partial determination of a man's choice, for this still permits his choice to be influenced by an ethical judgment. Our judgment could not lead him to do exactly what we wanted, but it could lead him roughly in that direction.

Partial determinism is a trivial assumption, too obvious to deserve proof. The only point of dispute has been about whether choice is completely determined or only partially so. Since either alternative is compatible with our explanation of how ethical judgments are related to avoidability, we may conclude that the dispute about determinism is irrelevant to ethics, so far as it deals with general presuppositions.

Why have so many theorists *thought* that ethics presupposed indeterminism? One reason, as has been intimated, is that they overlooked the quasi-imperative force of ethical judgments. They did not see that ethical judgments look to the future. Instead, then, of placing the connection between avoidability and ethical judgments in the future—instead of seeing that avoidable acts alone will subsequently be controlled by judgment—they looked to the past for a connection. Quite naturally, they could find an explanation only by making *choice* a mystery, as if it were somehow alterable even when it was irrevocably in the past. Some began to talk of indeterminism, and others, seeing that this really did not help, became unintelligibly metaphysical.

Perhaps an equally important reason for the confusion lies in the emotional state of mind from which ethical judgments proceed. The purpose of modifying actions, which attends an ethical judgment, is usually latent. Our introspectable state of mind may at times be one of indignation, fear, or even blind hatred. These emotions often help us to attain our latent purpose by giving our ethical judgment a forceful spontaneity. If we pause to consider the causes of the act judged, our feelings become stultified. Our ethical judgment becomes less convincing. What we are inclined to do, instead of finding causes, is to invent fictions, which strengthen our feelings by giving them semi-poetic expression. We pretend that the action came, without more remote causal antecedents, from the man we are judging himself. He is "just naturally mean." His conduct has nothing to do with social pressure or an unfortunate childhood. He dimly reminds us of the villain in an old-fashioned melodrama. Fictions of indeterminism, which give our feelings a more ready point of focus, are sometimes indispensable to the effectiveness of our ethical judgment. This may be an important source of error. How easy it would be to confuse these fictions, so prominent in consciousness, with the propositional meaning of the judgment. One might readily be tempted to say that the pre-supposition of indeterminism is found in the very "meaning" of ethical statements themselves. Perhaps theorists have been led in this way to give indeterminism an entirely unwarranted importance.

5

Several deliberate oversimplifications were made in Sections 2 and 3 which must now be corrected. The main simplification occurs in the definition of "avoidable." Let us see, by example, how the definition must be changed.

Suppose that our army officer would have prevented the failure only if he had given his men vigorous encouragement. He would not have had sufficient energy to encourage them unless he had had an extremely strong desire to do so. He would not, at the time, have had so strong a desire. Under these circumstances we should have to acknowledge, according to the definition, that the failure was "unavoidable." The officer would not have prevented it merely by *choosing* to encourage his men. He would have needed, as well, a strong desire to succeed in doing so, which he would not have had. A different choice alone would have been unavailing. And yet, although the failure was "unavoidable" according to our definition, it would not be called so by the commander, who would find no occasion for withholding ethical judgment.

In order to be more conventional the definition must be given as follows: "A's action was avoidable" has the same meaning as "if A had chosen a certain different alternative, and if he had had a particularly strong interest in bringing about what he chose, then his action would have been prevented." ("Interest" is here used, following R. B. Perry, to mean any kind of desire, aversion, etc.)

This new definition leaves the relationship between avoidability and ethical judgments essentially the same. In the above example the commander sees that failure may not occur in the future, other circumstances being roughly similar, if he can make the officer have a stronger desire to encourage his men. The commander's ethical judgment will serve to build up such a desire. It is likely to serve its purpose of preventing future failures.

We may now correct an unsound assumption made in Section 3. The main contention there was that avoidable acts alone are judged because they alone may be controlled by judgment. This required the assumption that ethical judgments control actions only through the mediating step of controlling a man's choice, for "avoidable" was then defined in terms of *choice* only. But at present "avoidable" is defined with reference to interests as well as choice. Hence we may replace the unsound assumption by the correct one: Ethical judgments control actions not only by modifying a man's choice, but in a more general way by intensifying his interests.

The definition of "avoidable" is still too simple, however, as may be seen from the following example:

A man is progressively becoming addicted to opium. At first we say that his taking it is "avoidable," but as he grows more and more addicted to it, we say that it is "less and less avoidable," until at last we say that it is "unavoidable." Our definition fails to provide a meaning for "less avoidable." It fails further in requiring us to say that the man's taking opium never becomes "unavoidable"; for at any time it remains the case that if he chose to stop, and desired to with *enough* strength, he would stop.

The definition is easily qualified: The stronger a man's interest must be in order to prevent the action, the "less avoidable" his action becomes. When it must be extremely strong the action ceases to be called "avoidable." These qualifications complicate our problem only very slightly. The less avoidable a man's action is, the more difficult it is for us to build up his interest in a way that would modify the action. Hence we parallel the decreasing avoidability by becoming increasingly more hesitant to make an ethical judgment. A low degree of avoidability becomes unavoidability when the intensity of the required interest becomes greater than any which our ethical judgment can build up. Judgment of avoidable acts still depends upon the probability of controlling the acts by judgment.

The example of the opium user raises a further question: If his action was avoidable, just when must the choice and interest have had to occur in order to have prevented it? Immediately before the action, or at *any previous* time? If we place no restriction on the time (and the definition does not) then his taking opium *was* avoidable even when he was in the last stages of the habit; for if he had chosen to stop taking it from the very beginning, even with a very slight interest in stopping, he would not have taken it thereafter.

The following qualification will suffice: When the conditions that existed at the time when the choice and interest would have prevented the action, and that were essential no less than the choice and interest in preventing the action, were of a sort that will not even roughly occur again, then the action is not called "avoidable." This obviously takes care of the above case. The opium user will never again be at the beginning stages of his habit if he is now in the last stages. The reasons for suspending judgment are equally obvious. If the beginning stages will not recur, and if they, no less than the effects of ethical judgment, will be essential to prevent his action, then his action cannot be controlled by ethical judgment.

We must next consider some more complicated cases. A man is sometimes excused from ethical judgment, though by no means always, because of his ignorance. If the failure of our army officer, for instance, would have been prevented by a certain choice, but if he had no reason to forsee that it would, even on the basis of excellent knowledge of the circumstances confronting him, his commander would probably make no adverse ethical judgment.

We need not trouble to decide whether this case requires us to revise the definition. It will be sufficient to see why the officer would not be judged. This is clear enough. A judgment would spur the officer on to make some change in his later procedure. The only significant change that he could make would be to acquire more knowledge thereafter. A judgment of the failure, then, would be tantamount, so far as its effective imperative force is concerned, to the judgment "you ought not to have been so ignorant." By hypothesis, however, the officer had taken great care in acquiring knowledge. Perhaps a certain amount of ignorance was unavoidable (in the sense as above qualified). Perhaps it was avoidable only to a low degree. Perhaps it was "avoidable only at too great a cost." (In other words, if the officer had taken steps to acquire more knowledge, he would have had to neglect something else and hence would have brought on even greater disaster.) For any of these reasons[5] the commander might suspend judgment of the failure. Judgment would make no desired change.

We have been assuming throughout that ethical judgments have no other purpose than to control actions of the kind judged. It is important to note that there are many exceptions to this. For example: A, whose social position is rivaled by that of B, makes many adverse ethical judgments of B's actions whenever he is talking to B's friends. His purpose is not to control these actions but rather to increase his own prestige by decreasing that of his rival. In general, an ethical judgment of a man's actions may be used to alter the man's social position. As in the preceding cases, however, such judgments usually serve no purpose when the actions judged are unavoidable. A will not induce B's friends to give B's social position to someone else unless someone else would have acted in a way more to their liking. If B's actions were unavoidable this would *usually* not be the case.

Yet the matter is not always so simple. Suppose B has become so strongly addicted to alcohol that his taking it is now unavoidable. A might then judge B's conduct, and with effect, even though the conduct was unavoidable. The reason is clear. A's judgment will

---

5. The last of the reasons I have mentioned is more interesting than it may seem, for it reminds us of an ambiguity. If we temporarily use "avoidable-I" to preserve the sense discussed above, we may describe the ambiguity as one arising from the possibility of using the term "avoidable-II," where to say that an action is unavoidable-II is a way of saying that it is avoidable-I but only at too great a cost.

Suppose, for instance, that a man became ill and consequently broke an appointment with a friend. Was his breaking the appointment unavoidable? It may have been avoidable-I, since he could perhaps have kept the appointment in spite of his illness. But even so the man may say, and honestly, that his breaking the appointment was unavoidable—i.e. unavoidable-II, and thus avoidable-I but only at too great a cost.

The example can be related to the withholding of blame in this way. What was unavoidable-I, we may assume, was a situation in which the man had either to break the appointment or to endanger his health quite seriously. Given these alternatives he chose what he considered the lesser evil. And his friend withholds blame, presumably, not because the man's *breaking the appointment* was unavoidable-I, but because he feels that the man, given the alternatives open to him, *should* have broken the appointment rather than endanger his health. We have in the end, then, a case where blame is withheld from a perfectly obvious reason: the man is felt to have done nothing wrong.

be tantamount in its imperative force to the combined judgment and reason "we ought not to give B a pre-eminent social position because he is a drunkard." In this form the judgment is of an avoidable act (our giving B a pre-eminent social position) and has the purpose of controlling actions of the kind judged. The latter judgment is not strictly identical with the former; hence the former constitutes a genuine exception to our previous account. But the reader will doubtless see for himself how a perfectly accurate account would have to proceed.

A final remark is pertinent, to summarize and extend what has been in question throughout the essay. We have asked the question "why, as a matter of fact, are ethical judgments commonly limited to avoidable acts?" We have found that this is because ethical judgments of unavoidable acts would serve no purpose. Apart from definitions our inquiry has been psychological. We have not asked the question "*ought* ethical judgments to be limited to avoidable acts?" This is an entirely different question. It is an ethical question, not a psychological question relevant to ethics.

In order to distinguish the latter question from the former, it may be well briefly to answer it. I answer, without hesitation, that ethical judgments *ought* to be so limited. It must be understood that this statement is essentially persuasive. I use it in order to influence people to disapprove of judging unavoidable acts. My purpose is to induce people to *continue* to judge avoidable acts alone, as they now usually do. In order to make my influence permanent I shall have to support it by reasons. The main reason is this: judgments of unavoidable acts do not serve their purpose. It so happens, in this case, that the causal explanation of why people now do restrict their judgments to avoidable acts, and the reason why they ought to, coincide. Perhaps this reason will be insufficient to make permanent my influence. Perhaps the reader has very curious purposes or approves of acting in a purposeless fashion. I should then have to point out other matters of fact, which might more successfully direct his approval in the way I wish. But I trust that in the present case this will not be necessary.

IX. Meaning : Descriptive and Emotive

I shall first discuss sign situations, or situations which frequently involve the sort of "meaning" that I call "descriptive." A discussion of the emotive aspects of language, and of the extent to which they resemble or fail to resemble the descriptive aspects, can conveniently be left until later.

In any sign situation there is one thing (a word, sentence, diagram, signal, etc.) which stands for another thing (an object, property, event, etc.). The analytic problem is one of defining the relational terms, "stand for." We all know roughly what it means but want to know more precisely.

Many writers have taken this relation to involve a conjunction of two others. Roughly speaking, when S stands for X, there is: (a) a relation between S and the *thoughts* of certain people, and (b) a relation between these thoughts and X, which is their object—or in other words, the relation named by "about" in such a context as "his thoughts were about X." I must confess (and in philosophy perhaps one should always "confess" to strong convictions) that I see no plausible alternative to such a view. I shall here accept it without attempting to defend it, hoping that the reader, even if he has doubts about it, will assume it as a basis for discussion.

We must realize, however, that when *stands for* is broken up in this way, only the very first step of analysis has been taken; for (a) and (b) contain indefinite and vague expressions that are of merely temporary use; they mark off the regions where further clarity must be sought, but do no more than that. We have still to ask just *what* relation holds between a sign and people's thoughts. We have still to ask what is designated by "thought," salvaging from the uses of that *omnium gatherum* term (and "cognition" is no better, by the way) something that is at once relatively precise and suitable for our purposes. And we have still to ask for an intelligible account of the relation between a thought and its object.

2

The last two of these questions—concerning "thought" and the relation of a thought to its object—are as old as philosophy; yet I know of no answer to them that I find satisfactory. In *Ethics and Language* my discussion of them was admittedly fragmentary. I maintained (and should still wish to maintain) that when we say, "Mr. A was thinking about X at t," we are not talking *exclusively* about A's experience *at t*—not exclusively about some image or unique feeling of his that resembles X or points to it by a unique self-transcendence. We are talking, in part, about what Mr. A *would* do or *would* experience if there were occasion for it;[1] or more specifically, we are talking about something that is "potential" or "dispositional."[2] But this establishes only the genus of the definition of "thought"; it does not cope with the more difficult problem of establishing the differentiae.

These are such large issues, however, that I am afraid they cannot profitably be discussed within the limits of the present essay. So I shall speak, with shameless freedom, of "thoughts" that are "about" their "object," of "cognition," of "beliefs," and so on. A sanction-

1. For discussions on the sense of "if" in question, see R. M. Chisholm, "The Contrary-to-Fact Conditional," *Mind* (October 1946); and Nelson Goodman, "The Problem of Counterfactual Conditionals," *Journal of Philosophy* (February 27, 1947). These papers do much to advance the analysis, even though in certain respects they are admittedly inconclusive; and they help to show how "would-if" statements are related to dispositional properties and to causal explanations more generally.

2. See *Ethics and Language*, ch. 3, particularly sect. 7.

ing of unclarity here, when acknowledged, may not be incompatible with an attempt to minimize it elsewhere.

My discussion of sign situations, accordingly, will be limited to the first of the above questions—that concerning the relation of signs to thoughts. It is less one question than a family of questions. We shall have the progenitor of the family if we understand "sign" and "stand for" very broadly, as in the context, "lightning is a sign which stands for thunder." The question can then be stated:

For what value of "R" will "S has R to Mr. A's thought about X" be an analysis of "S is interpreted by Mr. A as a sign which stands for X"?

In this general form the question may lend itself to analytical subtleties, but I am inclined to doubt that the subtleties are of much consequence. In a Humean sense of "cause" the R is pretty obviously a causal relation. One would have to go on, of course, specifying how a sign is to be distinguished from other part-causes of Mr. A's thought. But we are seldom perplexed by this distinction; a technical elaboration of it would do little to prevent confusion.[3]

We have a more interesting question when we look not to sign situations in general but to those of a special sort. If lightning stands for thunder, so also does the sentence "there will be thunder"; but we commonly say of the sentence, as we do not of the lightning, that it is a "conventional" sign, subject to "linguistic rules." It *is* of practical importance, in my opinion, to elaborate the distinctions that the latter terms introduce. So let us state our question more narrowly:

For what value of "R_1" will "S has R_1 to Mr. A's thought about X" be an analysis of "S is interpeted by Mr. A as a sign which stands conventionally for X, in accordance with linguistic rules"?

3

I shall christen the required R_1 in advance by the name "strictly evokes," letting the name have whatever sense I specify. (Although

3. The distinction is *roughly* provided by the first two sentences of condition (1) in the next section. (The third sentence would rule out the lightning-thunder example.)

an unfamiliar, technical term might be less misleading, this familiar one will do well enough for the present.) And I shall specify that S is "strictly evoking" Mr. A's thought about X if and only if the three conditions that follow are all of them fulfilled:

(1) S is causing Mr. A to think about X, and is a part-sufficient, immediate cause. As compared to the other causes, S is something conspicuous. It is of a sort that can be used (caused to exist) or not used at will, either by Mr. A or by others.

(2) If Mr. A's thinking about X, on experiencing S, has been "conditioned" by his past observations of relations between S and X, or if it is due to any beliefs that he has about relations between S and X, then these relations are not inevitable: they would not hold, in other words, if people chose to alter them. Moreover, people have in fact chosen to preserve them, with only slight changes, because they find them useful for purposes of communication.

Let me pause to illustrate this. When a man sees smoke and is caused to think of the fire that made it, his thought is not, by condition (2), "strictly evoked" by the smoke. His thinking about the fire depends upon his beliefs about certain relations between smoke and fire. And if some of these relations should happen not to be inevitable, they are none of them, at least, of a sort that people have chosen to preserve "because they find them useful for purposes of communication."

In general, "strictly evokes" will be inapplicable to sign situations that are not conventional—as is required. Condition (2) does not, however, exclude cases where smoke is used as a conventional sign in Indian fashion. If smoke then "strictly evokes" thoughts, the thoughts will not be about the fire that made it, but about something else; and any beliefs that are involved in interpreting the sign will be about relations of the sort that (2) permits. But the smoke will not "strictly evoke" any thoughts, of course, unless condition (3) is also satisfied; and this last condition must now be stated.

(3) S is related by syntactical rules to other signs; and these in turn, if A experienced them, would be related to other thoughts of his in the way specified by (1) and (2) above. For at least some of

these other signs, the "if" that begins condition (2) must not be contrary to fact. And: A's thought about X differs from any other thoughts he may have, on experiencing S, in that it is very strongly dependent upon his familiarity with these syntactical rules.

I shall delay any illustration of this condition, since I must return to it in another connection. For the moment it will be sufficient to say this: I have in mind not merely the rules of ordinary grammar, but all the rules that are built up by the use of analytic statements and definitions; and should signs other than words be subject to rules with a similar function, I should want to include them as well.

4

The term "strictly evoke" can now be used in defining "descriptive meaning." For the special, narrow sense in which I want to use the latter term, the statement:

S has a descriptive meaning, for A, that is about X,

will analytically imply the statement:

S *tends* to strictly evoke, in A, a thought about X.

This is not sufficient for a full definition, since it sees the situation from the point of view of the person interpreting, rather than the person using, a sign. But I shall be content with this limited point of view throughout this paper, since it will not prejudice my observations and will greatly simplify exposition.[4] With that understood, I can proceed as if the above two statements were synonymous.

A sign may continue to have the same descriptive meaning over a period of time, even though it is not strictly evoking anyone's thoughts during that period, for it may *tend* to do what it is in fact not doing. To know about tendencies of this sort is to know something important for communication, since the knowledge will apply not merely to some one sign situation, but to a great many. It is partly for that reason that "descriptive meaning" is a useful term.

Although I have defined "descriptive meaning" by a different

4. The topic is briefly developed in *Ethics and Language*, p. 57.

route, so to speak, than I did in *Ethics and Language*, I have not greatly altered its sense. My present use of "tendency," for instance, is an informal way of referring to what I previously called a "dispositional property." (Note, by the way, that the mention of tendencies or dispositions in connection with the sign-to-thought relationships is quite independent of any further mention of them in defining "thought.") There is only one change worth mentioning: I have altered condition (2) for "strictly evokes" in a way that seems to me a little more precise.

To simplify exposition, let me introduce two other terms:

Note that the descriptive meaning of a sign, as I use "descriptive meaning," is *not* that which the sign stands for. From the whole of the sign-signified relation it abstracts the "pragmatic" element, and it does so only for certain cases and in a special way. Yet the thoughts involved in descriptive meaning are always *about* something; and with the help of "about" the remaining part of the sign-signified relationship, though again only for special cases, can be re-established. To emphasize the latter point I shall use "strictly designates," defining it in this way: a sign "strictly designates" X if and only if it has a descriptive meaning that is about X. Hence: S strictly designates X, for Mr. A, if and only if S tends to strictly evoke in Mr. A a thought about X. (I did not use "strictly designates" in *Ethics and Language*, but my exposition would have been facilitated had I done so.)

When a sign does *not* strictly designate X but does tend to *cause* a thought about X, I shall say that it "suggests a thought about" X. And I shall sometimes say, for short, that the sign "suggests" X, but only when the context is sufficient to prevent misunderstanding. (In *Ethics and Language* I used "suggest" in the same sense.)

5

I must now consider whether my views on descriptive meaning (and on the neighboring topics mentioned above) can stand up under criticism; and I must also consider whether they help to reveal a sense in which meaning need not always be descriptive, but can also be *emotive*. Professor Max Black has made a number of interesting remarks in this connection, and I can best continue my elaboration and restatement of my position by arguing with him. I shall summarize Black's remarks as I go, but to make sure that I am not misrepresenting what he says, I quote, in footnote 18, the part of his article that is here relevant.

Let me begin with one of Black's objections to my conception of descriptive meaning—the one that in his list is numbered (3). It is a mistake, he says, to define "descriptive meaning" with reference to linguistic rules; and the first of his reasons for saying this (I shall mention the second presently) is that "some descriptive signs (say a traffic signal) have only the most tenuous syntactical connection with other signs."

He is assuming that "descriptive meaning" was intended as a rather broad term—one applicable to any case in which a conventional sign tends to affect cognition. It *could* be used more broadly, but I wished to use it narrowly, *excluding* such cases as that of the traffic signal.

To put the matter in another way: I should say that a green light *suggests a thought about* the safety of proceeding; but I do not want to say that it *strictly designates* the safety of proceeding.

The narrow sense of "descriptive meaning" (and of "strictly designates") is of practical importance, for it singles out the aspects of communication that are relatively precise and which require relatively little attention to the circumstances under which signs are used. We can see this if we attempt to "translate" the green signal, which does not have descriptive meaning, into ordinary English sentences, which do. Is the signal a way of saying "you may safely proceed," or "all is clear ahead," or "anyone who proceeds will be acting, all else being equal, in accordance with the law," or "if you do not proceed and are first in the line, the motorists behind you are likely to sound their horns"? (I do not include imperatives, for that would be irrelevant to Black's special point.) We can only answer that the cognitive function of the signal is more vague, though it causes us to let in the clutch no less readily, than *any* of these English sentences. One could, of course, stipulate that the signal *shall be* translatable as "it is safe to proceed," and by accustoming people to this translation one could *make* the signal have a precise cognitive function. But this stipulation would itself introduce a syntactical rule, relating the signal in a special way to a part of the English language; thereafter the signal *would have* a descriptive meaning.

If my definition of "descriptive meaning" is in accordance with my intentions, and if it is of practical importance, then the only remaining issue is whether my choice of this term, rather than another defined in the same way, is misleading—a point which I shall discuss implicitly in another connection.

The second reason that Black gives, in objecting to my reference to linguistic rules, is that they govern not merely our use of certain cognitive signs but also our use of epithets, interjections, and so on.

My reference to linguistic rules, however, is not a way of distinguishing between descriptive and emotive meaning. (That depends on my definition of the latter as a certain kind of tendency to express or cause attitudes, rather than thoughts.) It is only a way of distinguishing between the descriptive meaning of a sign and the thoughts that it *suggests*.[5] So if Black's observation were correct, it would not be a criticism of my definition of "descriptive meaning" but only a reminder that I could also have mentioned linguistic rules, had I needed to, in defining "emotive meaning."

And the example that Black gives—that of arranging disparaging epithets on a scale of increasing heat—is one of a sort that I have recognized and named. To arrange epithets in this way would be to "characterize"[6] their emotive meaning in a systematic way.

Are we to say, however, that interjections, epithets, etc., are subject to linguistic rules? The depends entirely upon how the term "linguistic rules" is to be understood. Consider the following statements: (a) Most people who use "2×50" freely interchange it with "100." (b) Most people who say "how amazing!" freely interchange it with "my goodness!" The second statement is inaccurate, but let us

5. *Ethics and Language*, p. 70.   6. Ibid., p. 82.

ignore that. Roughly speaking, both statements truthfully describe people's linguistic habits, and habits that they consciously or unconsciously try to maintain. Hence *in a broad sense* we may say that both describe people's way of following a "linguistic rule." For that sense Black's remark is correct.

But in *Ethics and Language* I was using "linguistic rules" in a narrower sense—a sense in which the rules must have the function that I there described. To repeat one of my examples:[7] When told that it is one hundred miles from one place to another, we are likely to refer back to other symbols to make our reaction (not an image but a dispositional property) more precise. We are referring back, in this way, when we say "100 = 2 × 50," or "if it is a hundred miles, it is the distance I would travel in two hours, at fifty miles per hour." These statements do not describe the world, even the world of numbers, according to my view, nor do they strictly designate (though they readily suggest) the habitual way in which people use language. Rather, they are symbolic exercises which build up or preserve linguistic habits. And their function is to help us—when we subsequently use symbols in other, synthetic, contexts—to think less vaguely and to relate some of our psychological reactions to a given sign more closely than we do others.

We may "calculate" with our signs, in this way, for many non-mathematical cases. When a student is asked whether Santayana is an epiphenomenalist, he may say to himself: "Epiphenomenalist—one who believes that bodily events cause mental ones, and not vice versa." And having cleared up his reaction to the question, he is in a better position to answer.

In the case of epithets,[8] interjections, and so on, there may be slight parallels to these "symbolic exercises" and their clarifying function, but they are scarcely worth mentioning. Perhaps we could devise a language in which they became important. We might accustom

---

7. Ibid., p. 68.
8. I speak of that part of the disparagement that is not "dependent" upon descriptive meaning. An epithet may *also* strictly designate, hence have a syntax of the sort required.

people to say, "*how amazing* equals *my goodness,*" and drill them on such utterances much as we might drill them on the multiplication tables. They might refer back to 'how amazing" whenever they suspected they were deviating from the standard reaction to "my goodness." In actual cases, however, this is paralleled only by the fleeting verbal connection that we make, for instance, when we learn a German interjection by equating it with an English one. And this does not help us much. To get the full flavor of an emotive term (or as Black wants me to say, a term that tends to have emotional influences) we must learn to react to it by hearing it used in living contexts; and any temporary variation from the standard reaction, should it really need to be corrected, would have to be corrected in the same way. (To "characterize" emotive meaning, by the way, is not to preserve or re-establish it, save incidentally; it is rather to take the emotive meaning as an object of cognitive study in which the terms *used* are emotion-designating but not necessarily emotive.)

6

Having now discussed the observations that Black has numbered as (3), I shall turn to those that he has numbered as (1), (2), and (4). There he is concerned not with "descriptive meaning," specifically, but with my generic sense of "meaning." And his observations on the generic sense apply chiefly to those "meanings" which I call "emotive." He objects to any use of "meaning" that makes it applicable to situations other than sign situations.

That my use of "meaning" is misleading is evidenced, I must confess, by the way people have been misled by it—and I speak not so much of Black as of certain others who have criticized my views. Having attempted to combat the current insensitivity, particularly in philosophy, to the flexibilities of language, I should have gone to greater lengths in protecting my use of "meaning" itself from this insensitivity. But I assumed that a term which is so obviously flexible—which so obviously must be either avoided or explicitly defined—would be understood throughout my somewhat technical discussion in the sense that I gave it. Is the *meaning* of "Queen Anne" dead? In one sense, yes; in many other senses, including mine, the question is nonsensical. Is anything "the" meaning of "meaning" or "the" natural one?

I chose the term in the spirit of choosing between evils. There was no ready-made, conveniently terse term for talking about what I wanted to talk about—the dispositional properties that relate a sign to the psychological reactions of those who interpret or use it. I might have chosen a term that was wholly unfamiliar; but that would have been opaque and might have given a pretentious, technical appearance to a relatively simple distinction. So I diverted the word "meaning" to my purpose, hoping that I had chosen the lesser evil.

The use of the specific term, "emotive meaning," is perhaps of more questionable advisability. In its popular sense, as Black has pointed out,[9] the term has become an epithet. And what is of more consequence, it has become an epithet which is used to condemn an aspect of our discourse that is imperfectly examined and which in fact we none of us really want to condemn in so sweeping a way. It often becomes a point of departure, moreover, for compartmentalizing beliefs and attitudes. We are not likely to remedy the situation, however, by avoiding the term. If we should introduce another, there would simply be two. Our new one, with exceptional good fortune, might be properly understood and serve some well-considered purpose; but the old one might still persist and go its usual way. A more effective remedy, as I see it, is to keep the familiar term and reject the ignorance and confusion that have led people to abuse it—to use it in a way that neither makes a sweeping condemnation of something imperfectly examined nor fosters a compartmentalized psychology. By pre-empting the term in this way one may at once call attention, by contrast, to its ill-considered usage and succeed in putting something else in its place. So having decided to use the term, I was accordingly insistent, throughout

9. See "Some Questions about Emotive Meaning," *The Philosophical Review*, 57 (1948), 112.

Ethics and Language, upon the abusurdity of condemning (persuasively) all persuasion and upon the necessity of seeing that our
beliefs and attitudes stand in an intimate and complicated relationship.

It is not that ethics becomes trivial through its connection with
"emotive meaning"; it is that "emotive meaning" becomes important through its connection with ethics.

There is a further point on which I find Black's observations of
particular interest. He remarks that my senses of "meaning" and
"emotive meaning" are very broad, applying to cases that could
more happily have been eliminated. Perhaps so. But to narrow them
profitably would require a detailed examination of the purposes for
which they are to be used; so I shall do less to repair my terminology
than to indicate some of the considerations that seem to be involved.
Although I should like to do this for the generic sense of "meaning,"
perhaps it will be sufficient to limit attention to "emotive meaning."

There is no convenience, I think, in restricting the application of
"emotive meaning" to *words*. I should want to say that a flag may
have emotive meaning, for instance. But there does seem to be an
inconvenient broadness in speaking of the "emotive meaning" of a
symphony, particularly when it is not program music. How do the
two cases differ?

We may first note that although the flag and the symphony are
both dispositionally related to our emotions, the former involves a
conventional element that is present in the latter to a much less
degree. It would be of interest to define "conventional" for this
context, and to note its family resemblance—I think there would
be *only* that—to the second of my conditions for "strictly evoke"
(p. 156). But that is a somewhat complicated topic that I shall not
pause to develop. The point I wish to emphasize is simpler:

In the case of the flag the emotions are directed to something else
—to the country that the flag represents or "stands for." In the case
of the symphony the emotions are not directed to something else but
involve a dwelling on the sounds that express them.

In all but highly complicated cases our *words* are more like the flag
than the symphony. They at once stand for something and direct our

emotions toward it. It often happens, of course, that certain of the words in a phrase express the emotion and *others* direct it, but the full context, at least, has both a sign function and an emotive function.

This connection between arousing and directing attitudes is essential to my account of ethics, for ethical judgments do not arouse our attitudes only to leave them undirected.[10] So if I wanted a sense of "emotive meaning" that best served my special purpose, I could narrow its definition by this qualification: Nothing will be said to have an "emotive meaning" unless it is *also* a sign of something else or is frequently used along with such a sign, and unless the attitudes that it tends to express and arouse are directed to whatever is thus signified.

If "emotive meaning" is to be a term useful in literary criticism, however, I suspect that the last clause in this restriction is too severe, or at least injudicious in its emphasis. In poetry, particularly, the relations between the emotional, the cognitive, and the musical aspects of language are so extremely subtle that I am inclined to keep silent about them. I suspect that "emotive meaning," whether used generically or specifically in literary criticism, should be supplemented by many other terms, else the poverty of our language about language may lead us to ignore important distinctions; and I suspect that my own distinctions between "independent," "dependent," and "quasi-dependent" emotive meaning are only the most obvious ones.[11] But however that may be, I think there can be no very interesting sense of "emotive meaning," in literary criticism or elsewhere, that makes it applicable to cases where sign functions are *totally* absent.

Let me now show how these remarks bear upon Black's criticisms. I have been acknowledging the inconvenience in speaking of the "emotive meaning" of things *other* than *signs*. I have also been suggesting that no such drastic revision of terminology is needed as that which he proposes. His terminology (which I shall discuss in my next section) is obviously a possible one; it may be important for

10. See *Ethics and Language*, particularly p. 227.
11. Ibid., pp. 72 ff., 78 ff.

some purpose, but it is simply foreign to my purpose. One can emphasize the relation of "emotive meaning" to sign situations, as he desires, without making the term *name* a sign situation. There is a use for the term in referring to attitudes that *accompany* sign situations.

This is not to say that emotive meaning is always dependent or quasi-dependent—that it is a by-product of cognition, so to speak, or that it is the result of a sign function *alone*. Such a view would make our attitudes a psychological anomaly. Roughly: every event has *many* causes. It would be very strange, then, if anything so complicated as our emotional reaction to signs should vary *only* with our cognitive reaction to them.

With regard to the definition of "emotive meaning" I have only this to add, and I am sure that Black will agree with me: It is less important to fix the term, whether in his sense or mine, than to cultivate a certain linguistic tolerance—a habit of mind that prevents divergent languages, so frequent in philosophy, from being a source of misunderstandings.

7

In the observations that Black has numbered (5), (6), (7), and (8), he proposes a sense of "meaning" in which the term becomes roughly synonymous with "that which a sign stands for." And emotive *meaning* becomes simply an emotion that is *meant*. In that sense "hurrah" has a *meaning* only in the way that "I am enthusiastic" does. Black adds, of course, that "hurrah" has a stronger tendency to exert "emotive influence"; but he considers that relevant to *meaning* only in that it enables "hurrah" to refer to the speaker's attitude more determinately—to point it out, so to speak, by arousing a similar attitude in the hearer.

Black suggests this terminology largely (though not wholly) because he thinks it will emphasize certain analogies that I have ignored and by doing so will help to provide ethics with "a basis of *rational* agreement." In this respect I think he is mistaken. The cognitive elements that he wants for ethics are not ignored in my analysis.

Nor do they need further emphasis; for whenever rational agreement is possible (and I have not denied the possibility but have only
said that it is subject to a certain condition[12]) it can be obtained not
by *these* cognitive elements, but by cognitive elements of a quite
different kind.

When a term is used to produce an emotional effect, may it also
give us information? No one, I think, has ever been in any doubt
about this. To return to our simple example: When a man says
"hurrah!" and says it convincingly, we not only have evidence to
believe that he is enthusiastic but have much better evidence than if
he had said "I am enthusiastic" in so many words.

So far as the "autobiographical" aspect of such a term is concerned,
only this distinction need be made, and I make it only to show that,
in this case, it is trivial: "Hurrah" *suggests* the speaker's enthusiasm
and suggests it very strongly. It does not, however, strictly designate
his enthusiasm.[13] In other words, it tends to *cause* thoughts about the
speaker's enthusiasm but does not tend to *strictly evoke* them. For the
interjection is not syntactically related, in the required way, to other
terms. If it were used in a telegraph code, with a code book expressly
equating it with "I am enthusiastic," it would then have the required
relationship. It would also cease to be our normal English interjection. Such remarks as "if hurrah, then I am not apathetic," or "if
hurrah, it is logically possible that *he* is not," are foreign to our
linguistic habits.

I have called the distinction trivial. There are *other* cases in which
it is by no means trivial. When an emotive term suggests thoughts
that are *not* about the speaker's attitudes, one must often take great
care to distinguish them from thoughts that tend to be strictly
evoked. For when thoughts are merely suggested, they are likely to
be attended by a belief that has not been scrutinized and tested and
are likely to lack precision, whereas when they are strictly evoked
they are likely to be scrutinized and to have precision to at least a
higher degree.[14] But in the present case the distinction is gratuitous,
for the thoughts in question (about the speaker's attitude) scarcely

12. Ibid., pp. 136 ff.   13. Ibid., pp. 95 ff.   14. Ibid., pp. 87 ff.

need to be tested, and precision is obtained by another device —normally by arousing a similar attitude in the hearer, just as Black says.

It was because of the triviality of the distinction, *in this case*, that I formulated my "first pattern" of analysis, for ethics, in a way that I hoped would avoid needless questions about it. I said that "good," for instance, has a descriptive meaning about the speaker's approval and also a laudatory emotive meaning. Since the emotive meaning in itself is sufficient to *suggest* the speaker's approval, and quite precisely, my reference to a descriptive meaning about his approval was a way of being more emphatic—though there was no impropriety, since "good" is syntactically less cut off from emotion-designating, nonemotive terms than is any pure interjection. So I left no doubt that "good" *meant* (in Black's sense) the speaker's approval. My procedure, if anything, was a little redundant, but it was convenient in freeing me from the need of reiterating the distinction between suggesting and strictly designating.

The term "good" likewise *suggests* the speaker's inclination to have others share his approval. I did not take it as strictly designating this inclination; but I might have done so (for "good" is vague in a way that makes it "naturally" take on any one of a variety of descriptive meanings that one assigns to it), and if I had, that would have made no significant difference to my account of first-pattern methodology.

Black's argument, in his footnote to his fifth observation, is one which, in my opinion, is without force. Having defined "meaning" in a way that makes "good," for the first pattern, *mean* only the speaker's approval and his inclination to have it shared, he immediately assumes that this *meaning* must be the only ground for ethical judgment; and he then points out that it is an inadequate ground. It is inadequate, beyond any question. But I have found the grounds for judgment elsewhere—in the reasons which support the tendency of the judgment to exert (as he wants to put it) "emotive influences." These "influences" have not been eliminated by Black's account. They may be self-persuasive or may persuade a hearer. The reasons that support them alter attitudes via alterations in belief (our attitudes and beliefs being psychologically related) and may remove conflicts or disagreements in attitude by strictly designating something that the ethical judgment itself does not strictly designate. I may be incorrect in my analysis, of course, but Black has not shown this by using a new terminology; nor can I see that his terminology calls attention to any cognitive element in ethics that I have not emphasized.

Let me be explicit on a somewhat different point: the ethical terms suggest *far more* than the speaker's attitudes and inclinations. To say that a man is "good" may be to suggest that he has such traits as honesty, humility, charitability, and so on.[15] These not only introduce a cognitive element but (in my terminology) make some of the emotive meaning "quasi-dependent."[16] Within communities with well-developed mores these varied suggestions become fixed, and people then tend to *define* "good" in a way that makes the word *strictly designate* what it formerly *suggested*. This is a perfectly natural thing to do, and I introduced my "second pattern" of analysis, with its emphasis on persuasive definitions, to account for it.

But whether these varied cognitive elements are suggested, or made evident from supporting reasons, or made evident from second-pattern definitions, they certainly exist. It is *they*, and not the autobiographical element that Black has attended to, that represent the important cognitive elements in ethics. And however they may enter into an ethical discussion, the net result, from a methodological point of view, is the same: one can always hope, and act on the heuristic assumption, that a rational agreement will be possible, but cannot be sure. For that depends on whether disagreements in attitude is rooted in disagreement in belief.[17]

8

The tenability of my analysis of ethics is a topic too large to be treated in this paper. Yet I should like to end with these remarks.

15. Ibid., pp. 85 ff.
16. Ibid., p. 78, bottom; pp. 87 ff.; and p. 257.   17. Ibid., pp. 136 ff.

My methodological conclusions center less on my conception of meaning than on my conceptions of agreement and disagreement. If the solution of normative issues requires agreement in attitude, if the relation between attitudes and beliefs is causal and possibly subject to individual differences, and if rational methods can effect agreement in attitude only through the indirect means of altering beliefs, then the essential features of my analysis remain intact. There will be important questions, of course, regarding the degree to which agreement in attitude is *in fact* secured by nonrational methods, and whether it *ought* to be; but those questions will not affect my discussion of the various *possibilities* of securing ethical agreement, with which the methodological part of my analysis is chiefly concerned.

Hence anyone who wishes to find, in normative ethics, a greater certainty than my analysis has disclosed may do one of two things:

He may endeavor to show that the principle which I recognize only as a heuristic assumption—that all disagreement in attitude is rooted in disagreement in belief—is not an assumption but a basic truth. That it holds for many cases, and perhaps for the most serious ones, is fortunately a tenable position; but does it hold for all cases? I have no reason to think so but should be happy to have any evidence that others may seek to provide.

To introduce a unique subject matter into ethics, so long as it is to be an object of our beliefs, is not sufficient to alter the situation. We must have reason to suppose that agreement in attitude will be consequent upon an agreement in belief about the unique subject matter.

There is this to be observed. For those cases, if they exist, in which disagreement in attitude is *not* rooted in disagreement in belief, we may be able to agree in attitude on a larger issue: we may come to agree that such cases are better left unresolved, or settled by compromise, than settled by war, with its increasingly devastating consequences. But although one may hope that that is true and exert every effort to make it true for the immediate future, one is scarcely justified in the tranquil conviction that its truth is preordained by a kindly providence.

The second approach, in seeking greater certainty for normative ethics, lies in questioning the distinction between beliefs and attitudes. One may hope, for instance, to show that "practical reason" is at once subject to rational proof and capable of giving a uniform direction to conduct. I know of no sense of "practical reason," half attitude and half belief, that I find intelligible. Yet since I have been able to distinguish attitudes from beliefs only by means of examples "together with admonitions not to hypostatize and oversimplify," I cannot be sure that a more careful examination of the distinction would be devoid of interesting results.

Meanwhile I have a strong suspicion (and perhaps I am entitled to no more) that my ethics does not suffer from the vagueness of its key terms and that by elaborating it I have done more to clarify the terms, indirectly, than I should have done by directly attempting to define them. My reason is this:

There are many occasions, throughout common life, when we use "thought," "belief," "doubt," and so on, without serious unclarity; we have no trouble in seeing how they differ, for important senses, from "attitude," "approval," "conflicting desires," and so on. Yet in ethics the distinctions *seem* in jeopardy—philosophical analysis there *seems* to encounter just those borderline cases where greater precision is necessary. Now that, I suspect, is not true. It seems true only because we approach ethics with a preconception: we suppose that moral problems are either wholly cognitive or else nothing. We are not willing, nor in sanity could we be, to accept the latter alternative. So whenever we encounter an aspect of ethics which in any other context we should unhesitatingly call "noncognitive," we forcibly *make* it a borderline case. And then we torment it further to make it "cognitive."

Perhaps my views on ethics, then, have done something to justify the very distinction on which they are based—not by exact definitions or dialectical arguments but by considerations that remove the psychological sources of an *apparent* unclarity. For I have maintained that the current preconception—the seeming dichotomy between a cognitive ethics and no ethics—is a false one: that normative ethics is in part noncognitive, and yet that its problems, for that very reason, are of deep and fundamental importance. And if its problems cannot always be insured the possibility of a rational solution, they are not cut off from reasoning; for in discussing them we can *make use* of knowledge and can derive far more strength from the sciences than moral philosophers are accustomed to suppose.

18. Black's comments, which I have dealt with in the present essay, appeared in his "Some Questions about Emotive Meaning," *The Philosophical Review*, 57 (1948). The following is quoted from Section VIII of that paper, most of the footnotes, however, being omitted.

> Stevenson's . . . view (highly condensed) amounts to this. A sign may be said to have meaning *for a hearer* when it has a disposition to cause him to respond in regular fashion to other stimuli, i.e., when reception of the sign regularly modifies his response to *other* stimuli. It is not necessary in this view that the "pragmatic meaning" of a sign shall be identified with any single response of the hearer. So long as reception of the sign induces a stable pattern of response, varying according to the attendant supplementary circumstances, the sign will have a meaning; and to say that the sign causes a "disposition to respond" is merely a convenient shorthand for referring to the modified routine of behavior (overt or covert) of which it is the precipitating cause. When the correlated responses are cognitive in nature the sign has "descriptive meaning"; and when the responses evoked by the sign are a "range of emotions" we have "emotive meaning." In either case, the sign functions only as a result "of an elaborate process of conditioning" which is taken to be the general defining characteristic of meaning. . . .
>
> I shall content myself with a catalogue of doubts about the correctness of this view.
>
> (1) I have some scruples about applying to correlated ranges of response the generic term "meaning." Certainly Stevenson guards his retreat by insisting that he is talking of "pragmatic meaning," yet it seems to me quite misleading to suggest (as his choice of language, for all its qualification, is bound to do) that speakers' responses (or the causal laws governing such responses) are co-ordinate with denotation or significance of symbols. If we talk in this way, shall we not have to admit that a sunset or a symphony "has meaning," inasmuch as they induce modifications of response to other stimuli? Ordinary people do talk in this way, but I suppose Stevenson wants a terminology less confused and confusing than ordinary usage can provide in this instance.
>
> (2) It will hardly do to reply that response to a landscape or a piece of music (or, for that matter, to an article of furniture or any natural object) is not "conditioned," and so outside the province of investigations into "meaning." For if "conditioning" means social or group modification of innate response, we shall need to include much more than interpretation of "words" as falling within Stevenson's definition. Stevenson's restriction of analysis to *verbal* meaning seems to need more justification than he gives; much behavior that makes no use of words undoubtedly

involves the use of signs, and a general linguistic theory should be able to include all signs within its scope.

(3) The suggested characterization of *descriptive* meaning needs more elucidation. Vagueness of reference to such a term as "cognition" may be unavoidable, in default of a more supple psychological terminology. Stress upon linguistic *rules* as a distinguishing characteristic of descriptive signs seems to me, however, definitely mistaken. Some descriptive signs (say a traffic signal) have only the most tenuous syntactical connection with other signs; while "emotive" signs display considerable syntactical complexity, as may be easily seen by the ease with which we can arrange disparaging epithets on a scale of increasing heat.

(4) What I miss most in Stevenson's analysis is any mention of the function of signs as representatives of or substitutes for that which they "mean" (in the sense of denoting or signifying). However hard it may be to give a satisfactory theoretical account of what is to be understood by "representation" (a word which is no doubt as hard to define as "cognition"), its use, or that of some approximate synonym, seems indispensable to any satisfactory analysis of symbolism. If we are properly so reluctant to say that a sunset "means anything," surely it is because we do not believe that it is indicative of anything outside itself. Whether as a result of previous conditioning (the prompting of nature-loving parents, reading Shelley, or what you will) we have *regular* or even stock emotional responses, seems beside the point. It seems only by a strained metaphor that we can regard the sunset as meaning anything, *in the absence of anything to be signified.* (As soon as we discover that red skies are followed by warm weather, or believe that God speaks in the rainbow, the situation changes. Immediately, the phenomenon becomes, or is supposed to become, representative, and we may properly refer to it as a "sign.")

(5) If the last point is sound, we shall be inclined to deny the status of signs to things which merely produce "emotive meaning" in Stevenson's sense. Insofar as an utterance, or some aspect of it (interaction, tone, rhythm, or other musical aspects) works *directly* upon our feelings, we might profitably speak of *emotive influences.* Such occasions should be sharply distinguished from those where the "emotive" utterance is interpreted as a *sign* of feelings and attitudes expressed by the speaker or intended to be aroused in the hearer. The second type of case seems to me at least as important as the first, and to be more directly relevant to Stevenson's ethical doctrines.

[Footnote here added: "Thus in Stevenson's 'first working model' (Chapter 2 of his book), 'This is good' is analyzed into 'I approve of this' (uttered with warmly expressed approval, equivalent to saying, 'Do so as well'). All that would seem to be *relevant* to the ethical issue (Was the speaker right in saying 'This is good'?) would seem to be *what we understand* by his utterance. On the analysis offered, the grounds for ethical judgment would seem to be (a) that the speaker approves the object, (b) that he wants us also to approve. And these grounds would seem quite inadequate, however 'contagiously' his judgment is expressed. I would go so far as to urge that submission to emotive influence is usually positively immoral!"]

(6) In this view, there will be but a *single* type of meaning and "descriptive"

will be distinguishable from "emotive" meaning only as American history from British history, i.e., in terms of differences between the respective *designata*.

(7) There remains the problems of accounting for the superior "vivacity" and "contagiousness" of "Hurrah!" over "I warmly approve!" This may perhaps be done in the following way: The "neutral description" of the alleged feeling is *descriptively* less adequate—it is easier to communicate the nature of feeling by giving *deliberate* vent to it than by "talking about it"; the use of aseptic language suggests (informatively!) a lack of sincerity in the alleged feeling; conversely, since emotion seems inseparable from its expression, the use of a symptom of the emotion as a *sign* for that emotion strengthens the presumption of its reality; finally, we must allow some importance (though not as much as Stevenson ascribes) to the direct influence of the more "poetic" sign (and its superior aesthetic appeal). With all this, we need not admit a special category of "emotive meaning," or overlook the amount of varied and compressed information conveyed by even the 'simplest" ejaculation.

(8) It may be that my disagreements with Stevenson are largely verbal. I agree warmly with him on the importance of the less obvious, "persuasive" employment of symbols which he has emphasized. But I remember also his wise remark about the prevention of "an inconvenient way of speaking." A way of speaking about "emotive meaning" which focuses attention upon the irrational aspects of ethical communication, and leaves ethical issues to be resolved by the interplay of generated emotive influence seems not merely inconvenient but almost mischevious. A reversal of emphasis, made possible by a fuller recognition of the informative aspect of utterances, however charged with feeling, may encourage some, perhaps, to search further for a basis of *rational* agreement on ethical questions.

X. Some Relations Between Philosophy and the Study of Language

Intellectual problems are of two distinct but related kinds. They require us to go either from false or doubtful views to those that are well established as true, or from confused views to those that are relatively clear. The latter task—that of going from confusion to clarity—is central to what Broad has called "critical" philosophy. And critical philosophy includes a vast number of the traditional problems.

The mind-body problem, for instance, when viewed in Descartes' way, is a problem of relating two diverse substances; but when viewed in Berkeley's way it is one of relating minds and ideas, and when viewed in the behavioristic way it is one of understanding the functions of the nervous system. Why, then, do we have *one* problem, rather than three independent ones? Simply because each way of formulating it purports to recognize the legitimate heir, so to speak, of a question that is asked at a less reflective level. Each purports to clarify our conceptions of mind and matter, preserving what can be preserved without confusion, eliminating only what is confused beyond hope of repair. Indeed, the essential question is concerned with how the mind-body question is to be interpreted.

In such a problem we are not describing the world but are preparing the way for subsequent descriptions. A growth of concepts is in question, rather than a use of old concepts in forming new beliefs.

This growth involves a shift in undertsanding that takes place beneath our words.

Now it is on this account that emphasis on language, in philosophy, becomes so important. The symbol itself is the most accessible point from which a shift in our concepts can be kept in view: it serves both to hold up the unclear concept for our attention and to provide a vehicle for expressing the clearer one. By presenting our problem as one of defining a familiar word (or of establishing its usage in some other manner) we shall likely profit in two ways. First, our definition will readily lead to the crucial question: whether or not the defined meaning can adequately *take the place of the old one*. It will show that growth from this rough concept to that more intelligible one is sought and not merely some fresh start from an unspecified point of departure. Secondly, the definition will show, in a way that a statement about the "nature" of so and so will not, that the problem involves a clarification of our views rather than an extension of them. And this last point must always be emphasized unless we are to have confusion worse confounded.

2

Let us now consider what kind of linguistic study is most needed in philosophy.

We might at first suppose that our problem is divisible into neatly isolated steps. We might hope to develop a broad, self-contained theory of how words are related to objects for which they stand—a theory that would lead us to general canons of symbolism, suitable for determining when word-usage is healthy and when it is pathological. Only then, we might suppose, would we be in a position to apply our results to the problems of philosophy; and we should have the relatively straightforward task of showing which views violate our canons and which do not.

If we reflect for a little, however, I think we must agree that this procedure is impracticable. It pretends that our initial study of the symbolic process can somehow stand above and apart from philosophy—that so long as we are developing *it* we stand on bedrock, whereas the regions of philosophy, as yet remote from us, are treacherous with swamps. And this will scarcely do. In point of fact, the perplexity and unclarity that hamper us in philosophy will appear beforehand, and in a serious form, within our very study of the symbolic process.

For it will be granted, no doubt, that the relation of words to their designata is never a simple thing. It always goes via the people who use the words and is intimately tied up with their thoughts. (I say "thoughts" where Ogden and Richards would say psychological "reference," and Morris would say "interpretant" or "process of taking account of"; but I cannot see that these new terms behave very differently from the old one.) If we are to develop a clear and adequate theory of the symbolic process, then, we shall immediately face the difficulty of clearing up the terms "thought," and "object of thought," and this will lead further into the long-discussed epistemological question about how thought and its object are related. I have a great interest in these matters, but when I discuss them I certainly do not feel that I am on bedrock. Consider, for instance, this parallel case from the history of philosophy: Descartes was emphatic in saying that a material substance must be distinguished from a pattern of sense-experiences, whereas Hume was equally emphatic in saying that a material substance could be nothing else than such a pattern. This divergence was largely a consequence of a prior one, which (roughly speaking) was concerned with the symbolic process: Descartes recognized imageless thought and Hume did not. Hence from Hume's point of view, though not at all from Descartes', any attempt to speak of a more-than-sensory material substance would involve a use of words without thoughts (or ideas) and so a use of meaningless words. Now if the two philosophers could have argued the matter out, they would very likely have found this question about meaningfulness their chief issue. Neither, I think, would have allowed the other to suppose that, when speaking about thought and meaning, he suddenly became immune from philosophical difficulties.

Nor is the situation any different when we turn to the issue, now well-worn with controversy, that has attended contemporary positivism. If a sentence is neither analytic, contradictory, nor empirically testable, is it devoid of cognitive meaning? Since the term "cognitive meaning" is commonly used in a vague, confused way, the answer will depend on how we decide to clarify its use. We cannot decide this all at once, so perhaps we shall hope to proceed like this: We shall take certain sentences that are not testable and whose classification as "cognitive" is in doubt and compare them first with those that are obviously to be called "cognitive" and then with those that are obviously not to be so called. If the nontestable sentences, on examination, show marked analogies to the obviously cognitive ones and marked differences from the obviously noncognitive ones, we may wish to call them "cognitive" as well; and in the opposite case we may wish to make the opposite decision. I am not suggesting that these considerations would force us to use one or the other of the term, but they would be helpful in guiding our decision.

In conducting such an inquiry, will we be on firm ground, safe from philosophical perplexities? I think not. For with what eyes, so to speak, are we to look for the analogies and differences that will be in question? If we look with severely empirical eyes we may find that the nontestable sentences differ greatly from the obviously cognitive ones. If we look with metaphysical eyes we may find that these differences are outweighed by analogies—we may find that the nontestable sentences, like the testable ones, reveal a kind of Platonic entity called a proposition, and that we have a power of insight which shows that they may correspond to metaphysical facts just as the testable ones may correspond to scientific facts. So the matter is likely to go on. We shall not be engaged in questions that are prior to philosophy but shall be in the midst of philosophy itself.

What, then, is to be done? Have we no better alternative than to lift ourselves up by our bootstraps? I think we are not in such a bad situation as we may seem to be, and in explaining why, I shall first try to indicate how we have been led into our seeming difficulty, and then indicate how we may hope to avoid it.

3

We have been led to our seeming difficulty by supposing that clarity must be obtained step by step, each successive step being taken with perfect security. Perhaps we can explain our inclination to suppose this by looking, once more, to the philosophy of Descartes. It is typical of the Cartesian approach to reverse our modern sense of justice and to hold all our ideas guilty until they are proved innocent. In particular there must be some one belief that can be established as perfectly and beautifully innocent from the start. This belief then turns witness for another and provides it with a watertight alibi; and by a series of such steps we are to ensure the innocence of a large body of beliefs.

Most of us have come to distrust this procedure. We have learned that the initial proof of innocence is hard to find and that even if we should find it, the belief it would establish is not likely to be a strong witness for anything else. Yet the old habits of thought are too much for us and continue to take us unawares. This may easily happen when we approach philosophy through a theory of language. Unless our linguistic theory can be proved wholly innocent, we feel, our start will be wholly guilty. But we cannot establish this initial innocence. So we seem to have one criminal providing unreliable evidence about all the others.

I can see only one way out of this difficulty: that of dropping the Cartesian approach altogether and of holding our ideas innocent— *innocent of unclarity, no less than of falsity*—until they are proved guilty. I say this not to propound a categorical imperative but to make an ordinary proposal—a proposal which simply emphasizes in philosophy a procedure that we have long taken for granted in science and in daily life.

If we follow this proposal what bearing will it have on the philosophical importance of a general theory of language?

It will not, of course, give us a theory of language that stands apart from philosophy as immune from the attacks of an imaginary sceptic. That asks for too much. But it will lead us to see that such a start is not a necessity. All that we need ask for is a conception of the symbolic process which, relative to our present knowledge, we can tentatively accept. You may not accept the same view that I do, but each of us can then trust to his own view and follow it where it leads. The interesting problems will arise when one view or the other, as we follow it out, begins to produce difficulties—begins to prove guilty. Only then will there be an occasion for altering or abandoning it.

But when does a view of language lead us into difficulties? Let us remember that by the above proposal—which suggests that we continue to accept until forced to reject—we shall be accepting not only a view of language but also much else. Most of us will be accepting, for instance, a good part of deductive and inductive logic, and the many beliefs that serve us in everyday life. So if our conceptions of language and meaning lead us, by steps of reasoning that we accept, to consider unintelligible certain views we have believed intelligible, or to consider intelligible those we have believed unintelligible, then we have a difficulty. I think C. I. Lewis encountered such a difficulty when his theory of meaning led him to say that our reference to past events is a special kind of reference to future ones: for one is puzzled to know what "future" could mean if it is to include the past, rather than stand in contrast to it.

In encountering a difficulty we shall not thereby locate its exact source or the means of surmounting it. Perhaps we must revise our views of language and meaning; perhaps we must reconsider our steps of reasoning; perhaps we must change our views about whether our old remarks were intelligible or unintelligible. But obviously our theory of meaning will have no privileged place; it too must now come under closer scrutiny and will not merely test, but will stand in need of being tested by, everything else that we accept.

How are we to decide, when a difficulty arises, whether our views about meaning must give way or whether something else must give way instead? I am unable to provide any rules for this and am inclined to think that we must decide as we go, rather than before we start. In scientific method one normally speaks, on parallel points, of the criteria of "theoretical convenience" or "simplicity" or "adequacy." Although I find these topics fertile in suggestiveness, I do not find it easy to be precise about them. I can only remark that, for philosophical cases, our conviction that a certain view *must* be retained will sometimes vanish when it has been carefully scrutinized; and one can proceed on the hope that by half-blind trials he can eliminate in this way one or the other of the views that compete for acceptance.

4

The net effect of these remarks is to suggest that a theory of language does not stand outside of philosophy but must be judged by its philosophical implications. I must now make clearer, however, that I have been referring by the term "theory of language" only to a *generalized* study of the symbolic process—to a study which is at pains to clarify the key terms of our language about language, such as "symbol," "cognitive meaning," "designatum," and "syntactical rule," and which goes on to consider certain principles of the psychology of language or to erect broad canons for determining when symbolism is successful. Now perhaps some are accustomed to use the term "theory of language" to include far more pervasive and detailed issues than this. More specifically.

If we should set up precise syntactical rules for a number of the broader terms of our ordinary speech, as distinct from our language about language, would we say that we were helping to develop a theory of language? Let me illustrate the question by returning to the topic of "time," which affords a convenient example. Is the theory of language concerned with the special syntax of the word "time"? We are of course, fully privileged to answer in the affirmative; but if we do we must sharply distinguish the inquiry from the more general one that I have been referring to. It is one thing to consider the meaning of "meaning" and another thing to consider the meaning of "time." It is one thing to *test* our general conclusions about meaning by applying them to the word "time," and another thing to expect them to *include* a study of all the detailed problems that that particular word may occasion. If the theory of language is to extend beyond the broad distinctions and principles that arise in studying the symbolic process and is to include an effort to systematize all the terms of our varied discourse, then it will cease to be an approach to philosophy. It will not merely lead to, but will actually include, the pursuit of clarity that I have characterized as typical of critical philosophy itself.

Let me reserve the term "theory of language" for the generalized study of symbolism, as before, and refer to the more detailed one as the "study of specific terms." I should now like to say a little more about how much a study of specific terms may involve.

If we take the conventional problems about time, say, and reformulate them as problems of establishing the syntax of the word "time," we shall, I think, do much to direct our efforts in an economical fashion. But the seeming simplicity of our approach must not deceive us into supposing that the old problems about time are easily settled. The reason is simply this: our syntactical rules are virtually destined to be trivial unless we consider the full set of purposes they are to serve and the full set of confusions they are calculated to eliminate. Indeed, the only difference between rules of syntax and rules for playing anagrams is that the former have a function which the latter have not. And the syntactical rules will immediately lose their function unless we continue to ask, "of what use is it to make *this* rule of syntax rather than that?"

The answer to such a question, so far from being simple, involves considerations of extraordinary complexity. I have never met anyone rash enough to pretend that he fully understood what was involved; nor shall I myself be so rash. But I should like to indicate, by example, a means that is useful in helping us approach the question.

Suppose that we should make a syntactical rule that excludes the expression "time can go backwards" as nonsensical. Someone objects, saying that the expression, though false, seems to him intelligible. In defending our rule we might resort to a familiar reply that runs like this: "When we say that an automobile can go backwards, we refer to a process that takes place in time. So if time were to go backwards there would have to be a second time, presumably, for the first time to go backward *in*."

Now the effect of such a reply, as I think one will immediately agree, is to call attention to a spatial metaphor, which we suspect is causing a confusion, and which may not do so when it is made blatantly manifest. But although this is how we may explain the effect of our reply, in retrospect, the reply itself does not explain this. In itself it is not a diagnosis but a kind of therapy. It is a verbal *device*, a sheer exercise with words, which stimulates our habits of looking to our way of speaking.

In addition to the device I have illustrated—which deliberately talks a greater nonsense to reveal a lesser one—there are many others; there is the device of making insistent use of simple contexts, both familiar and unfamiliar, to prevent a perplexing word from being studied with academic artificiality, or the device of putting seemingly parallel contexts side by side to accentuate any dissimilarities of function that may attend them, or the device of finding trivial cases that seem to illustrate the same difficulties that we find in more important ones. The great need of such procedures in philosophy is perhaps what led Wittgenstein to say that philosophy is not a theory but an *activity*.

If we want a traditional name for these devices we shall find no more fitting one than the term "dialectic." I do not want to be held responsible, to be sure, for everything that this name may suggest; in particular I do not want to defend Hegel's logic. And yet much of the traditional dialectic—from Plato's discussion of whether the whole of a universal (rather than a part of it) characterizes a particular to G. E. Moore's discussion of the naturalistic fallacy—has had the effect, though not always the calculated effect, of bringing to light the hidden complexities of our speech. I have no doubt that a dialectic which deliberately sought this effect would be doubly illuminating.

There is good reason to be suspicious of any kind of rule-making for words, no matter how rigorously its results are formulated, unless such a dialectic precedes it. For it is the dialectic that gives life to our linguistic habits and dispels the notion that our common speech, which alone preserves our cultural heritage, need only be half-examined, and that somehow we can make a fresh linguistic start. Dialectic is the first step, even if only that, in helping us to see why one syntactical rule is preferable to another. It does not systematize, classify, or in any way theorize about the considerations that are involved. It is only an involved way of saying, "notice this"; it provides evidence without stipulating the use that is to be made of it. But this is an important step if we are not to seek clarity in a vacuum, and it is the only practicable step so long as the criteria of clarity are themselves a subject of controversy.

5

Some may find my remarks disappointingly conservative. I have defended a kind of coherence test for a general theory of meaning and a dialectic for dealing with the study of special terms. These are old, and perhaps one will expect the linguistic approach to philosophy to provide something more exciting. But a note of conservatism, now that the linguistic approach has become well established, is greatly needed. When a movement is looked upon as new it is likely to bring unwarranted confidence and lead us to dismiss our problems prematurely. We are likely in our eagerness for a clarity that avoids pseudo-problems to attain only a pseudo-clarity that avoids problems. Meanwhile the old sources of perplexity remains with us, and if linguistic theory can resolve them it remains the case that many of them are not yet resolved.

A sense of our continuity with the tradition will serve to remind us how patiently the clarity of our views must be sought. Nor are we to suppose that this clarity can be obtained by a study of language alone, whether general or specific. Confusion springs from all manner of sources—from pretentiousness, vanity, and rhapsodic enthusiasm; from impatience, sterility, and lack of imagination; from excessive tenderness or toughness of mind; and from the all-pervasive drive that is found in the quest for certainty. The history of philosophy has known all of these forces and none has escaped criticism. I am confident that a careful attention to language will help us to detect them and to allow for them; but I do not expect it to work miracles.

XI. Retrospective Comments

I

The preceding essays in this volume seem to me to point in the direction, at least, of a tenable position, and it is on that account that I have been content to republish them. But they sometimes give me the impression, as I reread them, of being injudicious in emphasis or misleading in terminology, or, on occasion, perhaps a little more confused than an effort to clarify our discourse should be. So in the present essay I shall comment on what I have previously said. I shall attempt to write a review of my own work—though with digressions into any neighboring topics that I find of interest.

Instead of commenting on the essays one by one, I shall take up two of the questions that they all help to answer, the first dealing with the nature of ethical problems and the second with the meaning and function of ethical judgments. In discussing them I shall endeavor, though often by implication, to explain and clarify my answer to a third and central question, concerned with the way in which ethical judgments can be supported or justified by reasons.

2

Let me state the first question more carefully. Although it deals, as I have said, with the nature of ethical problems, it does so in a special and restricted way. It requires us to abstract from the detailed subject matter of the problems and to pay selective attention to the aspects of them that are most likely to prod us into problem *solving*. It requires us to see these aspects not from a moral point of view (which would attend any attempt to *settle* the problems) but rather from the point of view of an informal, common sense psychology. In effect, then, it asks for a generic description, given in psychological terms, of those ethical doubts and uncertainties, or discords and disagreements, that we often resolve by inquiry, deliberation, and discussion, but which on some occasions can lead us into an impasse, and on other occasions can induce us temporarily to suspend judgment, acknowledging that we are not yet in a position to come to a trustworthy conclusion.

In many cases, of course, ethical judgments are free from these problematical elements. Any society has its mores, which reflect its degree of conviction and accord. But for the purposes of ethical analysis the problematical cases are particularly instructive and must be singled out for special attention.

My answer to my first question, though scattered throughout the essays, is in essentials given partly in Essay I, which deals with ethical disagreement, and partly in Essay IV, which deals with what I now like to call *personal uncertainty*, but is there discussed with reference to the problematical aspects of a *personal decision*.[1] My present comments, in this connection, will be in the nature of a renewed discussion in which I shall mingle a summary of my views as previously expressed with a somewhat altered restatement of them.

Let me begin with an example. Suppose that a Congressional committee is considering a proposed bill, trying to decide in what respects, if any, it ought to be amended; and suppose that the bill is concerned with an ethical issue (e.g. civil liberties) on which a collective decision will be hard to reach. An initial exchange of views may then disclose a situation that lies somewhere between the following *extreme* possibilities.

On the one hand, each member of the committee may express his view with complete confidence: each may feel that he has "the

1. In *Ethics and Language* the first topic is discussed in chs. 1 and 8, and the second in ch. 5, sect. 3.

answer" to the question, holding that any other answer is "totally indefensible." If a collective decision is hard to reach, then, that will be because the confident answers are also divergent. Some members, perhaps, say that the bill should be recommended to Congress just as it stands, whereas others claim that exactly these amendments, or exactly those, are needed, and still others insist that the bill is so hopeless that it should virtually be rewritten. So for this possibility (which is not, of course, a probability) the problematical aspects of the question and the arguments to which they immediately lead are conspicuously connected with *disagreement*. They are not connected with *personal uncertainty*, that factor being excluded by hypothesis.

On the other hand, it is conceivable that each member is unable to express *any* view with confidence—finding the issue so difficult that he cannot even take a tentative stand on it without adding various "if's" and "but's" that disclose his inability to make up his mind. We then have the inverse of the above possibility. There is as yet no place for ethical disagreement, since no one has an opinion with which the others *can* disagree, and the problematical aspects of the question become evident only from repeated expressions of personal uncertainty. (I call the uncertainty "personal" in order to distinguish it from the "collective" uncertainty of the committee as a whole. The distinction is not of much consequence to the present example, but becomes useful elsewhere. A reference to the uncertainty of a group, for instance, is not necessarily a reference to the uncertainty of each and every member of it.)

Such examples as these readily serve, extreme though they are, to introduce the topics of disagreement and personal uncertainty and to remind us that neither topic can safely be neglected. If we want less artificial examples, however, we must look not to these cases—which misleadingly suggest that uncertainty and disagreement are governed by "all or none" laws—but rather to cases like the following:

Mr. A begins by proposing that the bill should be amended in these or those ways but makes clear that his proposal is a tentative one. Mr. B expresses his surprise at A's proposal, and mentions aspects of it that he is inclined to consider unsound. So far, then, there is an element of disagreement; but the disagreement is far from being a sharp one, since each man (as the terms "tentative" and "inclined to consider" readily disclose) is indicating his partial uncertainty about the issue. This partial uncertainty may continue to be evident, moreover, as others enter into the discussion. Thus Mr. C may come to A's defense, though again without full confidence. Mr. D may then do the same with regard to B's position. And Mr. E, though more inclined to the one side than to the other, may for the moment speak noncommittally, his opinion on the issue being so provisional that he wants to think further before expressing it.

What I want particularly to emphasize, in connection with this example, is the way in which personal uncertainty can serve to *moderate* or *temper* disagreement. The personal uncertainty in question, which I have described as "partial" and might alternatively have described as "present to a limited degree," is no longer of the sort (as in the second of my extreme cases) that prevents the men from forming any opinions whatsoever. It simply causes their opinions to be of the "so far as I can now see" variety rather than of the "beyond any shadow of a doubt" variety. So when the opinions are submitted to the group for discussion, to this or that extent leading to disagreement, the disagreement is not likely (in contrast to the first of my extreme cases) to represent a clash or a dissention. It may do no more, indeed, than transfer to the group a prod to problem solving that each man has felt, though in a different form, in the course of his own reflections on the issue. The presence of an element of personal uncertainty, in short, makes the disagreement no less "tentative" and "provisional" than the expressions of opinion that provoke it.

Let me develop the example a step further. Mr. A, we may assume, subsequently discusses his proposal at length, acknowledging some of its weaknesses, but arguing that they are outweighed by its strengths. He is then trying, in part, to win further support from the other members of the committee; but we must not conclude on that account that he is doing nothing else. He may still be wondering whether he can convince *himself* that his proposal is a sound one. He may survey the issue, as he speaks to the others, because he wants to keep its various aspects clearly before *his* mind, no less than before *theirs*, and he may freely invite criticism not because he is confident that he can "answer" it but because he half-suspects that it may later become part of his own self-criticism. To ask, in such a case, whether Mr. A's arguments are prompted by a concern with disagreement, or whether, *instead*, they are prompted by a still lingering element of personal uncertainty, is simply to ask a poor question. *Both* factors prompt his arguments, and they may be so intermingled that Mr. A himself scarcely knows which is the predominating one.

The "intermingling" of the two factors and the importance of taking both into account become particularly evident from such a possibility as this: Suppose that Mr. A, having concluded his remarks, finds to his surprise that he has convinced almost everybody and there is even a sentiment in favor of putting the matter to an immediate vote. It may easily happen, in that event, that he will consider his victory too easily won and will attempt to avoid a premature decision by calling renewed attention to the several *weaknesses* of his proposal. His efforts to secure an immediate agreement, in other words, may be offset by his uncertainty—an uncertainty that temporarily leads him to "take sides against himself," but is attended, of course, by a hope for a greater certainty and a more carefully considered agreement later on, either with regard to his original proposal or with regard to some alternative proposal to which it gives place.

In giving this extended example I am not suggesting that it illustrates the way in which *all* issues are discussed or even the way in which *most* are discussed. Ever so many examples lie closer to (and some may even reduplicate) my extreme cases—which is only to say that men are of many sorts, some holding adamant opinions on the most complex of issues, and others being unable to make up their minds on the simplest of them. Nor am I suggesting that the example typifies the way in which issues invariably *ought* to be discussed. That would raise a question of some little difficulty, and one that stands apart from the point that I am preparing to make.[2] I am suggesting, merely, that the example has counterparts in everyday life that are entirely familiar and that it must not, accordingly, be allowed to escape our attention.

3

Let me now explain how these remarks bear on the preceding essays and consider to what extent they implicitly criticize them.

In some of the essays, particularly the earlier ones, I was so intent on emphasizing the topic of disagreement that I said too little about the neighboring topic of personal uncertainty. The first essay, for instance, which here appears as Essay II, barely hints at the latter topic. When it says that each man in a discussion "may be willing to give ear to the other's influence" (p. 26), it refers by implication to the way in which personal uncertainty (as I now put it) may moderate or temper disagreement, but it does not develop this implication. Much the same is true of Essay III, where a persuasive definition is seen with insistent attention to its potential effect on a hearer, who may or may not "agree" in accepting it. Too little attention is given to the speaker, whose personal uncertainty may have led him to deliberate at length before arriving at his definition, and who may wish, even so, to submit it tentatively rather than announce it with conviction. Essay I is more careful in its emphasis (see p. 5), but it is not at all an essay that could bear the title, "The

2. If, in my studies in the meta-theory of value, I seem surprisingly reluctant to evaluate, that is simply because I deliberately limit myself to the aim of *clarifying* issues. Evaluations would be in the nature of digressions, and digressions that would have to be either impossibly long or unpardonably dogmatic. Thus if I were inclined to suggest, above, that my example shows how people invariably *ought* to discuss their issues, I should be troubled by the counter-example (among others) of Thomas Hart Benton's stand against slavery—a stand that provoked disagreement to the point of violence and showed no element of personal uncertainty whatsoever. President John F. Kennedy has discussed Benton in a book entitled not *Profiles in Prejudice* but rather *Profiles in Courage*; no one, I think, is likely to question his title.

Nature of Ethical *Uncertainty and* Disagreement." And so on. Personal uncertainty receives its due share of attention, as I now see it, only in Essay IV, whose content might happily have been portioned out among the other essays.

I tolerated the misemphasis in order to get on to the topics that most interested me—the topics of *meaning* and *method.* Finding that I could introduce these topics by discussing disagreement, I assumed that my conception of personal uncertainty, being parallel to it, could be handled by brief comments. But that had the unfortunate effect of making my view of the problems appear one-sided. More specifically:

My brief examples, overemphasizing disagreement and underemphasizing personal uncertainty, too easily seemed to emphasize my first *extreme* case as described above. They too easily seemed to suggest that men are careless in forming their ethical opinions and inflexible in defending them. For such men, of course, any question of the form "ought X be done?" would be problematical only insofar as it gave place to the half-question, "I have no doubt that X ought (or ought not) to be done, so how can I get others to share my view?" Now in examining ethical problems and in describing them as they are rather than as they ought to be, I considered it essential to take such "half-questions" fully into account, no matter whether they led to the topic of reasons or to the topic of rhetoric; for some cases *do* correspond to my first extreme case, or at least approximate it. But my essays were nevertheless at fault—and I speak primarily of those that were written prior to Essay IV and prior to the parts of *Ethics and Language* that were akin to it[3]—in being open to a misinterpretation that made the "half-questions" seem more important than they are and made the "full questions" of ethics (where a man scarcely knows, in answering, whether he is addressing his arguments to others or to himself) seem proportionately unimportant.

The nonextreme example that I have given above speaks for itself

3. In *Ethics and Language* I was attempting to correct the misemphasis of my early essays but must acknowledge that I did not go far enough in that direction.

in showing how my early essays should be corrected; but I should like, even so, to add the three observations that follow—observations that I shall simply state in order, without transitions.

(1) Personal uncertainty can easily be illustrated, as in Essay IV, by problems that occasion an individual's "private" deliberations and inquiries (i.e. those that he has not yet communicated to others). An exclusive use of such examples, however, would again be misleading. Personal uncertainty has its manifest effects on interpersonal discussions, as is evident from Mr. A's "so far as I can now see" opinions, and his temporary willingness to "take sides against himself." In this respect, then, even Essay IV was remiss: it tended to separate the topics of personal uncertainty and disagreement, whereas it should have gone on to explore their connections.

(2) My misemphasis had nothing to do with the fact that it introduced a so-called noncognitive conception of ethics. It would have been equally misleading if it had introduced, say, a form of naturalistic ethics or a form of intuitionistic ethics. For in the latter views, too, there would have been a need of showing that uncertainty, no less than disagreement, is a prod to problem solving; and there would also have been a need of distinguishing the full question, "ought X to be done?" from the half-question, "I have no doubt that X ought (or ought not) to be done; so how can I get others to share my view?"

Throughout the essays, of course, I defended a special analysis of what "disagreement" and "uncertainty" mean in ethics. I denied, in contrast to both naturalism and intuitionism, that ethical disagreement involves only opposed beliefs, holding, rather, that it at once involves opposed beliefs (usually) and opposed attitudes, the latter being predominant in the ways mentioned on pages 4 f. And I conceived of ethical uncertainty in a parallel way, taking it to arise when these same opposed beliefs and attitudes are present in one individual (who is in ethical disagreement with himself, so to speak) rather than in several individuals. My conceptions had many implications with regard to the methods by which *either* disagreement *or* personal uncertainty could be resolved; but they had no connection, let me repeat, with my inadvertent tendency to say more about the former than about the latter.

(3) A number of contemporary writers, though basically in sympathy with my position, have nevertheless felt that there is "something more" in ethics than I have managed to find; and being suspicious of nonnaturalism, they have tried to effect a compromise between my type of view and naturalism.[4] I very much doubt, however, that a satisfactory compromise of that sort is possible. Naturalism is usually introduced by a persuasive definition (or if you will, by a norm-preserving or norm-altering definition); and when such a definition purports to belong to *analytical* philosophy it confuses the aim of meta-ethics with that of normative ethics. Or alternatively, naturalism becomes relativistic and encourages a confusion (see pp. 90-93) between "good" and "considered good." I should like to suggest, then, that the "something more" of ethics can be found not in a compromise with my view but rather in a more detailed development of its psychological background, beginning, as above, with a greater emphasis on personal uncertainty.

4

Since a complete study of the problematical aspects of ethics would be extremely complicated, I have been selecting from it the special topics that best serve my analytical purposes. It will not do, as we have just seen, to select merely those aspects that bear on disagreement. But we must also remember that a joint emphasis on disagreement *and uncertainty*, though less misleading, is still far from handling all the aspects of the problems. Let me restate this a little more emphatically:

It will be evident that a discussion comes to an end and is felt by

4. The compromise in question is curiously evident in Bertrand Russell's *Human Society in Ethics and Politics* (London, 1954), which begins with a position like my own, and like his own at the time he wrote ch. 9 of *Religion and Science* (New York, 1935), but afterwards veers off into naturalism and stays there. I find elements of the same tendency in Stephen Toulmin's *The Place of Reason in Ethics* (Cambridge, 1950), in R. M. Hare's *Language of Morals* (London, 1952), and in Patrick Nowell-Smith's *Ethics* (London, 1954).

those who take part in it to have "gotten somewhere" when the disagreement or uncertainty that originally prompted it gives place to agreement and certainty. It will be equally evident that this "happy ending," though it is now described in a way that does not neglect uncertainty, is still only a part of what is sought in a discussion. Many other things may be sought as well.

Mr. X, for example, is advising his son to go into a certain profession and is perfectly confident that his advice is good. He suspects that he could argue "effectively" by telling his son lies, or by giving him a one-sided description of the facts of the case (weighting rather than weighing the evidence), or by constantly repeating to him, with enthusiasm, favorable judgments of the profession, and so on. But Mr. X may in fact repudiate these methods. Although he is himself free from personal uncertainty and can accordingly bring about a "happy ending" of the discussion by securing his son's agreement, he may refuse to purchase the agreement at anything like *so high a price*. His aim of securing the "happy ending," accordingly, is to that extent counteracted by other and broader aims.

It is easy to see what sort of "price" may be in question. Although Mr. X is confident (by hypothesis) that his advice is good and suspects that lies and the like would lead his son to make the right decision in *this* case, he is presumably looking ahead to *further* cases. He may feel that such methods, by encouraging a habitual blindness, would affect many of his son's subsequent decisions, and affect them in a way that both parties would ultimately come to regret. Or he may feel that such methods would give rise, when later detected, to a strong resentment. He wants not merely a son in the given profession but also a son who continues to trust and respect him. And so on.

Mr. X himself, of course, may not bother to tell us these things and may not bear them explicitly in mind. If asked why he does not use the above methods he may reply that he simply is not made that way. And note that his reply, though it may for the most part indicate his impatience with the question, may also indicate something further: perhaps he finds truth telling and, in general, efforts to deal with others on equal terms rather than efforts to "manipulate" them, to be valuable *partly for their own sake*. There would be nothing anomalous in this. Mr. X did not, to be sure, have such a sentiment at birth; but no matter when he acquired it there is always the possibility that it now takes an "autonomous"[5] place in his personality and serves to guide his discussions in partial independence of any anticipated consequences.

As a further example let us take the case of Mr. Y, who frequently discusses politics at his club. The other members of the club are all confident Republicans, but Mr. Y is given to political doubts and wavers between a Republican and a Democratic position. This disturbs him because he has either to conceal his doubts or risk offending his friends. But he can easily take steps to "remedy" this situation. He can take care to read only Republican newspapers and attend only Republican rallys; and if through an inadvertency he turns on his television set when a Democrat is speaking, he can turn it off before he hears what the speaker is saying. By that means he can do at least a great deal toward transforming his uncertainty into certainty, and thus toward insuring that his discussions at the club will have "happy endings."

Now I am unable to maintain that the voting public includes no one who follows such a practice. But all the same, I shall not be making Mr. Y superhuman if I assume, for the purposes of this example, that he is not only reluctant to follow it but is at pains to avoid it. For although a freedom from uncertainty, permitting a full agreement with his friends, must be numbered *among* his aims, his other aims (as in my previous example, *mutatis mutandis*) have also their force in directing his procedure. These other aims, being rather like those that prevent him from avoiding danger in the manner of the ostrich, will need no special analysis. But note (once again) that they need not be wholly concerned, though they will doubtless be mainly concerned, with anticipated consequences. Mr. Y may

5. See *Ethics and Language*, pp. 194–98, where the functional autonomy of motives is discussed with references to J. S. Mill and G. W. Allport.

find that a careful attention to both sides of an issue is valuable partly for its own sake.

Let me point out that both of my examples, illustrating as they do the complexity of aims (or of motive, wants, and attitudes of all sorts), are in accord with a familiar principle, and one that has often been emphasized in the preceding essays. A man's aim in a discussion—i.e. what he wants to get from the discussion or give to it—is no simpler than any other aim. It too is an attitude and can be strengthened, weakened, or redirected by other attitudes, the latter having their effect through the mediation of a growing body of beliefs. And it can be taken as an *end in view*, as I have described in Essay VI (where my interpretation of Dewey leads his conception to become mine by adoption).[6] The attainment of certainty and agreement in a discussion, in fact, is *at most* an end in view, and it may cease to be even that when the available means are thought not to be justified by the end. So all that I am doing in this connection is to apply to discussion conduct, so to speak, the same principle that applies to ordinary conduct, the latter providing a discussion with its subject matter. Or if you will, I am describing the way in which a man might discuss discussions.

A further development of this topic could profitably deal with the *varying* things that people try to get from or give to a discussion; for individual differences in motivation are there enormous, ranging from modesty to egotism and from concealed selfishness to altruism. For the moment, however, I wish only to point out that my selective attention to uncertainty and disagreement is not to be confused with a psychological naiveté: I have not held that a discussion of ethics is guided *solely* by an effort to eliminate these factors, and I have repeatedly implied that it is not.

5

In concluding my remarks about the problematical aspects of ethics I want to go a little further into the *analysis* of personal uncertainty.

6. See pp. 110–113. For parallel remarks, developed with attention to the topic of disagreement, see *Ethics and Language*, ch. 8. What I there call a "focal aim" is akin to a large and important end in view.

In Essay IV,[7] where I took it to involve conflicting attitudes and to provoke reflections intended to resolve the conflict, I was obviously and avowedly borrowing from the views of John Dewey. I was trying to show, in effect, that his description of ethical problems pointed not to *his* account of meanings and methods, which were never clearly distinguished from those of science, but rather to *mine*. Beyond that (as is evident less from Essay IV than from the other essays) I amended Dewey by *generalizing* his references to conflicting attitudes, letting the conflict be social, as in disagreement, as well as personal, as in uncertainty. But with regard to the presence of conflicting attitudes in one individual and its correlation with ethical uncertainty, I had no quarrel with Dewey at all.

It is quite possible that I still have no quarrel with Dewey in this respect and that the remarks I am about to make, though seemingly at variance with him on points of detail, serve only to make explicit what he took for granted. But however that may be, I want to emphasize some distinctions that may help to make the ethical aspects of personal uncertainty more clearly understood. Once again, I can best proceed by example.

Mr. Z is convinced that he ought to vote in the next local election. He has until now, however, paid so little attention to local politics that the rival candidates are little more than names to him, and he doesn't know for whom to vote. He accordingly reads up on the candidates, listens to their speeches, and in general takes steps toward making a decision.

In such a case his inquiry does *not* begin with a conflict in his attitudes. He has so little knowledge about the candidates that he has no attitudes to them at all, nor is there any conflict (by hypothesis) that attends his felt duty to vote. There is indeed personal uncertainty, but it arises from a desire (itself an attitude) that is directed toward *developing* attitudes to the candidates. The desire in question, which establishes his end in view, involves no conflict simply because it is not for the moment being called into question, either with

7. See also my earlier and similar account in *Ethics and Language*, ch. 5, sect. 3.

regard to its cost of purchase or its cost of maintenance (see Essay VI, p. 109). Now it will not do to classify Mr. Z's inquiry as lying just outside ethics rather than within it; for it attends the question, "for whom *ought* I vote?" So when I said (Essay IV, p. 56) that personal uncertainty arises from a conflict and involves a consequent effort to make one's attitudes "speak with one voice," I was neglecting this sort of example.

But the example requires me only to qualify and not to repudiate my views. It continues to bear out my contention that ethically relevant beliefs serve to *guide* attitudes—as is here still the case, since Mr. Z's attitudes to the candidates develop in response to his growing body of beliefs about them. And it illustrates something that can arise, at most, only in the very first stages of an ethical problem, immediately giving place to a more complicated situation. To understand the latter point we need only go on with the example.

As Mr. Z learns more about the candidates he finds that he cannot give his unqualified support to any of them. He cannot get the political measures that he is *for* without accepting some that he is *against*. So a conflict in his attitudes immediately arises, and one of the sort that I have emphasized in Essay IV. Mr. Z partly does and partly does not want to vote in a certain way and is prodded into further inquiries and deliberations on that account. He may thus, via beliefs, connect his vote with still other attitudes, which in turn may lead him to make his decision one way or another. His uncertainty, prior to his decision, is in good measure an "uncertainty in attitude" —that term usefully paralleling my term "disagreement in attitude."

Not all cases, however, are so simple as this; so it is important to carry the example a step further. Suppose that Mr. Z, as he continues his inquiries, finds that one of the candidates is working for a measure that will be of interest, financially, to Mr. Z himself, but will be financially disadvantageous to the community as a whole. He is inclined to vote for this candidate but is again subject to a counter inclination. And the counter inclination, though it partly arises from his concern for the community, partly arises from something else. Being accustomed to take pride in his altruism (let us assume), he is ashamed at the thought of voting selfishly; and his desire to cast such a vote is to some extent blocked on *that* account.

It is of particular interest, here, to consider the sense in which a man can take pride in certain desires and be ashamed of others. As I see it, we have a situation in which certain attitudes have others as their objects. That is in principle nothing unusual: we have just seen that Mr. Z began with a *desire* directed to developing *attitudes* to the candidates. In that part of the example, however, we had a situation that did not as yet give rise to conflicts, whereas now, and in a different way, we have a situation that often does give rise to conflicts —the conflicts being between attitudes that are on different levels. But let me explain.

A man's attitudes are frequently directed to, and thus have as their object, this or that aspect of his environment; they can be correlated (though only roughly, to be sure) with his efforts to change his environment or to keep it from changing. Within limits he can thus "mold" his environment. But it is not only his environment, of course, that is of concern to him; for within limits he can also "mold" himself: he can eliminate certain traits from his personality and make other traits a permanent part of it. So when he is ashamed of some of his desires and proud of others, there is a point in saying that his second-level attitudes have first-level attitudes as their objects—the former being correlated, as before but *mutatis mutandis*, with his efforts to change the latter (i.e. the objects of the former) or to keep them from changing. One part of his personality attempts to control another and perhaps resisting part of it; and we have a special manifestation of the situation, decidedly familiar, that led Freud to say that the ego involved the super-ego and the id, and led Plato, two thousand years earlier, to use the figure of a charioteer with a white horse and a black horse.

It is foreign to my present purposes to comment on the *normative* implications of this aspect of psychology, save to say that they must not be exaggerated. If Mr. Z, for instance, ends by favoring one of the candidates with pride rather than with shame, we are not logically obliged to conclude, merely for that reason, that he favors the best candidate; nor is there any absurdity in our saying of a man (however much he may disagree with our judgment) that he is proud of his vices and ashamed of his virtues. But I do wish to point out that attitudes *to* attitudes, as above illustrated, must certainly be included in a description of personal conflicts, and thus in a description of ethical uncertainty. When Mr. Z cannot easily decide for whom to vote (in the last version of my example), his selfish desire is blocked by an altruistic desire *that is strengthened by his pride*; or what amounts to much the same thing, it is blocked, in part, by his second-level attitude of shame, which tends to give his first-level attitude, selfish desire, a more vulnerable place in his personality.

I have emphasized "pride" and "shame" in this connection but could also have used a number of alternative terms. Thus one may say that Mr. Z is inclined to "have contempt" for certain of his desires, regarding their objects as "temptations" that he is "struggling to resist"; or one may say that he considers them a part of his "lower" nature and not of his "higher" or "ideal" or "true" nature, or that he "feels cheap" when he "yields" to them. And so on.

It will be evident then, if I may now recapitulate, that personal uncertainty in ethics may take various forms. Sometimes it involves only the absence of certain attitudes together with a desire for knowledge that will help to develop them. But it usually involves a conflict of attitudes, and the conflict may be either between attitudes on the same level or between attitudes on different levels.

My passing comments on second-level attitudes—which deserve far more elaboration than is here possible—help to reinforce my answer to those who seek for "something more" in ethics than my view provides. They can best find it, let me repeat, by supplementing my view with a richer psychological background.[8] A psycho-

8. Professor David Falk, whose views on ethics belong to the same family as mine has discussed various aspects of the psychological background of ethics in a way that I find illuminating. He has said less about the point I here mention than about a quite different point—one concerned with the factual reasons that may support a judgment. These reasons, he reminds us, do not necessarily have to introduce beliefs that are *new*

logical background is needed for *any* type of meta-ethics, and in my opinion is too much neglected in contemporary philosophy. But I have paused to examine personal uncertainty for other reasons as well. An understanding of it, particularly with regard to second-level attitudes, has its obvious bearings on the methodological aspects of ethics. And the quite disparate forms that it may take roughly correspond to the varying degrees of complexity that are found in ethical problems; for as we all know, and as the above remarks do something to explain, some of our ethical problems present only minor difficulties, whereas others become overwhelmingly perplexing and can pervade the whole of our emotional and intellectual life.

It will be evident that if personal uncertainty involved only first-level attitudes, F^1, F^2, etc., directed to the objects O^1, O^2, etc., then the ethically relevant reasons, helping to remove the uncertainty, would need to explore only (!) the nature and consequences of the O's; for the new F's that were thus brought into play would need no special scrutiny. But when second-level attitudes also enter, directed to the F's, then the reasons must also explore the F's and the consequences of letting them continue as parts of one's personality. Nor is there any objection, in principle, to the recognition of third-level attitudes, and so on. The complexity of an ethical problem, then, is not only potentially unlimited, but potentially unlimited in more than one direction.

For the moment I need make only one further remark about personal uncertainty—a remark that deals with its relation to the socially shared attitudes that make up the mores of a community. It is well known that anyone's attitudes are strongly influenced by these mores, sometimes being a mirror image of them. And it is important to see that my account of ethics must not and need not forget that. In discussing personal uncertainty, of course, I have been emphasizing only the attitudes of the man who feels the uncertainty,

to this or that person; they often serve to drive home a person's old beliefs, or to make him bear them fully in mind, or to make him take them to heart. Only then do the beliefs become likely to affect attitudes. (I refer to papers that are still in manuscript but will soon, I hope, be published.)

taking his relationship to his community for granted. But that is feasible simply because the effect of his community, insofar as it bears on his personal uncertainty, always takes the form of influencing and reinforcing some attitude of *his*. He is likely to find his uncertainty particularly troublesome, for instance, when he begins to question the mores and feels a conflict between the attitude that he "inherits" from his society and some new attitude that is "peculiarly" his own (the latter being one that, if expressed, may have its element of force in bringing about a *change* in the mores). Or again, he is likely to find his uncertainty particularly troublesome when the mores of a part of his society differ from those of another part and force him to choose between them. And I am mentioning, it must be remembered, only the problematical cases. There are countless times when a man's attitudes are in full accord with his mores, his experience giving him no occasion for questioning them; in those cases he makes ethical judgments without any sense of uncertainty at all. The mores come into view, in short, as soon as we look behind the individual's uncertainty or certainty and consider its origins.

To say that the mores are usually right is to state a conservative position, and to say that they are usually wrong is to state a radical one; but neither position, it must be understood, is implied by the wholly descriptive, nonnormative meta-theory that I am trying to develop.

I emphasize an individual's attitudes, in dealing with personal uncertainty in ethics, for the same reason that I would emphasize an individual's beliefs in dealing with personal uncertainty in science. When a scientist hesitates between alternative hypotheses, his uncertainty arises from the state of *his* beliefs. That is compatible with the observation that he has "inherited" ever so many of his beliefs from the scientific tradition; it in no way attempts to estimate the extent to which the scientific tradition is defensible or indefensible.[9]

9. For some further remarks about the mores and their relation to an individual's judgment, see *Ethics and Language*, p. 94.

6

I must now leave the first of my broad questions, which deals with ethical problems, and turn to my second one, which deals with the meaning of ethical terms.

Since the problems are connected with attitudes, and in a way that distinguishes them from factual problems, I have taken the ethical terms, which formulate them, as being likewise connected with attitudes. More specifically, I have emphasized their *emotive meaning*—that being a tendency, arising from the history of their usage, to express the attitudes of the speaker and to evoke those of the hearer or hearers.[10] The terms accordingly become "laudatory" or "derogatory," or terms "of praise" or "of disparagement," depending on whether their emotive meaning is favorable or unfavorable.

I shall not pause to discuss whether or not my semi-technical senses of "emotive" and "meaning" foster a misleading way of speaking (see Essay IX) but instead shall attempt to clarify my view by emphasizing such neighboring terms as "tends to express," and "tends to evoke," and by comparing or contrasting the typical functions of factual sentences with those of evaluative sentences. In that way I can connect my view with those of Russell, Ayer, Carnap, and others[11] (for I have sought only to qualify and supplement, not repudiate, what they have said) and can also call attention to the simple and obvious but nevertheless important observation that underlies my view—one to the effect that our language has functions over and above its cognitive functions.

10. See Essay IX, p. 165, for a needed qualification of this definition of "emotive meaning." In *Ethics and Language*, pp. 59 ff., the term is defined with reference to *feelings* or attitudes. I think that that more generic sense of the term is for many purposes convenient; but for ethical purposes the present, more specific sense is also useful.

11. See List of Works Cited. For a discussion of various early contributions to the so-called noncognitive theory, see *Ethics and Language*, pp. 265–68. I regret that my discussion there neglected the ethical writings of A. Hägerström, now available in C. D. Broad's translation from the Swedish, and R. B. Braithwaite's remarkably penetrating paper, "Verbal Ambiguity and Philosophical Analysis," *Proceedings of the Aristotelian Society*, n.s. 28 (1927–28), 135–54.

It will be evident that factual sentences, in which cognitive functions are primary, are normally in declarative form, rather than in interrogative or imperative or exclamatory form; and they have in common a *tendency to express* the speaker's belief. Nor is that a linguistic accident. If a person regularly (as distinct from occasionally, as in rhetorical questions) attempted to express his beliefs by sentences not in the declarative form, those who managed to conjucture what he was driving at would immediately proceed to correct his English. But only rarely does a speaker use factual sentences to talk *about* his beliefs (or to *refer to* them, or to *designate* them, etc.). If he says "I used to believe that Jones insulted Smith," he is indeed talking about one of his beliefs, though one different from any that he thereby tends to express. If he says "Jones insulted Smith," however, he is not talking about his beliefs at all (though he presumably *is* expressing one) but is simply talking about Jones and Smith and an insult, or more specifically, about Jones' having insulted Smith.

There is a distinction, then, between what a sentence tends to express and what it is about, and the distinction helps us to see what "tends to express," in one of its important senses, commonly means. Similarly, "If only Jones would insult Smith!" tends to express a wish but is not about that wish; whereas "I used to wish that Jones would insult Smith" *is* about a wish but does *not* tend to express it. Here we have much the same express-versus-about distinction, save that a wish rather than a belief is in question. I should add that the distinction (or at least neighboring forms of it) can be found in a number of writers. It is preserved in W. E. Johnson's[12] terminology by "assertive attitude" and "assertum," in H. N. Sheffer's[13] by "prescript" and "ascript," and in R. M. Hare's[14] by "neustic" and "phrastic."

Let us now turn to evaluative sentences, with attention to the

---

12. *Logic* (Cambridge, 1921), I, ch. l, particularly pp. 3 ff.

13. I hope I remember correctly the terminology used by Professor Sheffer in his courses at Harvard, 1933–34.

14. *Language of Morals*, p. 18.

same distinction. What shall be said of "Jones ought not to have insulted Smith"? Since the sentence is in declarative form, we may be inclined to assume that it too tends to express a belief; and to a limited extent, to be sure, we are not unjustified in that assumption. The sentence is commonly used to imply strongly that Jones *did* insult Smith and can accordingly be taken as tending to express a belief to that effect. And it may tend under certain circumstances to express other beliefs: as has been explained in Essay VIII, "ought not" brings with it certain factual *suggestions*, and these, when "promoted" by a persuasive definition to the status of *meanings*, may make the sentence tend to express, say, some belief about the consequences of the insult in question. In such ways the declarative form of the sentence serves helpfully rather than misleadingly to show that its functions resemble those of a factual sentence.

There is no reason to suppose, however, that an evaluative sentence is limited to these cognitive functions, and that (as naturalism would have it) it is accordingly indistinguishable from a certain kind of factual sentence. We would not classify it as "evaluative," in my opinion, unless it tended also to express the speaker's attitude. In the present example it tends to express disapproval of Jones' having insulted Smith. Of course it is *about* Jones, Smith, and the insult, etc., since in that way it provides the disapproval with a specified object. But it is not about the disapproval any more than "Jones insulted Smith" is about a belief. It "tends to express" the attitude, rather than just this or that belief, because its component evaluative term, "ought not," permits the declarative form of the sentence to take on an added function, and a function that is embodied in our customary habits of speaking.

The word "express," when used with reference to attitudes no less than to beliefs, is not, I think, being diverted to a misleading sense. For suppose that a man says "Jones insulted Smith" without believing that the alleged insult took place. That is comparable, *mutatis mutandis*, to his saying "Jones ought not to have insulted Smith" without his really disapproving of the alleged insult. Given certain attendant circumstances, the first case involves lying and the second involves, if not lying, then hypocrisy. Although lying and hypocrisy differ, they obviously belong to the same family. There is in both cases a (potentially) deceptive use of words, arising from the fact that the words don't *express* what they *tend* and thus *seem* to express. So the terms "express a belief" and "express an attitude" represent parallel locutions.

Other examples point in the same direction. Thus the sentence, "it will rain, but I do not believe that it will," is self-defeating (or one that formulates a "pragmatic contradiction") because, if it does what it tends to do, it will first express one of the speaker's beliefs and then go on to express a second one, to the effect that he does not have the first one. We have a similar absurdity in "he is good in all respects, but in no respect whatsoever do I approve of him." If this does what it tends to do, it will first express the speaker's *attitude* and then go on to express a belief (about the attitude) to the effect that he does not have the attitude.

In spite of their absurdity such examples suggest various other points that deserve attention. Note that it is *not* self-defeating to say, "it will rain, but not long ago I did not believe so"; nor is it self-defeating to say, "he is good in all respects, but not long ago I approved of him in no respect." So far from being self-defeating, such sentences merely indicate (without saying so in so many words) that the speaker has recently changed his mind. Their "innocence" arises from the fact that the second verb in each is in the past tense and accordingly makes the second part of the sentence refer to a belief or attitude that the first part has *not* expressed. A belief or attitude, insofar as it is expressed, is necessarily contemporary with the utterance of the sentence that expresses it; and its existence is not denied, of course, by any reference to a different belief or attitude that existed previously.

Somewhat similarly, it is not self-defeating to say, "it will rain, but my friend Robinson does not believe that it will"; nor is it self-defeating to say, "he is good in all respects, but my friend Robinson approves of him in no respect." The sentences would be self-defeating only if the last part of each of them denied the existence of a belief or attitude *of the speaker*, as *expressed* in the first part; but here the last part refers only to *Robinson's* belief or attitude. (Trustworthy utterances of such sentences, then, indicate merely that the speaker disagrees with Robinson.)

So much, then, for the similarities that help to justify my generic use of the term "express." I mention them in order to clarify what I mean when I say that evaluative sentences may be distinguished from factual sentences in that they (in part, at least) tend to express attitudes, rather than merely to express beliefs. In Essay V, Section 5, having perhaps too briefly made a similar distinction, I went on at greater length to discuss its importance and need here only review my conclusions. The broad nature of a *problem* is evident from what sentences tend to express, rather than from what they are about. I.e. the extent to which they express attitudes, and not just beliefs, indicates the extent to which any uncertainty or disagreement that attends them is *in attitude* and not just in belief. And this in turn determines the broad sorts of *reasons* that are needed in handling the problem, which may be either reasons for approving (or disapproving) or else reasons for believing (or disbelieving). If we should misconceive the function of our evaluative sentences, then, supposing that they expressed only beliefs, we should give a confused impression of the reasons that can be used to support them. We should hide, rather than reveal, the variety of factual knowledge that can relevantly be brought to bear on our attitudes, and which alone (in a familiar sense, but not the sense of the logicians) can provide them with a *rational* guide.

The word "express" emphasizes the relation of a sentence to a *speaker*, dealing with its relation to a *hearer* only by implication. If we turn more explicitly to the latter relation, however, we shall see that it introduces much the same considerations. Just as factual sentences bear on the hearer's beliefs, so evaluative sentences bear, beyond that, on his attitudes. Or as I am accustomed to put it, the sentences respectively tend to "evoke" the hearer's beliefs or attitudes.

But the term "evoke," let me immediately acknowledge, is not altogether a suitable one. (I have used it in want of a better one and because I have felt that the introduction of a new term would be needlessly technical.) The inadequacy of the term is no less evident with regard to beliefs, of course, than it is with regard to attitudes. To say that a factual sentence tends to evoke the hearer's beliefs is to say little more than that it tends to produce or recall it; and although "tend," here, avoids the absurdity of implying that the hearer always believes what he is told, the word "evoke" still misses something that is essential to the situation. It fails to emphasize the *intent* of the speaker with regard to the hearer (for even a liar intends his factual remarks to be believed), and it fails to emphasize the many conventions and customs by which the communication between a hearer and a speaker is normally governed.

I am indebted to Mr. J. O. Urmson for pointing this out to me in personal discussions, and also for suggesting that a more suitable term, if one were available, would belong to the same family as "invite." To say that a factual sentence normally "invites" the hearer's belief is not, to be sure, *just* what I want to say. For certain cases the term would be too weak, much as "demands" (replacing it) would for certain cases be too strong. But I think Urmson is perfectly right about the family connections of the needed term. It must, *like* "invites," be related to a hearer in a way that takes account of the speaker's intent and of the conventions and customs that bear on the situation. If it causes a hearer to accept a belief, it does so *in that special way.*

An official term is fortunately not indispensible, however; and if for the moment I may be permitted to use the makeshift term, "invites-so-to-speak," then I can make my point thus: Just as a factual sentence typically invites-so-to-speak the hearer to share the speaker's expressed belief, so an evaluative sentence (though it may in part do the same thing) typically invites-so-to-speak the hearer to share the speaker's expressed attitude.

In regard to its relations to a speaker *and* to a hearer, of course, a sentence lends itself to "so far as I can now see" remarks and thus does not stand apart from the uncertainty or the merely tentative disagreement (or agreement) that I have illustrated previously. Much depends on the speaker's tone of voice or on his use of such a word as "perhaps." Thus "perhaps Jones insulted Smith" tends to express a belief that is not free from uncertainty and invites-so-to-speak the hearer to share a belief *of that sort*. And "perhaps Jones ought not to have insulted Smith" tends to express, in part at least, an *attitude* that is not free from uncertainty (the uncertainty being *in* attitude, of course, though it can be largely due to one in belief), and sends out its invitation-so-to-speak in a corresponding way.

7

Having restated my view I can now call attention to a needless and unwanted complexity that made its way into some of my earlier essays, particularly Essays II and VII. According to those essays "X is good" can be taken, in part, to have the same meaning as "I approve of X" and thus (again in part) to have a certain "auto-biographical" function. The emotive function (concerned with expressing and so-to-speak-inviting attitudes) was taken not as replacing this autobiographical one but only as supplementing it. In effect, then, "X is good" was said (1) to express the speaker's approval of X, and (2) to express, over and above that, his belief that he has this approval—in each case, of course, with corresponding so-to-speak invitations to the hearer. Now my view becomes more plausible when, as in the preceding section, (2) is deleted, leaving the connection between "X is good" and the speaker's approval to be specified by (1) alone. The need of this deletion was pointed out to me by G. E. Moore;[15] and although I once thought (and said in Essay IX, p. 168) that it would merely free my analysis from a pardonable

15. In his reply to Essay VII (see *The Philosophy of G. E. Moore*, ed. P. A. Schilpp, pp. 537–54), Moore said that he was uncertain whether to accept his old position or to accept one *like* mine, and went on, with the analytical acumen and detachment for which he was always so admirable, to suggest that mine needed to be amended. I am here accepting his proposed amendment; and my grounds for doing so, which I am about to give, may be of a sort that Moore had in mind—though as to that I cannot, of course, be sure. In any case, my indebtedness to Moore, here and elsewhere, is a great one.

redundancy, I have subsequently come to consider it more important than that.

It is important, in my opinion, because of its bearing on the general topic of *reasons*; and to explain what I mean let me return to my comparison between factual and evaluative sentences, developing my examples a little further.

Suppose that "Jones insulted Smith" is said by Mr. X, who, though not exactly lying, is nevertheless speaking deceptively. He neither believes nor disbelieves what he says (knowing nothing at all about the insult); but as a man accustomed to take part in gossip, he feels that he is expected to have an opinion on the matter, and he says what he says in order to simulate an opinion. His simulated opinion is not necessarily a false one, however, so he is still free to look for reasons that will substantiate his remark; and if by good luck he can find these reasons, they will be apropos because, and just because, they help to show that Jones insulted Smith. They will *not* have to show that his initial remark really expressed the belief that it seemed to express. In other words, his reasons for his remark have only to substantiate that remark and do not have to free him from a suspicion of having made it, initially, without any real conviction.

Those to whom Mr. X is speaking may of course see through him: they may be able to describe just what he is doing and give reasons to justify their description. But that is only to say that their interests extend to a further topic—one that is no longer about the ways of Jones but is instead about the ways of Mr. X. And their reasons, it must be particularly noted, go beyond those mentioned above; for they are no longer reasons for or against any assertion formulated in the words, "Jones insulted Smith," but are instead reasons for the quite different assertion that can be formulated in such words as "when Mr. X initially said that Jones insulted Smith he did not particularly believe it."

The example readily illustrates my simple point. We must not suppose that it would be merely gratuitous, as distinct from incorrect, to claim that

(a) "Jones insulted Smith"

has in part (and thus includes) the meaning of

  (b) "I [the speaker] believe that Jones insulted Smith."

For we should then be claiming not only that (a) tends to express the speaker's belief but also that it is in part about that belief, as (b) is. And that would be more than a harmless redundancy[16] in the analysis of (a). It would imply that the reasons needed to substantiate (a) include those that are needed to substantiate (b)—an implication that we have just seen to be incorrect. Parallel remarks could be made, of course, about any other factual sentence.

If we now turn from factual sentences to evaluative sentences we shall find that we need much the same distinction and for much the same reasons—though we must, as usual, substitute the word "attitude" for the word "belief."

For suppose that Mr. X, having discovered that he was telling the truth when he said that Jones insulted Smith, goes on to say that Jones *ought not* to have done so. And suppose that he is still so ignorant of the details that he really neither disapproves nor approves of the insult but is again merely saying the sort of thing that he thinks is expected of him. As before, his as yet unsubstantiated remark has a chance of being substantiatable; and in going on to look for reasons he need only consider those that bear on an evaluation of the insult. That is to say, he is called upon to justify what he said, namely, "Jones ought not to have insulted Smith." And *apart from a change in topic*, he is not called upon (fortunately, for him) to establish the (factual) statement, "when I said that Jones ought not to have insulted Smith I was not simulating my disapproval."

We can thus repeat, *mutatis mutandis*, the conclusion drawn above

16. If we call "Jones insulted Smith but I do not believe that he did" a *pragmatic contradiction*, then we may with equal propriety call "Jones insulted Smith and I believe that he did" a *pragmatic redundancy*. But a pragmatic contradiction is not (as is a statement of the form "p and not-p") the genuine contradiction of logic; and similarly, a pragmatic redundancy is not (as is a statement of the form "p and p") the genuine redundancy of logic. In a pragmatic redundancy the second part-sentence (as illustrated above) *adds* something to what the first part-sentence says: it talks *about* what the first part-sentence tends to *express*.

and thereby correct the assumption that was embodied in some of my early papers. It will not do to claim that

(a) "Jones ought not to have insulted Smith"

has in part (and thus includes) the meaning of

(b) "I [the speaker] disapprove of Jones' having insulted Smith."

For we should then be claiming not only that (a) tends to express the speaker's attitude but also that it is in part about (i.e. is in part expressing a belief about) that attitude, as (b) is. And that would be more than a harmless redundancy in the analysis of (a). It would imply that the reasons needed to support (a) include those needed to support (b), as is not the case.

This conclusion, requiring the deletion of what I have above called the "autobiographical" element in my analysis of ethical judgments, does much to simplify the analysis. I discussed the possibility of just such a simplification (though without seeing that it was mandatory) in my *Ethics and Language*,[17] and then went on to say: "If we are to have a full understanding of the flexibilities of language, [an emphasis on] this simplicity is not desirable. We must deal with all the important possibilities; and the purely emotive senses of the ethical terms [i.e. those not introducing the autobiographical element], though among these possibilities, are not complicated enough to require any attention beyond that which our general study of emotive meaning has provided." But I am now convinced that I exaggerated, to say the least, when I said that the simpler senses needed no further attention; and the various complexities that attended the autobiographical element,[18] which I worked out in full detail, now impress me, so far as ethics is concerned, as being aside from the point. Having incorrectly admitted them, I had to take care to bow them out again. (Happily, however, I excluded the autobiographical element from my "second pattern of analysis," and from the essay in the present volume that parallels my second pattern, namely Essay III.)

17. P. 95, bottom, p. 96, top, and note 13, p. 96.

18. Incidentally, what I took to be the autobiographical element does not always attend the words "I approve" or "I disapprove." See Essay V, p. 80, note 13.

When my analysis takes a nonautobiographical form it requires me, of course, to alter the "models" that I have used (particularly in *Ethics and Language*) in comparing evaluative sentences with those that are partly in the imperative mode. (That is true quite apart from the rich meanings of evaluative sentences that are taken up in Essay III.) My (first pattern) model for "X is good," namely, "I approve of X; do so as well," is more instructive when changed to "Let us approve of X." But it must be remembered that imperatives, in this connection, are useful only for the purpose of analogy, and indeed, only for the purpose of cutting through the supposition that ethical sentences can express nothing but beliefs. If expected to do more than that, imperative models will be misleading.

Note, for instance, that "X is good" is no closer to "let us approve of X" than "X is yellow" is to "let us believe that X is yellow." The latter model, unlike the former, is altogether useless, since it cuts through no supposition that needs to be cut through. But in other respects the two models are alike.

It is impossible, in my opinion, to "translate" an evaluative sentence into either an imperative or a factual sentence—or even into a gerundive sentence. One can clarify it only by describing or "characterizing" its typical functions. I myself think that the term "emotive meaning," so long as it is kept in a technical sense, can be helpful rather than misleading in such an undertaking; but that, as I have said, I do not want to discuss here. Meanwhile such terms as "tends to express attitudes" and "tends to invite-so-to-speak attitudes" are available; and they serve well enough, I think, to dispel the preoccupation with beliefs that underlie both naturalism and (in its standard forms) nonnaturalism.

8

Having mentioned the imperative models I want to point out a respect in which they have been *decidedly* misleading. They have caused people to claim that ethical judgments, when analyzed as having functions that differ from cognitive functions, are thereby marked as being "neither true nor false." And that claim, though no less characteristic of those who have defended the analysis in question than of those who have criticized it, does nothing to clarify the issue and does much to confuse it.

It is perfectly obvious, of course, that "true" and "false" are not used in connection with *imperatives*. There is a certain intelligibility (though also an oddness) in saying "let us approve of him"; but there is none in saying "it is true that let us approve of him" or "it is false that let us approve of him." And when Mr. X says, "John, close the door," John may reply by saying "yes" or "no," but not by saying "that is true" or "that is false." Such an observation cannot, however, be transferred without more ado to contexts in which ethical sentences are used. There is at most an *imperfect* analogy between imperatives and ethical sentences; and if we want to understand how "true" and "false" are related to the latter, we cannot go by this analogy alone. We must take into account how "true" and "false" actually behave in our ethical discourse.

Now an attention to our ethical discourse—and indeed, to any sort of evaluative discourse, no matter whether it is concerned with morality or beauty or (even) the "good manners" of etiquette— shows that it allows us to introduce "true" and "false" with full linguistic propriety and without any trace, in practice, of making our judgments obscure. Thus when Mr. A says, "on the whole, he is a good man," Mr. B can readily answer, "that is true"; nor will A be likely to accuse B of speaking oddly or unintelligibly. We should have a parallel situation if B were to reply, alternatively, "although it is true that he is a good man *on the whole*, it is also true that he has some all too human frailties." And if Mr. C, now joining the conversation, should say, "if you listen only to the favorable judgments that his political allies make of his character, you may indeed suppose that he is a good man; but in my opinion their judgments are for the most part false," he too cannot be accused of speaking oddly or unintelligibly. It is idle, then, to say that ethical judgments can be neither true nor false. Such a view would represent not an effort to preserve our normal habits of speech but rather an effort to reform them. And although it must be granted that our habits of speech, on occasion, are in need of reform, this particular reform shows every sign of being so inconvenient that its advantages (if any) would fail to justify it.

So let us agree, in deference to our language, to say that ethical judgments *are* either true or false; and let us go on to the further question: "Since they are either true or false must we assign them a function that is exclusively, or at least primarily, cognitive?" This is in effect to ask whether our customary use of "true" and "false" runs counter to the analysis that is here being defended. The answer, as I see it, is very simple. It is definitely a "no," and for the following reason:

The words "true" and "false" become appropriate or inappropriate to their context, with regard to the point now in question, on account of a linguistic rule that is *purely syntactical*. In expressions of the form, "it is true that p," for instance, the rule stipulates nothing about the *function* of the sentence that replaces "p," but has entirely to do with the grammatical structure of that sentence. It requires nothing more, in fact, than that the sentence be in the declarative mood. So when a sentence is evaluative and when, accordingly, it introduces such terms as "good," "wrong," etc., *without ceasing to be in the declarative mood*, the possibility of putting "it is true that" in front of it shows nothing whatsoever about its cognitive or noncognitive function—i.e. nothing whatsoever about whether it expresses a belief or an attitude or both or neither. The same can be said, let me add, about the reply, "that is true." It is *linguistically* permissible if and only if the antecedent of the demonstrative pronoun "that" is a remark in the declarative mood.

We can readily see this in a case that does not involve ethical judgments. Suppose that a certain historian has often made undocumented statements. Having pointed this out for past cases we might go on to say, "can we suppose, then, that he can document his present statement?" Here our question, being rhetorical, has a function resembling that of the declarative sentence, "we cannot suppose, then, that he can document his present statement." But in spite of its function it is *formulated* as a question. And so long as that is the case, one cannot reply by saying "that is true." Only a *declarative reformulation* of our rhetorical question can prompt such a reply.

Or consider a case in which a declarative sentence does the work of an epithet, as in "he's a stinker." Here we are linguistically free to reply, "how true," or "that is simply not true," etc.—and just because of the grammatical structure of the initial remark. Our reply, moreover, will in no way suggest that we have missed the epithetical function of the remark.

Now (to return to my central topic) it is precisely this rule that makes us feel so comfortable, in our ordinary discourse, about calling *value judgments* true or false. And it is a rule that cannot, in the very nature of the case, run counter to the analysis that I am defending; for my analysis deals only with the function of value judgments (or rather, with the *tendencies* of words that fit them for a certain function), whereas the rule deals only with the grammatical structure of the judgments. Thus when the analysis points out a (slight) functional resemblance between value judgments and imperatives, the rule simply reminds us that the judgments, being formulated in the declarative mood, can be called true or false even so.

An attention to the rule is useful, however, in helping us to see that imperative models for value judgments are likely to be misleading. The rule *does* prevent us from calling *imperatives* true or false. And if we exaggerate the accuracy of the models, taking them not only to hint at the function but also to preserve the grammar of value judgments (the latter being an absurdity, of course) we shall be tempted to draw the conclusion that I am here repudiating—namely, the conclusion that the judgments, like their models, are neither true nor false.

We have still to ask, to be sure, *in what sense* a value judgment is true or false. But perhaps a few examples will help to clear up that matter as well.

When Mr. A says "Jones ought not to have done it," and Mr. B replies, "that is true," what is the force of B's reply? Rather obviously he too has said, in abbreviated form, the equivalent of "Jones ought not to have done it." His "that is true" permits him as it were to repeat A's remark, thus expressing an attitude (apart from hypocrisy) that is in agreement with A's. The extent of their agreement in *belief* will usually not be evident until they go on to give reasons for their judgments. Note, by the way, that if B had answered, "no, that is false," he would in effect have said, "Jones ought to have done it, or at least, it was all right for him to have done it."

To continue: when Mr. A says "Jones ought not to have done it," and adds "yes, it is true that he ought not to have done it," just what does this linguistically permissible but rather unusual addition amount to ? So far as I can see it amounts to very little. Mr. A is in effect repeating himself, perhaps in an attempt at greater emphasis. (But his attempt at greater emphasis may not help him, of course, since his protestation of truth may suggest that his judgment is attended not by an earnest conviction but rather by an uncertainty that he is combating within himself.)

We have a little more complexity in the example that follows. Mr. B takes Mr. A as his ultimate authority on politics. He acknowledges that he has not read Mr. A's article about the present administration, but he does not hesitate to say in advance: "Whatever A says in his article about what the administration ought or ought not to do is true." Now what he is saying, in effect, could also be said in such words as these: "Whenever A says in his article that the administration ought to do so and so, then the administration ought to do so and so; and whenever he says that it ought not to do so and so, then it ought not to do so and so." It will be noted that B's use of "true" does not enable him to repeat, in effect, A's judgments; for he does not yet know know what A has said. It does, however, commit him to sharing these judgments if or when he finds out what they are, and in the same manner, it invites-so-to-speak others to share them. So the example, in spite of its initial appearance, is very like my first one.

I would have to give further examples, of course, if I wanted to cover all the typical cases; but perhaps I have now said enough to establish my point. In emphasizing the noncognitive aspects of ethical judgments my analysis does not cause the terms "true" and "false," as commonly used in connection with the judgments, to become unintelligible or obscure.

One may at first suspect, in view of my remarks, that ethical judgments are true or false only in atypical senses of the terms—in senses that have little or nothing to do with those that are appropriate to factual contexts. But I am myself inclined to doubt that. I am inclined with Frank Ramsey to think that "true" and "false," even in factual contexts, have a far simpler function than philosophers have usually supposed. When Mr. A, for instance, makes the factual remark, "Jones did it," and Mr. B replies, "that is true," what has B done, essentially, other than reaffirm what A has said? (He expresses a belief that concurs with A's belief, just as in the ethical case he expresses an attitude that concurs with A's attitude.) And when Mr. A, having said that Jones did it, goes on to say, "it is true that Jones did it," what is he doing other than giving his initial statement an added emphasis? (His "it is true that" here accentuates his expression of belief, just as in the evaluative case it accentuated his expression of attitude.) But these are matters that lead too far into epistemology to permit me to develop them here. I must be content to refer the reader to my all too brief discussion of the topic in *Ethics and Language*, and to the various articles developing Ramsey-like theories of truth that have appeared in the past several decades.[19]

For the present I need only say that my examples point to a sense, whether typical or atypical, in which the remark, "ethical judgments are neither true nor false," is absurd. Those who have insisted on the remark have spoken with an insensitivity to the ways of our language. Nor can I, in spite of my critical discussions of the remark in *Ethics and Language*, pretend to have been entirely free from such

19. See *Ethics and Language*, pp. 169–71 (where my discussion needlessly dwells on the "autobiographical" element that I introduced into ethics) and p. 267, bottom. See also Frank Ramsey, *Foundations of Mathematics* (New York, 1931), pp. 142 ff.; A. J. Ayer, *Language, Truth and Logic* (London, 1936), pp. 122 ff.; Alfred Tarski, "The Semantic Conception of Truth," *Philosophy and Phenomenological Research 4*, (Mar. 1944), pp. 341–75; and the symposium between P. W. Strawson and J. L. Austin on "Truth," *Proceedings of the Aristotelian Society*, supp. vol. *24* (1950).

an insensitivity. But it remains the case that the general sort of analysis that I am defending remains intact when "true" and "false" are restored to their proper place in ethics. The answers to the central questions—whether they are concerned with the nature of ethical problems, terms, or reasons—can all be stated in a way that takes truth and falsity into account.

It should be particularly noted that the remark, "ethical judgments are neither true nor false," is so contrary to our linguistic habits that it leaves us perplexed about its meaning; and to resolve our perplexity we may be inclined to interpret it as meaning that ethical judgments are neither to be defended nor to be attacked. We may suppose that no attitude, according to the analysis in question, is worth expressing or worth being guided by a knowledge of the factual situation in which it might arise. Once this supposition is formulated, of course, no one in sanity could take it seriously or even suppose that anyone else ever took it seriously. But when the supposition is only half-formulated and comes to mind in an imperfect way, it may trouble our common sense with hidden, artificial worries. So an attempt to dismiss "true" and "false" from ethics, though absurd, is something whose absurdity needs to be pointed out. It may otherwise seem to give a "philosophical" inevitability to the genuine worries of everyday life and thus cause us, in certain moods, to have a "profound" sense of insecurity. Much the same can be said, I suspect, of our alleged lack of a free will, and our alleged inability to know about other people's minds, and various other confusions that must be combated in philosophy—confusions that do not, of course, spring wholly from our language, but which an attention to our language may help to dispel.

9

An analytical study of values can profitably begin with such judgments as "he ought to do it" and "his character is good"— judgments that are at once generic and simply worded. Many additional questions arise, however, with regard to judgments that are more specific and judgments that involve special idioms. I can here do no more than consider samples of the latter sorts of judgment; but that much, at least, I now want to do. The samples promise to be of interest in themselves, and they are also needed in order to show that the preceding essays, which have rarely dealt with them, do not attempt (and could not reasonably have attempted) to present a complete study of our evaluative discourse.

Consider, then, "he is courageous," where "courageous" yields a (prima facie) favorable judgment that is rather specific. In rough approximation, we may take it as equivalent to "he habitually makes a stand against danger in a manner that is admirable." I speak of a rough approximation largely because there should be some reference to the man's intent, and about his awareness of the danger and the circumstances attending it; but if such matters are allowed for, the approximation will serve its present purpose.

It will be evident that the evaluative force of "courageous" is preserved solely by "admirable." The first part of the proposed analysis has no evaluative force but simply gives a half-indeterminate factual description of the man in question. (If we should couple the first part with "not admirable" we should suggest rashness rather than courage and thus reverse the evaluative force of the sentence— though of course there would quite possibly be an implied change in the [factually describable] *manner* in which the stand against danger was made.) So by my proposed analysis, "he is courageous" is of a hybrid character: its meaning has at once an important factual component and an important evaluative component. And there can be little doubt, I think, that the factual component does more than the evaluative component to make its meaning specific rather than generic.

My example is not unrelated to the considerations of Essay III, where I have explained that a persuasive definition may cause virtually any value judgment to contain a factual component. But it emphasizes a point that Essay III did not make sufficiently explicit. In "he is courageous" the factual component, so far as it includes some or another habitual stand against danger, plainly and simply *belongs* to the sentence, being fixed by the conventions of our language. If we tried to remove it by a persausive definition—saying, for instance, "the truly courageous man invariably becomes paralyzed in the presence of danger"—we should leave others at a loss to see what we were driving at. In general, a hybrid judgment (which may with equal propriety be called a hybrid *statement*, but might more happily be called a hybrid *remark*) has an evaluative force that attends a "core" of factual description, the latter being not merely permitted by the rules of language but actually required by them.

The core of factual description does something to complicate the reasons that bear on such judgments, but only in obvious respects. In considering whether a man is courageous, for instance, we must first determine whether he habitually makes any sort of stand against danger at all. That much is a straightforwardly empirical matter. If observation shows that he does not do this, then the judgment becomes untenable. But if it shows that he does, then the judgment is only partly established; and it continues to be only partly established, of course, even if we go on to describe—in factual terms, and again with empirical evidence—the exact ways, including the attendant circumstances, in which he makes his stand against danger. For there will still be a question as to whether these ways are *admirable* ways. From there on we are dealing with values; and our reasons, which previously have been inductively related *to the judgment*, become related to it in another way. They are no longer reasons for believing that the man has certain characteristics, but instead are reasons for (or against) admiring them. (Cf. my parallel distinction, pp. 82 f., between reasons for believing and reasons for approving.) As in any example that bears on values, of course, we may here introduce persuasive definitions into our discussion. That is only to say that some of the reasons of the sort last mentioned can temporarily be built into the meaning of "admirable," and can thereby be built into the meaning of "courageous" as well. Note, however, that they can be built in only temporarily, and for this sort of context only. They can readily be "built out" again by anyone who rejects the persuasive definition. So we must not confuse the factual component introduced by a persuasive definition with the core of factual meaning that is established by fixed rules of language.

What I say of "courageous" can for the most part be repeated, *mutatis mutandis*, for the various virtue-terms of our language—a family of terms that includes "temperate," "considerate," "charitable," and so on. And with appropriate changes in both factual and evaluative components it can be repeated for the opposites of these terms, such as "cowardly," "intemperate," and so on. We must remember, however, that the terms do not always behave quite so simply as my example of "courageous" (which itself has been analyzed somewhat schematically) may at first suggest. The core of their factual meaning may specify, for instance, only the presence of one or another *subset* of a *group* of qualities, as in Wittgenstein's "family resemblances."[20] It may involve, as well, meanings that are *almost* fixed to the terms, or in other words, meanings that can be removed without doing positive violence to our language but cannot be removed without occasioning a strong sense of linguistic discomfort. When a definition deals with these almost fixed meanings its function becomes evident only when close attention is paid to its context. It may be a persuasive definition, but it may also be a definition that simply records or misrecords common usage.

I have mentioned only *one* of the ways in which value judgments can become specific. There is also another way: they can express (and invite-so-to-speak) not just favor or disfavor but rather a special sort of favor or disfavor. An example is provided by the term "admirable," which I used just above. (I may not have been accurate in using just that term to analyze "courageous"; but my general point can be made independently of that.) It will be evident that "admirable" is at most a *near* synonym of "desirable," and that both these terms are at most *near* synonyms of "worthy of respect." They are all three favorable terms, however; so they presumably differ in that they permit us to express (and invite-so-to-speak) different and relatively specific "shades" of favor.

20. *Philosophical Investigations*, p. 67.

It would be perhaps impossible to indicate, save by example, just what different "shades" of favor are in question. But the need of recognizing the differences becomes evident when we remember that an attitude is of a dispositional nature, involving a variety of responses that may progressively attend a variety of stimuli. Among the responses, in particular, there are various differences in *feeling* between admiration, desire, respect, etc.; and as I need scarcely add, these differences have their behavioral correlates.

The terms "morally good" and "morally wrong," which are usually more specific that "good" and "wrong," seem to me to illustrate a combination of the factors that I have been mentioning. In Essay IV I suggested that they became specific by their connection with a peculiarly moral sort of approval or disapproval (involving such responses as feeling indignant, shocked, etc.).[21] I should have added, I suspect, that they also become specific on account of a core of factual meaning—not a simple one, however, but rather one involving a "family resemblance," and involving also what I have just called "*almost* fixed" meaning. And besides, various *ambiguities* of "morally" must presumably be taken into account. I say this for a negative reason. Various efforts that I have made to handle "morally" in a simpler manner impress me as being inadequate.

If complete profiles of such terms are eventually to be obtained, with illustrations of *just* how "admirable," "desirable," "morally good," etc., differ in their use, they will presumably be obtained by those who continue in the type of analysis now current at Oxford. I for one would be interested in the various minutiae that the profiles would reveal, but at the same time I wonder whether they would be of much importance. I doubt, for instance, if they would free us from any tempting confusions with regard to the reasons that we give for our judgments: they would bear on the precise content of this or that reason but would not be likely to disclose anything new in principle. In that case they might turn out to be less of philosophical than stylistic interest.

21. Also cf. *Ethics and Language*, pp. 90 ff.

There is no ground for supposing that full profiles of such evaluative terms, by revealing their core of factual meaning, would afford us a "linguistic protection" against those who evaluate very strangely. The terms "courageous" and "rash," for instance, do not force anyone to evaluate various stands against danger in disparate ways. A man can always say "all so-called courage is really a kind of rashness," or "all so-called rashness is really a kind of courage," or "any stand against danger is neither right nor wrong, but simply indifferent." If he holds the latter view (and I am singling out strange views deliberately) he will find that the terms "courageous" and "rash" tend to become useless to him; but he can then, if he wishes, take an alternative tack, saying that courage is not a virtue and rashness is not a vice. He will have his difficulties in remaking our language to suit his evaluations; but there may be nothing to prevent his attempt from being a concerted one, and meanwhile he has other locutions that readily permit him to state his opinion.

The same is true with respect to any core of factual meaning that may be thought to attend the words "moral" or "morally." It could not protect us from the strange judgment, "no one should respect moral obligations," or from the judgment, "so-called moral obligations ought always to be greeted with contempt." Linguistic analysis can hope to rid us of certain confusions, but it cannot hope to rid us of men whom we consider socially irresponsible.

10

I have still to consider judgments that involve special idioms. Of the many that I might mention I shall deal only with those that arise in certain contexts containing "good."

Since a car is a vehicle, a red car is a red vehicle, and since a mouse is an animal, a hungry mouse is a hungry animal; but we must not suppose that we have here a rule that holds without exception. It clearly will not do, for instance, to say "since a father is a man, a good father is a good man."[22] So it is of interest in this latter case to consider how our words are behaving.

22. I take the example from Paul Ziff's *Semantic Analysis* (Ithaca, N.Y., 1960), p. 223.

The expression that most needs attention is "good father." For note that we fail to preserve the meaning of "X is a good father" when we attempt to paraphrase it as "X is good and X is a father." In the former expression the adjective and the noun collaborate, so to speak, whereas in the latter they work independently. We have less of this collaboration in "good man"; for when we paraphrase "X is a good man" by "X is good and X is a man" there is at least no very striking error. And we have none of the collaboration in "red car," since "X is a red car" can quite readily be paraphrased as "X is red and X is a car." We must ask, then, of "good father," what sort of collaboration between the adjective and the noun is typically involved.

In any full context—and let us for the moment select the context "Charles I was a good father"—it will be evident that the "good" of "good father" still yields a judgment that normally expresses and invites-so-to-speak a favorable attitude. And we can take an important step toward answering our question by considering the *object* of this attitude. Its object is not specified, of course, by the term "Charles I" alone. If we supposed so, we should take the judgment as favorable to *various* characteristics of Charles I, most of them having nothing to do with what he did as a father: so we should overlook the limited scope of the judgment. The object of the attitude, then, is in part indicated by the term "father." And it will be noted that this term has two functions: it not only enables the judgment to affirm that Charles I *was* a father but also insures a restricted reference to certain of his characteristics (namely, those bearing on what he did as a father) which *alone* are being *commended* by the judgment. The faulty paraphrase, "Charles I was good and Charles I was a father," is faulty because it preserves only the first of the functions of "father," entirely ignoring the second.

We shall accordingly stay closer to the meaning of "Charles I was a good father" when we paraphrase it as "Charles I was a father, and what he did as a father (i.e. what he did in the capacity or role of a father) was good." I do not wish to suggest that this is a fully accurate paraphrase. The expression "what he did" may be putting too little emphasis on purposes or intentions, and the words "capacity" and "role"[23] clearly deserve further examination. But it is a sufficiently accurate paraphrase to be instructive. The second, evaluative part of it is of the form "X was good"; and that form I have handled previously. So "good father" is of interest only for illustrating a special locution, used in specifying *what* is being judged.

It is easy to see why the special locution is convenient. In estimating a man's worth we normally feel that he has his good points and his bad points and that these have to be weighed against one another. So we proceed piecemeal, separately evaluating each of the "points." Now "good father" simply helps to isolate some of these points, just as "good son" or "bad son" helps to isolate others and "good king" or "bad king" helps to isolate still others, etc. It will be evident that our language contains other locutions that belong, closely or distantly, to the same family. We are likely to proceed in a piecemeal fashion when we evaluate, say, a proposed law; and we can do so by saying, "it would be good *so far as* its effects on the laborers are concerned but would be bad *so far as* its effects on the capitalists are concerned." Similarly, we may say that such and such an armed base is good *with respect to* military strategy but bad *with respect to* diplomatic relations. Alternatively, and in at least *one* familiar sense, we can say that the armed base is good from a military *point of view*, but bad from a diplomatic *point of view*.

But let me continue with the "good father" locution. If we were asked to enumerate some of the *factual* characteristics that make a man a good father, we should presumably mention a care for his children's health and education, a sympathy with their problems, and so on. And we might be inclined to think that we were mentioning some of the qualities that a good father must have *by definition*. But we need not be doing that. We may simply be mentioning some

---

23. "Role" is one of the large family of terms that must be defined with some or another reference (a purely factual reference) to social customs. The importance of such terms has been emphasized by Jack Rawls in his paper, "Two Concepts of Rules," *The Philosophical Review*, 66 (1955), 25 ff.

qualities for which we are prepared to express and invite-so-to-speak approval, though with exclusive attention, of course, to qualities that are relevant to the role of a father. Or if we insist on adding "by definition," then our definition will be persuasive. It may often seem gratuitous in its persuasive (or normative) aspects, for it may be attended by no uncertainty or controversy; but it may serve, even so, to prevent our converging evaluations from becoming half-hearted. And the *possibility* of controversy becomes apparent from such a question as "under precisely what circumstances does a good father withhold advice with the intent of increasing his children's self-reliance?"

When we turn to contexts that are grammatically similar to the "good father" example, we must be careful not to generalize the above analysis without providing qualifications. Here in particular "the silent adjustments to an understanding of colloquial language are enormously complicated."[24] Consider, for example, the judgment, "that is a good road."[25] If we treat this like the preceding example we shall take it as a favorable judgment of *certain aspects* of the road. One does not question the judgment in pointing out that the road was too expensive or that it spoiled an otherwise beautiful little town. That would be irrelevant, showing only that the road, if a good road, may nevertheless not be a good thing. The judgment, in other words, evaluates the road *as a road* and not as an economic venture or as a community project in aesthetics. And to that extent it *seems* only to reduplicate our previous considerations. (The phrase "as a road" specifies the object of favor in a way that is certainly vague; but it is vague only, perhaps, in the way that "good road" is vague. To insist on precision would be comparable, perhaps, to insisting that *many* must be equated with a definite number.)

But we must remember that "good road" is reminiscent not only of "good father" but also of "good money" (the latter term belonging to a family that includes "good electric light bulb," "good spark

---

24. L. Wittgenstein, *Tractatus Logico-Philosophicus*, 4.002.

25. I take the example from a paper by J. O. Urmson—a paper that has not, to my knowledge, been published.

plug," and so on). In most contexts "good money" behaves very much like such *factual* terms as "money that can serve its usual purposes," and "money that has purchasing power," and (in particular) "money that is authorized and backed by a solvent government." It is somewhat arbitrary, here, to draw a line between what our term strictly means and what it merely suggests. But the point to be noted is that in a sentence like "this is good money" any tendency to express the speaker's favor and to invite-so-to-speak the favor of others) the favor being directed, of course, only to *certain aspects* of money, and having nothing to do with whether or not money is the root of all evil) becomes of minor importance. It is residual, so to speak, and can easily be counteracted by one's tone of voice. The context-bound, idiomatic references to purposes and purchasing power, etc., take precedence over it and prevent the term from having a potential use, even, in *strengthening* or *modifying* attitudes. And in that respect the term "good money" *differs* from "good father."

We can see this in the following cases. When a man says "a good father must always be harsh to his children," we object (if we do) on ethical rather than on linguistic grounds. The speaker indicates favor where we are inclined to indicate disfavor; and if that is due to his believing something that we consider false (e.g. to his believing that harsh treatment gives the children great strength of character), that is only to say that we question the truth of a reason that he might give for his judgment *as well as* the judgment itself. But when a man says (without joking) "good money must always lack purchasing power," we are likely to object, in the first instance, on linguistic grounds. However much (in his unworldly way) he may be against the purchasing power of money, and however much he may want to deny it a prima facie claim, even, to anyone's favor, we expect him to say that good money must have some or another posititive connection with purchasing power—and to say it in deference to what is commonly *called* "good money." Seeing this, he may subsequently be content to restate his view (in a way that is more or less, if not exactly, faithful to what he was first driving at) in such words as these: "In no respect is good money any better than bad money." But here his attempt at reforming our attitudes—his protestation against people's usual concern with the purchasing power of money—is evident from his quite standard use of "in no respect . . . better than." It has nothing to do with any laudatory or derogatory force of the terms "good money" or "bad money"; for these terms have at most, being special idioms, only a residual force of that kind, and a force that is here wholly counteracted by the accompanying context.

Thus "good father" gives us some little linguistic freedom, though always within limits set up by our conception of the role of a father, in enumerating the factual characteristics that *make* a man a good father: and diverging enumerations of this sort represent diverging evaluations. But "good money" allows us no such linguistic freedom; and in cases where diverging evaluations might arise (as they *very* rarely do) they would virtually require us, in deference to our language, to introduce our evaluations by means of other terms, using this *idiomatic* term in an evaluatively neutral way.

And what shall be said of "good road" in this connection? The example is interesting, in my opinion, because it stands between the other two. We are very likely to press it into the "good money" pattern; but the flexibilities of our language half permit us, at least, to press it into the "good father" pattern. Let me develop the example further:

A certain man says that Middlevale Pike is no longer a good road. This surprises us, because we know and suppose him to know that it has been rebuilt in a smooth, hard, durable manner, etc. But we get his point when he goes on to comment on the difficulties of the many farmers who drive their horses along it. We tend to reply, "I see what you mean; you are not questioning that it is a good motor-highway but are simply saying that it is no longer a good farm road." Thus we *avoid* the term "good road," thinking that it raises unnecessary difficulties. Shall we spell out its meaning with reference to smoothness, hardness, etc., just as we can spell out the meaning of "good money" with reference to purchasing power, etc.? If so we shall have an "ambiguity," and one too troublesome to explain. So we drop the term as we do any ordinary factual term whose meaning proves too unstable for its special purpose. The terms "good motor-highway" and "good farm road," meanwhile, restore communication without raising an evaluative issue that (we suspect) would here be out of place. But on the other hand we could urge that Middlevale Pike *is* a good road, adding that the needs of the farmers, who are a minority group, cannot easily be taken into consideration when roads are built. That would treat "good road" like "good father," letting it be central to a *discussion* of values. Linguistic considerations do very little to prevent this; and if it seems strange in the present case, that is largely because we normally would not want to "make an issue" of the matter.

I give these examples less to show their importance than to show their unimportance. They usefully remind us of the flexibilities of our language and of the absurdity of seeking "the" meaning of a common term. But they leave us, from there on, with the central ethical distinctions on which I have previously insisted—those between uncertainty or disagreement in attitude and uncertainty or disagreement in belief, and between expressing attitudes and expressing beliefs (etc.), and between reasons for favoring and reasons for believing. So the examples simply help us to recognize these factors in cases where colloquial language tends to conceal them.

Ethical naturalism falls well short of a triumph when it points out that questions of the "good money" family are amenable to empirical solutions. Such solutions are always theoretically possible when disagreement in attitude is rooted in disagreement in belief or when uncertainty in attitude is rooted in uncertainty of belief. And terms of the "good money" family are useful only when this "rooting" occurs, and indeed, only when the beliefs in question are so simple that they can be specified in advance. When these conditions are not fulfilled then the terms are dropped in favor of others. So we must look well beyond such terms if we are to envisage a methodology appropriate to the really difficult questions of ethics—questions that permit us to hope for empirical answers but require us to hope with empirical caution, and questions so pervasive that the very *sorts* of information that bear on them, so far from being specifiable in advance, can bewilder our imagination.

II

In the course of this essay I have discussed (1) the manner in which ethical disagreement can be "tempered" by uncertainty; (2) the nature of ethical uncertainty; (3) the sense in which ethical judgments express and invite-so-to-speak attitudes, with particular reference to (a) the inappropriateness of including an "autobiographical" element in the analysis of the judgments, and (b) the appropriateness of calling ethical judgments true or false; and (4) the function of relatively specific judgments, in cases where they use special terms and in cases where they use special idioms.

If I conclude my comments at this point, that is only because the remaining topics are so numerous. They force me to choose my stopping point somewhat arbitrarily. My unfinished business includes an analysis of the distinction between beliefs and attitudes; it includes an inquiry (only touched upon in Essay VI) into the role of generalizations in ethics; and it includes a host of comparative studies relating ethics to psychology, legal theory, linguistic theory, aesthetics, and (in particular) epistemology.

The magnitude of this unfinished business effectively prevents me from thinking that I have "settled" matters. Ethics is as difficult as it is important; and it would be an impertinence to suggest—even for the limited part of the subject that lies within analytical philosophy —that its problems can be settled by one book, one writer, or one generation. But however inadequate or incomplete the essays in the present volume may be, I hope they do something to establish this simple but curiously neglected point:

Our ethical judgments represent our personality in all its complexity. However much they may be guided by a full use of our intelligence, they do not spring from the intellect alone.

List of Works Cited

Aristotle, *Nicomachean Ethics*, ed. and trans. H. Rackman, Cambridge, Mass., Harvard University Press, 1939.

Austin, J. L., and P. W. Strawson, "Truth" (symposium), *Proceedings of the Aristotelian Society*, supp. vol. *24* (1950).

Ayer, A. J., *Language, Truth, and Logic*, New York, Oxford University Press, 1936.

Barnes, W. H. F., "A Suggestion about Values," *Analysis*, *1* (1934), 45–46.

Bentham, Jeremy, *An Introduction to the Principles of Morals and Legislation*, London, 1789.

Black, Max, "Some Questions about Emotive Meaning," *The Philosophical Review*, *57* (1948), 111–26.

Bloomfield, Leonard, *Language*, New York, Holt, 1933.

Braithwaite, R. B., "Verbal Ambiguity and Philosophical Analysis," *Proceedings of the Aristotelian Society*, n.s. *28* (1927–28), 135–54.

Brandt, Richard, *Ethical Theory*, Englewood Cliffs, New Jersey, Prentice-Hall, 1959.

Broad, C. D., *Determinism, Indeterminism and Libertarianism*, Cambridge, Cambridge University Press, 1934.

—— "Is 'Goodness' the Name of a Simple, Non-natural Quality?" *Proceedings of the Aristotelian Society*, n.s. *34* (1933–34), 249–68.

—— "Some of the Main Problems of Ethics," in *Readings in Philosophical Analysis*, ed. H. Feigl and W. Sellars, New York, Appleton–Century, 1949.

Carnap, Rudolf, *Philosophy and Logical Syntax*, London, Kegan Paul, Trench, Trubner, 1935.

Chisholm, R. M., "The Contrary-to-Fact Conditional," *Mind*, 55 (1946), 289–307.

Dewey, John, *Human Nature and Conduct*, New York, Holt, 1922.

—— *The Quest for Certainty*, New York, Minton, Balch, 1929.

—— *Reconstruction in Philosophy*, New York, Holt, 1920.

—— and James H. Tufts, *Ethics*, New York, Holt, 1908.

Field, G. C., *Moral Theory*, 2d ed. rev. London, Methuen, 1932.

Goodman, Nelson, "The Problem of Counterfactual Conditionals," *Journal of Philosophy*, 44 (1947), 113–28.

—— *The Structure of Appearance*, Cambridge, Mass., Harvard University Press, 1951.

Hägerström, A., *Inquiries into the Nature of Laws and Morals*, trans. C. D. Broad, Stockholm, Almqvist and Wiksell, 1938.

Hare, R. M., *The Language of Morals*, Oxford, Clarendon Press, 1952.

Hart, H. L. A., "Ascription of Responsibility and Rights," *Proceedings of the Aristotelian Society*, n.s. 49 (1948–49), 171–94.

Hobbes, Thomas, *Leviathan*, London, 1651.

—— *The Questions Concerning Liberty, Necessity, and Chance*, London, 1676.

Hume, David, *A Treatise of Human Nature*, London, 1739–40.

Huxley, Aldous, *Brave New World*, Garden City, N.Y., Doubleday, 1932.

—— *Eyeless in Gaza*, New York, Harper, 1936.

Johnson, W. E., *Logic*, 3 vols. Cambridge, Cambridge University Press, 1921–24.

Lanz, Henry, *In Quest of Morals*, Stanford, Calif., Stanford University Press, 1941.

Lewis, C. I., *Knowledge and Valuation*, La Salle, Ill., Open Court, 1946.

Moore, G. E., *Ethics*, New York, Holt, 1912.

—— "Is Goodness a Quality?" in *Philosophical Papers*, New York, 1959.

—— *Philosophical Studies*, New York, Harcourt, Brace, 1922.

—— *Principia Ethica*, Cambridge, Cambridge University Press, 1903.

Nowell-Smith, P. H., *Ethics*, London, Penguin Books, 1954.

Oertel, Hanns, *Lectures on the Study of Language*, New York, Scribner's, 1901.

Ogden, C. K., and I. A. Richards, *The Meaning of Meaning*, 2d ed. London, Kegan Paul, Trench, Trubner, 1927.

Perry, R. B., *General Theory of Value*, New York, Longmans, Green, 1926.

Plato, *Theaetetus*, trans. Francis M. Cornford, London, Kegan Paul, Trench, Trubner, 1935.

Pottle, Frederick A., *The Idiom of Poetry*, Ithaca, Cornell University Press, 1941.

Ramsey, Frank, *The Foundation of Mathematics*, ed. R. B. Braithwaite, New York, Harcourt, Brace, 1931.

Rawls, Jack, "Two Concepts of Rules," *The Philosophical Review*, *66* (1955), 3–33.

Ross, W. D., *The Right and the Good*, Oxford, Clarendon Press, 1930.

Russell, Bertrand, *Human Society in Ethics and Politics*, New York, Simon and Schuster, 1955.

——— *Religion and Science*, New York, Holt, 1935.

Schilpp, P. A., ed., *The Philosophy of G. E. Moore*, Evanston, Ill., Northwestern University Press, 1942.

Schlick, Moritz, *Fragen der Ethik*, Vienna, Springer, 1930.

Stace, W. T., *The Concept of Morals*, New York, Macmillan, 1937.

Stevenson, Charles L., *Ethics and Language*, New Haven, Yale University Press, 1944.

Tarski, Alfred, "The Semantic Conception of Truth." *Philosophy and Phenomenological Research*, *4* (1944), 341–75.

Toulmin, Stephen, *An Examination of the Place of Reason in Ethics*, Cambridge, Cambridge University Press, 1950.

Urmson, J. O., "On Grading," *Mind*, *59* (1950), 145–69.

Westermarck, Edward, *Ethical Relativity*, New York, Harcourt, Brace, 1932.

Wittgenstein, Ludwig, *Philosophical Investigations*, trans. G. E. M. Anscombe, New York, Macmillan, 1953.

——— *Tractatus Logico-Philosophicus*, New York, Harcourt, Brace, 1922.

Ziff, Paul, *Semantic Analysis*, Ithaca, Cornell University Press, 1960.

Index

Admiration, 221–24

Alas, emotive meaning of, 9, 21, 64

Allport, G. W., 196 n.

Ambiguity, of ethical terms and questions, 9–10, 12, 15, 52–54, 224

Analysis, emotive (so-called noncognitive view): summary of, 15–18, 71, 79–80, 186–87, 193–94; function of, 17, 137, 175–76, 184, 191 n., 200, 203; patterns of, 23–31, 48–56, 60–62, 79, 182–85, 294–10, 213, 221–32 (*see also* Good, Signs); role of cognition in, 28, 60, 99–100, 168–72 (*see also* Attitudes); criticism of, 60, 64, 79, 117 ff. (*see also* Black, Moore); defense of, 64–70, 170–72 (*see also* Emotive meaning, importance in analytical ethics); view of relation between factual reasons and judgment, 66–67, 84–93, 208 (*see also* Reasons); contrasted with relativism, 80, in identification of issues, 81–82, in relating reasons to judgment, 82–84, in methodology, 84–93, 194; of sign situations, 153 ff. (*see* Signs); further development of, 194, 201–02, 232; correction to, 210–14 (*see also* Autobiographical element in emotive analysis). *See also* Disagreement, Emotive meaning, Language, Personal decision

Analytical ethics: defined, viii–ix, 114; function of, 17, 175–76, 184, 191 n.; criticism of nonemotive views, 60–63, 78 (*see also* Interest); evolutionary school, 61–62; need for psychological background, 201–02, 232; Oxford

school of, 224. *See also* Analysis, emotive, Naturalism, Nonnaturalism, Relativism

Approval: as attitude, 2, 9, 16, 56, 79–80, 117 n., 206; ethical statements defined in terms of, 11–14, 76, 79, 91, 96, 117–36, 168, 210–14; effect of reasoning (consequences) on, 14, 45, 47, 49–52, 57–58, 66–70, 82–86, 90–93, 95–96, 99–114, 135–36, 170, 196–97, 199–202, 222; as influence, 16–18, 79, 134–35 (*see also* Emotive meaning, laudatory); feelings associated with, 25, 59, 142–43, 147, 224–25; decision to grant, 56 (*see* Personal decision); secondary, 59; complexity of, 61–62, 84, 100, 199–202; as attitude-designating, 76, 79–82, 117 n. (*see also* Introspection). *See also* Judgments

Arguments, ethical. *See* Disagreement, Emotive meaning, Personal decision

Aristotle, 139

Attitudes (interest): defined, 1–3, 12 n., 26; judgment as expression of, 2, 9, 80–82; use of empirical method, cognition (reasoning) for reconciling, 6–8, 27–28, 49–54, 56–58, 63, 66–68, 80, 83–85, 90, 95–96, 99–100, 129–30, 134, 164, 168–72, 197–99, 208 (*see also* Approval, Beliefs); judgment as description of, 9, 16, 65–66, 80, 117 n., 130, 157–60, 167; redirection through approval, judgment, 9 (*see* Influence); relation to emotive meaning, 21 n. (*see* Emotive meaning); feelings associated

237